R I V E R   T H A M E S

these Woolwich Marshes are occupied by the ordnance of John Watts Esq[?]

ORDNANCE *LANDS*

GS at WOOLWICH

July 1806.

Geo. Wayston
Capt. &c R[?] Engineers
Woolwich 20 Aug 1806.

The Royal Artillery, Woolwich
A Celebration

The Royal Artillery, Woolwich

A Celebration

Consultant Editor:
Brigadier Ken Timbers

THIRD MILLENNIUM
PUBLISHING. LONDON

The Royal Artillery, Woolwich: A Celebration

© The Royal Artillery and
Third Millennium Publishing Limited

First published in 2008 by

Third Millennium Publishing Limited,
a subsidiary of Third Millennium Information Limited.

2–5 Benjamin Street
London
United Kingdom
EC1M 5QL
www.tmiltd.com

ISBN 978 1 903942 73 4

British Library Cataloguing in Publication Data
A CIP catalogue record for this book is available from the British Library.

Edited by Ken Timbers
Designed by Matthew Wilson
Production by Bonnie Murray

Reprographics by Studio Fasoli, Italy
Printed by Gorenjski Tisk, Slovenia

Queen Elizabeth II, by David Poole, 1975.

CONTENTS

QUO   FAS ET GLORIA   DUCUNT

The stained glass window that graced the Church of St Michael and All Angels at the Royal Military Academy, Woolwich, now transferred to the Church of St Alban the Martyr at Larkhill.

So-called 'Coffee Table Books' abound these days, well illustrated with a reasonable story to tell. But it would be wrong to categorize *'A Celebration'* in this way – the picture it paints through a shrewd assembly of images and the tale it tells in a very fresh way mark it out from the crowd. There are some charming anecdotes too. This is a book to be savoured – not just by members of the Royal Regiment but those with enquiring minds who want to know how this Island developed as it did and why that matters today. Woolwich may be less on the map than it once was (though the Olympics may see to that), but it goes very deep into the Nation's heritage and that of one Regiment – many regiments have links with towns and regions, but I venture that none has been as significant as that which the Royal Regiment has forged with Woolwich over almost 300 years.

Woolwich also housed The Royal Arsenal which in its heyday was at the forefront of military science and technology and in the bloodstream of the Royal Navy and the Gunners. It became home to a vast arsenal, manufacturing everything to do with guns. It is a sobering thought that this Island's remarkable place in the world depended on its firepower as much as its fighting men. Without high quality guns, the Royal Navy's ships could not have protected the established trade routes. Without the weapons to defend the trading ports in far away parts of the Empire, there would have been no Garrison Gunners. Without guns, there would have been no Empire. In 1741, the Royal Military Academy was established in the Royal Arsenal (moving in 1806 to Shooters Hill where the buildings still stand) to educate, until 1939, officers of the Gunners and Sappers. It was commonly acknowledged that officers from 'The Shop', as it was known, were prominent amongst the movers and shakers of the Army. And throughout its history the Regiment has played a decisive part in the advance of military thinking: in 1778, by Captain Congreve's development of the first proper School of Artillery for *'the instruction of young officers and men of the Regiment'*; by the foundation of the Royal Artillery Institution in 1838 for the purpose of studying the science of artillery, particularly survey and astronomy; and by the foundation of a library and observatory. These were significant developments which led to the formation of a nucleus of well-trained competent officers, promoted on merit, when advancement by purchase still held sway in much of the Army.

Woolwich was home to Regiment from 1716 until last year. It was considered home by many Commonwealth Gunners too. Royal families of many countries were entertained and the Regiment demonstrated its skills in displays on Woolwich Common, the largest of which attracted 100,000 spectators. Batterys and regiments departed from Woolwich to fight – not least in the Crimean War, the Boer War and both World Wars. At the height of the Second War, over a million men were Gunners, many of them passing through the Depot at Woolwich.

We are a smaller Regiment now, but we continue to play a major part on the battlefield, deploying a range of systems at the leading edge of technology, enabling the long-range precision attack of targets. Gunner officers still exert influence across the Army at every level. What has characterized the Gunners over the centuries – a preparedness to embrace technology, a determination to apply it intelligently on the battlefield and essential competence in all that they do – owes much to what happened at Woolwich. A regiment needs to understand its antecedents and Brigadier Ken Timbers, the Consultant Editor, and all those who have contributed have done us a real service in this respect. I congratulate them.

Master Gunner St James's Park

TIMELINE OF EVENTS

Left: Model of a seven-barrelled machine, believed to date from the early 17th century.

Far left: The Tudor cipher on one of the Mary Rose guns, held by the Royal Military Museum.

1667 Dutch wars: Prince Rupert's Fort built at Woolwich.

1500   1600

1485 Board of Ordnance appoints Master Gunner with 12 'fee'd' Gunners to train artillerymen.

Board of Ordnance provides storehouses for guns and powder needed for fortresses and warships. First Gunners in Woolwich.

1512-3 Henry VIII establishes Royal Dockyards at Woolwich.

1600 Storehouse of guns and powder at Woolwich the largest in the country.

1670s Storehouse at Gun Wharf moved to The Warren. Master Gunner and staff move into Tower House.

Left: A 17th-century view looking south towards the dockyards.

The Goodwood Cup of 1864, a magnificent trophy that shows a scene at the Battle of Namur in 1695.

Royal Artillery, 1743.

1702–13 War of Spanish Succession.

1739 War of Jenkins's Ear.

1742–8 War of the Austrian Succession.

1700

1695 Greenwich Barn moved to the Tower House site.

1716 By Royal Warrant two companies of field artillery, each 100 strong, raised at Woolwich.

1722 Royal Regiment of Artillery commanded by Col Albert Borgard.

1741 Royal Military Academy established. Cadet company formed.

Right: Lieutenant General Albert Borgard. This portrait by an unknown artist was placed in the Military Repository in 1785.

Above: These kettledrum banners are among the oldest possessions of the Royal Artillery, dating from the early years of the 18th century. They were draped around the two kettledrums, the beating of which controlled the train of artillery in the field. The drums were mounted on a four-wheeled cart, drawn by a team of six grey horses. The damask and gold fringes were made in Italy between 1680 and 1740.

Above: The final scene of the siege of Gibraltar (1779–83) after a battle of fire from ship to shore, and from shore to ship, which lasted throughout the day and into the following night. Watercolour by Lieutenant G.F. Koehler, Royal Artillery.

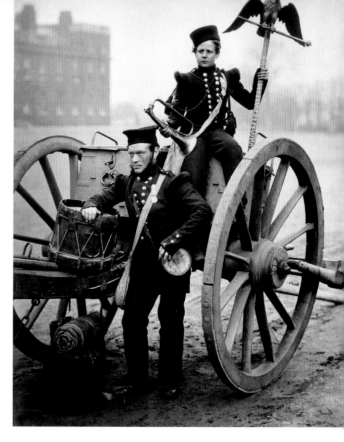

Right: Soldiers of the Royal Artillery who served in the Crimea: George Gritten, 11th Battalion, and W. Lang, Bugler, 12th Battalion, pose with war trophies, including a Russian eagle flagstaff, probably at Woolwich Barracks. Aged twelve, Lang was thought to be the youngest soldier in the British Army at the time.

1756–63

The Seven Years War.

1776–1815

American War of Independence 1776–93.

French Revolutionary and Napoleonic Wars 1793–1815.

The Napoleonic Wars: Peninsular Campaign 1808–1814; Waterloo 1815.

1854–6

Crimean War.

1800

1772–88

Total strength 32 companies in four battalions, plus two Invalid Companies for garrison duties.

RA barracks built in two main stages on Woolwich Common. Started 1772, first half completed in 1788. Royal Military Repository established in 1778.

Left: A jacket and shako of the Royal Horse Artillery, 1828.

1793–1803

Royal Horse Artillery formed in 1793 to provide added mobility, used mainly to support cavalry.

Royal Irish Artillery absorbed in 1801. By 1812 RA strength was total of 12 RHA troops and 100 RA companies in 10 battalions.

RA fully established on Woolwich Common in 1802. New Officers' Mess opened 1803.

The Riding Establishment RHA formed in 1803, forerunner of The King's Troop RHA.

1822–56

Corps of RA Drivers disbanded in 1822, ending the system of separating guns from the teams that drew them. Regimental strength significantly reduced after Napoleonic Wars.

In 1833 William IV grants RA its mottoes Quo fas et gloria ducunt and Ubique, which becomes its universal battle honour. Regular royal visits to Woolwich throughout the reigns of William IV and Victoria.

RA Institution established in 1838 – genesis of further science education for officers and forerunner of Royal Military College of Science.

Regiment strength increased after period of peace, 1854–6, to 112 companies in 14 battalions.

Right: The Empress Eugénie Shield (detail). The Prince Imperial, son of Napoleon III and the Empress Eugénie, attended the Royal Military Academy, Woolwich, in 1871–5 and was killed while serving as a staff officer in South Africa in 1879.

1855–63

Board of Ordnance abolished, 1855. Regiment comes under War Office as part of regular Army.

Reorganization into brigades and batteries, with equipment permanently allocated, 1859. Depot brigade formed at Woolwich.

Firing practice moved to Shoeburyness in the 1860s; other ranges were developed later, as needed.

Garrison Church of St George established in Woolwich, 1863.

Above: The remaining gun and its detachment of L Battery in action against German guns at Néry on 1 September 1914. Drawing by Fortunino Matania.

Right: A 105mm light gun of 40th Field Regiment RA, on operations in Iraq, 2007.

1882–1918

Egyptian War 1882.

Sudan War 1884–5.

Omdurman 1898.

Boer War 1899–1902.

First World War 1914–18.

1939–45

Second World War 1939–45.

1982

The Falklands War.

1990–

The First Gulf War 1990–1.

War in Afghanistan 2001–.

Invasion/occupation of Iraq 2003–.

1900 · **2000**

1899–1924

Regiment divided into Royal Field Artillery (including RHA) and Royal Garrison Artillery in 1899.

Woolwich becomes fully identified with its 'depot' function, 1922.

Woolwich Stadium opened on Woolwich Common, 1924.

1938–45

HAA and LAA guns on Woolwich Common, Z-rocket battery on Shooters Hill. RAI building destroyed by bombing and Royal Garrison Church destroyed by V1 'doodlebug'.

1954–92

RA awarded the Freedom of the Borough of Woolwich, 1954.

20 Regt RA returns to UK from Korea and goes into Cambridge Barracks, 1955.

Rebuild of RA Barracks accommodation in 1964.

17 Training Regt moves to Woolwich and takes on all basic training, later adding the role of managing the Depot, 1968–92.

1993–2007

200th anniversary parade of RHA in Woolwich, 1993.

HQ DRA moves to Larkhill in 1994.

16 Regt RA in Woolwich, 1995–2007 – the first service regt to serve there since 20 Regt RA.

Regt moves its 'home' from Woolwich to Larkhill, 2007.

Above: Housewife, containing sewing kit and other essentials of the Second World War period.

Right: The King's Troop RHA, performing at an At Home event in Woolwich.

EDITOR'S NOTE

In preparing this book, it became clear that the best approach would be an informal illustrated history, with none of the references and footnotes normally associated with years of research: there was not enough time for that. The problem was in trying to tell the many different stories that overlap one another, making it impossible to keep the sequence chronological. I chose to retain the individual stories as entities and simply place them as close to the historical timeline as I could. However, I had to divide some of the longer stories to enable the parts to be placed in at least the correct century. There is inevitably some overlap between the different contributions, but this has been necessary in order for the articles to stand alone.

I aimed to bring in as many others as I could persuade to help, and I am grateful to all those who responded so willingly: their contributions give the book its breadth of story. I have listed them along with their articles, so I will refrain from naming them all again here. Material without by-lines has been written by me.

Aside from the writing, the task has also been to find suitable pictures. Here I am indebted to the Librarian at the RA Library, Paul Evans; further invaluable support has come from the staff of *The Gunner* and the publishers, Third Millennium Information Ltd. Many others have chipped in and I cannot thank them enough: picture credits are shown where possible, but some have no clear provenance and I beg forgiveness if I have breached anyone's copyright. Sadly, the poor state of some of the old photographs is such that they do not provide the sort of quality that a book like this expects:

sometimes it has been a question of using them or foregoing any relevant image.

Indeed, some of the articles cannot be supported by directly relevant pictures or maps. Where this is the case, I have used other pictures from the compilation in the hope that, for many people, the old saw about a picture being worth a thousand words holds true. It also allowed me to include pictures that would otherwise not appear at all.

I can claim little credit for the Section dealing with the transfer of the Regiment's home to Larkhill. That Section has been produced under the aegis of the Regimental Headquarters and shows that, despite having to leave Woolwich, the Regiment continues to hold true to its history and traditions.

Given the number of people who have contributed, it seems invidious to pick out individuals, but thanks are due especially to the Regimental Colonel, Col Chris Nicholls; Lt Col Will Townend; Major Denis Rollo: Col Nick Richards; Col Bob Jammes; The Rev. Dr Michael Gilman; Maj Eddie Ellis Jones; and in particular, Col Martin Cooper. I want to add that I thoroughly enjoyed working with the very supportive team at Third Millennium: it has been a happy and productive relationship. Last, I want to thank my wife, Bridget, whose patience and support have been invaluable. Her 23 years of service to the RAI as the chief clerk to the Historical Secretary has given her an amazing insight into the question of 'where to go for honey', and she frequently produced guidance without which this book would be a great deal the poorer.

Ken Timbers

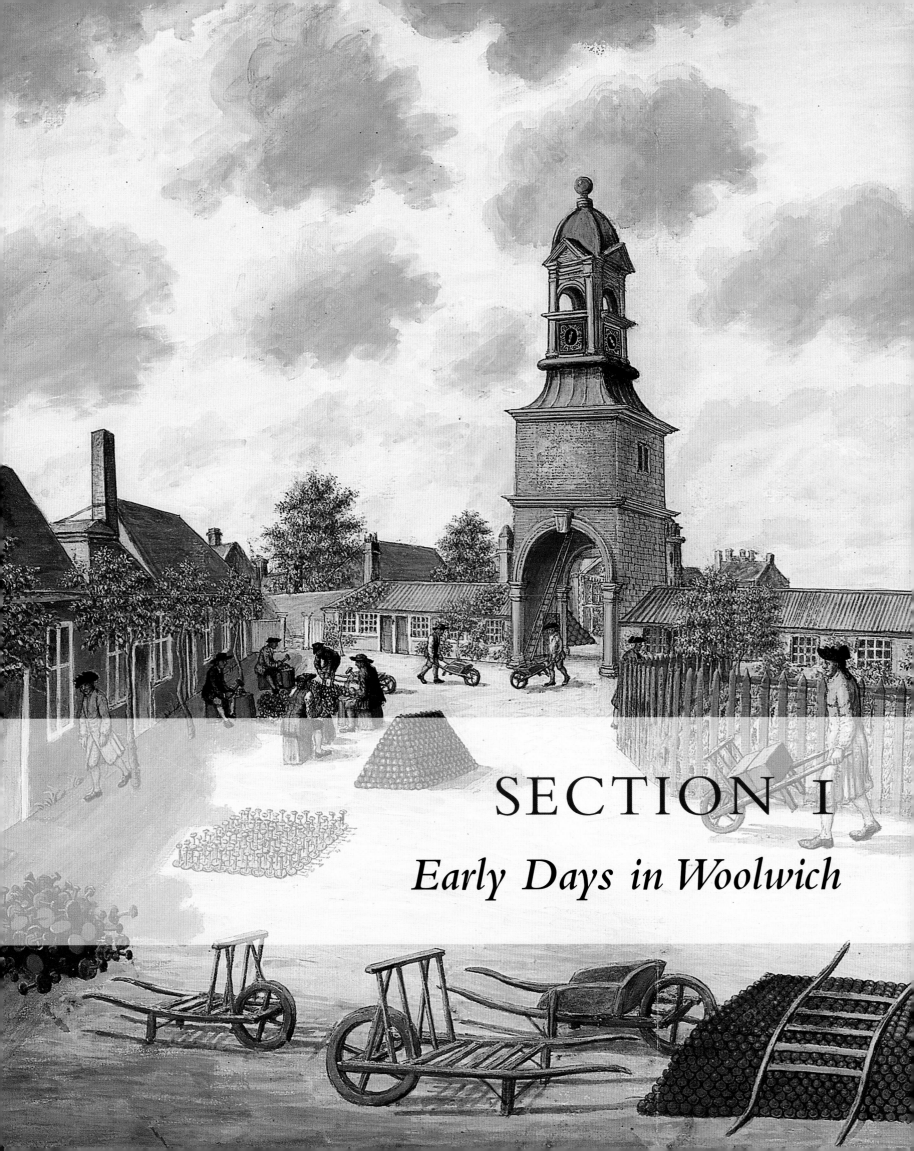

SECTION I
Early Days in Woolwich

INTRODUCTION

How the Gunners came to Woolwich

Within living memory, the Royal Regiment of Artillery has been larger than the Royal Navy and, with over 800 regiments, has had close to a million men under arms, drawn from across the entire United Kingdom. Yet for 291 years it regarded Woolwich, once a small Kentish town, as its home. This is the remarkable story of the Gunners in the context of that home town and begins with a look at how they came to be there, shortly after the accession of King Henry VIII to the throne of England. It seems entirely appropriate that the King should have had such an influence on what was to become the Army's principal source of firepower.

Power was Henry VIII's birthright. Succeeding Henry VII in 1509 at the age of 18, talented, secure, buttressed by the wealth amassed by his father, Henry could afford to be ambitious and to look beyond his own realm for glory, especially against England's traditional enemy, France. But adventures overseas needed warships, and the Royal Dockyard at Portsmouth lay dangerously close to the French shore. In 1512–13, for better

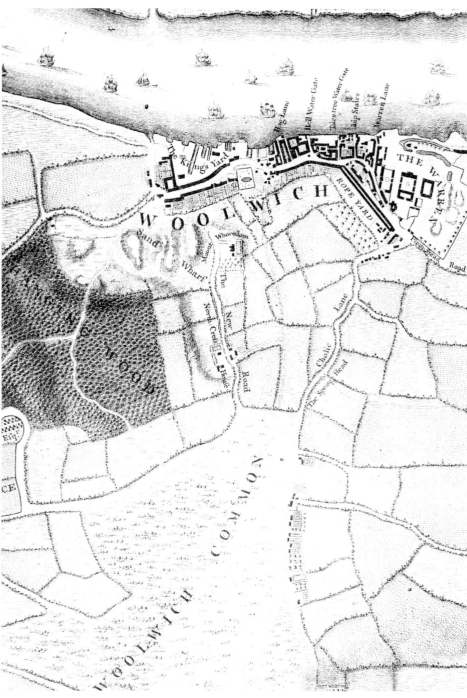

A general map of Woolwich and its environs c.1720.

The Great Harry was built at Woolwich and launched in 1514, during the reign of Henry VIII. She was one of the first ships of war to carry gun ports. These allowed her to fire a broadside. The Great Harry was accidentally destroyed by fire in 1553.

ESTABLISHING GUN-FOUNDING IN ENGLAND

Previous page: This depicts the southern entrance to the Royal Laboratory in The Warren at Woolwich, c.1700.

Right: One of the Mary Rose brass guns salvaged in the early 19th Century and held by the RA Museum. The cipher shows the Tudor rose of Henry VIII.

Below right: One of the guns made exclusively for the Sovereign of the Seas, Charles I's great warship, built at Woolwich. This gun is in the Regimental museum in Woolwich.

Henry VIII had another great influence on artillery: the development of English gun-founding in order to provide a secure source for guns, most of which had hitherto been bought from Continental sources. He brought gun-founders, such as the Arcana family from Venice, and established them in England, making guns for warships like the *Mary Rose* – one of her great brass guns is in the Royal Artillery Museum.

organization that began in Plantagenet times as the King's personal accounting system, known as the *Privy Wardrobe*. This evolved into the *Great Wardrobe* and eventually, as the complexities of running the country grew, split into different agencies. One of these was responsible for all the logistics of war and was called the *Office of Ordnance*, based in the Tower of London. In due course, this became the *Ordnance Department*, managed by the *Board of Ordnance*.

In the reign of Henry VII the Ordnance Department sought better control over the increasingly important power of artillery, both as an established naval weapon and as a growing threat on the battlefield. In 1485 it obtained authority to appoint a Master Gunner of England with 12 'fee'd' (paid) Gunners. These officials provided expert advice on everything to do with artillery and organized the training of gunners for duties in coast artillery and on the battlefield. Their duties included supporting the storehouses for guns and powder that were needed to stock fortresses and warships, especially in the Royal Dockyards, and by the time of Elizabeth I's reign the storehouse at Woolwich was the largest in the country.

It was the Gunner link with the Board of Ordnance storehouses that was the genesis of the Gunner presence in Woolwich at the beginning of the 16th century, almost 500 years ago. They may have been visiting inspectors – the records are

Below: 1630, a barge arrives at Greenwich Palace on the Thames east of London, during the reign of Charles I. During Christmas 1594 William Shakespeare and the Chamberlain's Men were paid to perform two separate comedies at the palace before Queen Elizabeth I, who was born there in 1533.

security, Henry founded Royal Dockyards in the Thames at Woolwich and Deptford.

In those days, guns were purchased by the Crown from manufacturers at home and abroad. The agency for this was an

vague – but their role continued throughout the life of the Royal Dockyard and into the foundation of the new arsenal in Woolwich, overlapping the foundation of the Royal Artillery in 1716, so the continuity was unbroken.

We may never know the name of the first Gunner to set foot in Woolwich, but he began a connection that was to endure, linking the Royal Regiment of Artillery with a small Kentish town that was to become its home. Woolwich itself went on to become the site of a vast arsenal manufacturing everything to do with guns, so much so that its coat of arms proudly bears three guns as the principal charge. It is a sobering thought that this small island's historic place at the top table among much bigger nations depended on its firepower as much as its fighting men. Without high quality guns, the Royal Navy's ships would have been toothless and could not have protected the established trade routes. Without the weapons to defend the trading ports in faraway parts of the Empire, the Royal Artillery would have had no need for garrison gunners. Indeed, without guns, there would have been no Empire.

While this is not the story of the Royal Dockyard in Woolwich, it is in itself a fascinating subject. It continued to produce warships throughout the Elizabethan era and, in the reign of Charles I, built the *Sovereign of the Seas*, the greatest and most successful warship of her day and by far the most expensive. She was the first warship with three full decks of guns and these

GUNPOWDER

Gunpowder, used both as an explosive and a propellant, has a long history, dating back to China towards the end of the first millennium. It did not make an appearance in Europe until the 13th century, since when it has been associated with guns, mines and fireworks. In the early days the men who used it in these forms were private individuals and were hired when needed. They were often the same people who made guns and projectiles. Even when the Tower of London began making guns in about 1370, there were still many private manufacturers.

were of particular interest, made especially for that one ship. (One of them is on display in the Regimental Museum.)

As a direct consequence of its Royal Dockyard, Woolwich began to grow in both size and stature, though its population remained tiny by comparison with today. It had very little in the way of fine buildings and remained in essence a riverside village until the middle of the 17th century, when converging factors – the government's need to remove noisy and explosive activities from larger centres of population, together with the sudden threat of Dutch naval attack – brought a significant change.

KAT

The Royal Dockyard at Woolwich was built in 1514, one year after the Deptford Yard, and closed in 1869. The yard was originally built by Henry VIII for the construction of his famous ship Harry Grace a Dieu, *known more colloquially as the* Great Harry. *The last ship to be built in this yard was HMS* Thalia.

Developments in Greenwich and the Move to Woolwich

King Charles II's cousin, Prince Rupert, an experienced campaigner both at sea and on the land, who made the first military use of the Tower House site.

By the middle of the 17th century, Greenwich had long been involved with making arms and armour, some of its most famous products being armour for Henry VIII and Charles I. As the wearing of armour died away, the workshops began to make gunpowder and associated products, like quick match for the firelocks of muskets. With the closing of the Royal Palace at Greenwich, the population became more aware of the danger in having a gunpowder mill in the middle of the town, and it was moved out to the peninsula (close to where the southern entrance to the Blackwall Tunnel is today).

By this time, the Royal Dockyard in Woolwich was well established and successful. The township lay on its eastern borders, but at this time was very small, occupying the area between the Dockyard and the Tower House estate, also known as Tower Place. This estate was somewhat run-down and, in 1667, found itself the focus of attention when the threat of a Dutch naval raid led to its becoming the site of Prince Rupert's Fort.

Prince Rupert's Fort

Rivalry between the European nations led to three Anglo-Dutch Wars during the 17th century. England had the better of the conflict in the first and third of these, but the second took place with the kingdom suffering the after-effects of the Great Fire of London and an outbreak of plague. In June 1667 a triumphant Dutch fleet sailed into the River Medway and devastated the shipping at Chatham – a feat comparable with Sir Francis Drake's famous exploit at Cadiz 80 years earlier. The Dutch then moved to the mouth of the Thames, poised to attack up the river to the heart of London.

It was the threat of such an action that led to the rapid building of a fort at Woolwich, alongside the great basin on the Thames known as Gallion's Reach. King Charles II ordered his cousin, Prince Rupert, an experienced campaigner both at sea and on the land, to carry out this task. A simple triangular-shaped embankment was hurriedly thrown up, providing platforms and embrasures for up to 60 guns. Not all of these

were trained on the entrance to the basin: some faced across the Plumstead marshland to guard against a land approach to the fort. However, the main threat lay in a strong attack up the river itself, so the bulk of the guns would have trained their fire at the point where the enemy came into view around the bend. With limited room for manoeuvre thanks to several large ships deliberately sunk in the river, and with their broadside guns facing the wrong way as they turned south, enemy warships would have made easy pickings. It was sufficient to deter attack and the fort was never put to the test.

Nonetheless, the stockaded fort had an important role in the development of Woolwich as a military town. Prince Rupert's use of the riverside gave him ample opportunity to look at suitable land on what was, at that time, a quiet stretch of the Thames. The gathering of guns and gunners at the fort with their need to train and practise encouraged the Board of Ordnance to implement plans to move some of its activities out of built-up areas nearer London.

Tower Place – also known as 'The Warren'

All this activity on the estate did nothing to enhance it as a private property and its owner was awarded damages. Shortly afterwards, it was snapped up at a bargain price – interestingly enough at a time when the Crown was beginning to survey the property's potential for development. Its new owner was William Prichard, a merchant tailor from Eltham in Kent, who was also a supplier of many commodities, including construction materials, to the Ordnance Office. In the light of what was to follow, his purchase of the estate was either a shrewd investment or an early example of 'insider trading'.

In 1671, Prichard agreed to exchange the estate's 31 acres for the Gun Wharf, which lay alongside the Royal Dockyard, plus a substantial sum of money (£2,957 – some £380,000 today). This wharf, which also housed the Ordnance storehouse, had become run down and was in need of much refurbishment. History does not relate why Prichard wanted the wharf, but it was certainly in a convenient place for a

Below: This site alongside the Royal Dockyard was where guns and munitions for warships were stored. It was exchanged by the Board of Ordnance for the site at Tower Place.

merchant using the river to trade. The storehouse at the Gun Wharf was transferred to the new site.

The Ordnance Office began soon afterwards to use the estate as an ammunition storage depot; the Master Gunner of England moved into Tower House itself, accompanied by staff from the Tower of London. It was the beginning of expansion on a site that was to become the Royal Arsenal and the first headquarters of the Royal Artillery.

One of the first new developments, in 1695, was the move of one of the Tower of London's workshops, the 'Greenwich Barn', which stood in the Tilt Yard (jousting track) of the old Royal Palace of Placentia (Greenwich). Its removal was necessary in order to facilitate the construction of the Royal Naval Hospital, and the Greenwich Barn was re-erected on the Tower House estate the following year. It remained for many years alongside the western wall of the complex of buildings that formed the Royal Laboratory, eventually being knocked down to make way for the Royal Brass Foundry in 1716.

There had been some refining of saltpetre and manufacture of fireworks on land to the south of the manor

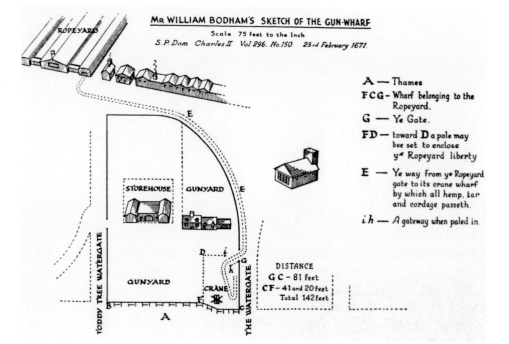

A 1701 drawing by Borgard of the site in the Warren, with Prince Rupert's Fort shown clearly as the triangular structure in the centre. The Royal Laboratory and Tower House can be seen on the lower right of the drawing, which is oriented with east at the top.

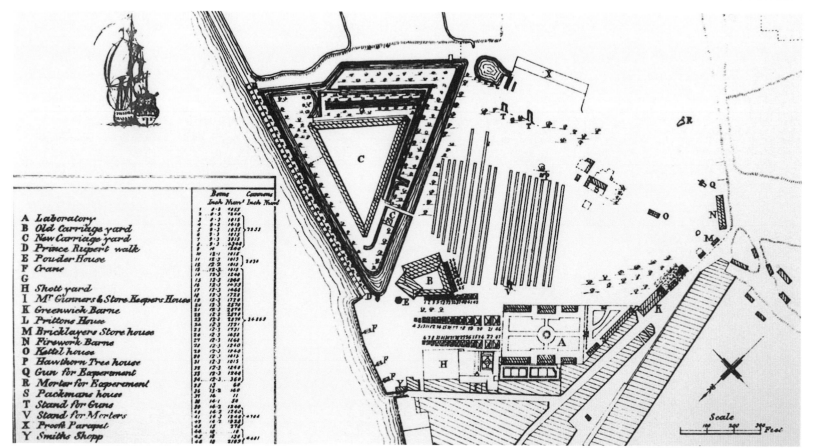

house since 1662 and this, along with fuze filling, became one of the roles of the new Royal Laboratory when it was established in 1695. Shortly afterwards, Prince Rupert's Fort found a new use as the site for repairing or scrapping old carriages. Sheds for the work were built, and the site became the 'New Carriage Yard'.

By the turn of the 18th century it was clear that everything was coming together: senior artillery figures in the Board of Ordnance had taken up residence, the Royal Laboratory was producing ammunition and there was an embryo carriage factory in being. Proof firing was well-established on the site and there were considerable storage facilities. All that was missing to make it a proper arsenal was a foundry for gun-making, but that was soon to be remedied.

The Royal Laboratory (re-founded 1696)

As part of its move out of Greenwich, the Board of Ordnance moved the laboratory known as 'the Great Barn' from the Tilt Yard of the Palace to its new site at Woolwich. The move itself reflected the Board's parsimony, saving the building materials from the laboratory and shipping them downriver to the Tower estate. Here it was re-erected alongside the new buildings which became the Royal Laboratory and the home of ammunition manufacturing for more than 250 years.

Initially based on the Greenwich Barn, the Royal Laboratory grew into a 'cottage industry' style of ammunition production, where there were Gunners deployed in the refining of saltpetre as well as the more dangerous tasks, such as fuze-filling. The Royal Laboratory was set up immediately to the south of Tower House (which later became the Royal Military Academy), its northern gate less than 40 yards from that building. Early prints show that this gate boasted the figures of a lion and a unicorn on the gateposts.

The layout consisted of two pedimented buildings (the oldest buildings on the site of the Royal Arsenal today) facing each other across a courtyard, with smaller workshop buildings alongside grouped to form an enclosed area, gated at the north and south entrances. It was an attractive site, complete with a central fountain and fine gates. Contemporary pictures show that it was also used to store ammunition that was either being filled with explosive or undergoing cleaning: the great piles of cannonballs shown in the pictures were typical of the method of storing ammunition at the time. Indeed, there were specific formulae for calculating the number of rounds stored in a pyramidal structure of this type – a piece of information that would have been part of the mathematical knowledge expected of aspiring gunners in those days and certainly part of the training of cadets at the Royal Military Academy (RMA) when it was formed in 1741.

The Royal Laboratory retained its name throughout the history of the Royal Arsenal and continued to play an important

role in the development and manufacture of ammunition. The initials 'RL' stamped on its products were a proud mark of its long history. When the RMA ceased to operate in the Royal Arsenal, the building itself was absorbed within the ammunition department and, for many years, housed the patterns for its products. Most of those patterns are now in the ammunition collection of the Royal Artillery Historical Trust and on display in the Regimental Museum.

Tower House and the Royal Military Academy Building

Although nothing remains of the original Tower House, probably built in the late 15th century, an artist's impression of the Tudor mansion, based on a floor plan drawn in 1682, gives a good idea of what it looked like. It was built as a family home, unlike its successor on the site, so it was not suitable for the purpose of the Ordnance Office and was, in due course, replaced. However, it was used initially to house officials of the Board of Ordnance, notably the Master Gunner of England who, until this point, had a house in the Minories, close to Artillery Gardens in the City of London. The first Master Gunner to live in Tower House was Richard Leake (1629–96).

The hexagonal tower from which the estate got its name was five storeys high, its open floors linked by simple ladders. It formed part of the Tudor building, though it is not clear whether it had a specific purpose. There was a similar Tudor tower at the Tilt Yard in Greenwich. Either or both may have had some sort of defensive role, perhaps acting as a watchtower to provide early warning of hostile ships sailing up the river, but there does not appear to have been an official role as such and it may have been merely the original owner's equivalent of a 'folly'. The tower was isolated from Tower House as that building was gradually pulled down and finally replaced in 1719 by the structure now known as the Old Royal Military Academy (RMA). The tower (by this time called 'the turret') remained in place for another 67 years and was demolished in 1786.

The Old RMA building is now considered to have been designed by Nicholas Hawksmoor, who had done a lot of his early work under the eye of his more famous contemporary, Sir John Vanbrugh, who is credited with the Royal Brass Foundry in the Royal Arsenal. Its main features were the two large rooms on the ground floor: on entering, the room on the left was the academy; that on the right was the Board of Ordnance committee room. The academy room was originally the same height as the Board room and may have had a gallery for observers. In 1778 the room was redesigned, with a new ceiling inserted at the level of where a gallery might have been, providing another large room above the original.

The rest of the building contained offices and some accommodation, together with two small gardens. It looked out upon an area immediately to the north of the Royal Laboratory, which was bounded by high walls and serviced by an imposing gateway. When this gateway was demolished during changes many years later, the figures of a lion and a unicorn that had stood upon the gateposts were removed and placed on the entrance to the RMA.

The Brass Foundry (built 1716–17)

The Brass Foundry was the second of the major works on the site of the embryonic arsenal. It appears to have been in the minds of the Ordnance Office for some years before, but it was brought forward by the accident that took place in the gun foundry at Moorfields on 10 May 1716. This was a brass foundry belonging to the Crown, sited at Windmill Hill in Upper Moorfields, near the modern Finsbury Square in the City of London. Cannon were cast from new metal and from old pieces no longer serviceable; at that time all pieces manufactured for the government were cast in bronze.

A drawing of the Old RMA in the early part of the 18th century, drawn by Paul Sandby, showing the tower that had characterized the original Tower House. It remained in being until it was demolished in 1786.

The Royal Brass Foundry is a Grade I listed building, designed by Vanbrugh and still in much the same condition as in its heyday. It is owned by the National Maritime Museum and used to store ship drawings. This drawing by Paul Sandby shows some of its castings lined up on the ground.

Mathew Bagley was the gun-founder at Moorfields in 1716 when it was decided to recast some of the guns captured from the French by the Duke of Marlborough. The whole procedure was one that always attracted visitors and there was a distinguished group present on the day to watch the metal poured into the moulds. Among the onlookers was the celebrated Danish-born Gunner Colonel Albert Borgard, Chief Firemaster of England, the official in charge of artillerymen, their training and their equipment.

The *Mercurius Politicus* of 18 May 1716 reported as follows:

Several gentlemen were invited to see the Metal run, which being a very great and curious Piece of Art, a great many Persons of Quality came to see it, and some General Officers of the Army among the rest; but whether it was some unusual hindrance in the Work, or their better Fate that occasioned the Metal to be longer preparing than usual, we know not, but be that as it will, the Gentlemen waiting past Ten a Clock went all or most of them away. About 11 at night the Metal being ready, was let go … the burning Metal no sooner sunk down to the Bottom of the Mould, but with a Noise and Force equal to that of gunpowder, it came pouring up again, blowing like the Mouth of a Vulcano, or a little Vesuvius. There was in the place about 20 Men, as well as Workmen as Spectators, 17 of whom were so burnt that nothing more horrible can be thought of, neither can Words describe their Misery. About 9 of the 17 are already dead, the other 8 are yet living, but in such condition that the Surgeons say they have very small hopes of above 2 of them.

Borgard himself received four wounds from this accident, which took place while casting one of his own designs. One of the failed castings was kept as an example and is now in the Regimental Museum in Woolwich.

The loss of Moorfields and Bagley was the spur to building a new foundry in Woolwich. Given the state of Europe, these were dangerous times to risk being without a secure source of guns. Building began almost immediately and the Board advertised for a founder. A 24-year-old Swiss foundryman at Douai (one of France's principal gun foundries), Andrew Schalch, answered and, after the selection process, was appointed to the post, one that he held for almost 54 years.

The design of the building has long been attributed to Vanbrugh, although no signed drawing of it by him exists: the attribution is based on his relationship with several senior members of the Board of Ordnance and a style which was unmistakably his own. Clearing space for the new building meant the demolition of the Greenwich Barn, but the work proceeded apace and, by the late spring of 1717, the building was finished and ready for the installation of its two furnaces. The finishing touch was the installation of the great stone representations of the Royal Coat of Arms and, just below them, the Arms of the Duke of Marlborough, Master General of the Ordnance. The first guns to be cast were two 24-pounders.

The Board now came to an agreement with Schalch for the continued casting of guns of all the types required and permitted him to employ the necessary staff, including as many as he could use from the marching company of the Royal Artillery. It is not clear how many became permanent artificers and the practice did not continue for long, but Gunners were certainly employed in the early years of the Royal Brass Foundry, just as they were in the Royal Laboratory.

KAT

FORMATION OF THE ROYAL ARTILLERY 1716

Fortress Artillery and Trains of Artillery

From the time of the earliest guns in the 14th century, artillery was either assembled when needed for war or was emplaced in fortresses for defence. In a fortress, the guns came under the control of master gunners, assisted by gunners and matrosses of the Ordnance Office. (Matrosses were the unskilled gunners of that period, much like a 'plumber's mate', learning his trade.) For war, guns would be assembled into either a 'field train' to support an army or a 'siege train' to batter a fortress, depending on what was required – sometimes both.

In the early days of warfare, armies were raised in an ad hoc manner, but even after the formation of regular infantry and cavalry, it was not considered necessary to provide a large regular body of artillerymen. The existing system of raising 'traynes of artillery' had been tried and proved in several campaigns, and in those days warfare was a more leisurely business, when both sides would stop fighting during the winter or in bad weather by mutual consent. This usually meant that there was plenty of time to decide whether or not to go to war, giving time to recruit the necessary manpower and to equip the troops for fighting.

However, a train of artillery was quite an undertaking, consisting not only of the weapons and men to serve them, together with troops for protection, but all the impedimenta of war – ammunition, baggage, pontoons for bridging, tentage, facilities for cooks, farriers, blacksmiths and other trades, plus of course, all the animals needed for hauling the wheeled vehicles and to provide seats for riders. For example, the train prepared for action in Ireland towards the end of 1688 included no fewer than 26 guns, 1,500 horses, 532 drivers and an enormous number of officials as well as the men to serve the guns. It was to be accompanied by the Master Gunner of England as well as the Chief Engineer, together with paymasters, commissaries, provost-marshals, firemasters, petardiers (men who handled small bombs made of wood or metal filled with gunpowder), conductors, tent-makers and so on. Given the costs, it is hardly surprising that, as soon as possible after any campaign, the trains would be disbanded, the temporary troops paid off and the equipment returned to stores.

A proportion of the men who served the guns on campaign during the four centuries leading up to the formation of the Royal Artillery came either from the infantry or as recruits, pressed into service for the duration of the war. They were licked into shape by

Colonel Albert Borgard became the first Colonel of the Royal Artillery when it was formed in 1716. By this time he was probably the most experienced artilleryman in Europe with an illustrious record of battles and sieges to add to his immense technical expertise in munitions and as a gunfounder.

the professional master gunners who together with the gunners provided by the Ordnance Office, took charge of the business of handling and firing. The others did the strenuous, but less technical tasks of moving the guns, running them up after each round fired, fetching ammunition, swabbing and loading.

Forming a train, together with the necessary training of gunners (and it is no coincidence that both words have the same root), took time as well as money. The decision to do so was not taken lightly and was a matter of high policy. As a result, a proper artillery train was not always ready for action in time, and this happened at the time the Jacobite Rebellion broke out in September 1715.

BRONZE KNOWN AS BRASS

It is worth noting that all British guns cast in bronze (a mixture of copper and tin) were called 'brass guns', although brass is actually a mixture of copper and zinc, which was the favoured metal for French guns. A gun was a piece of ordnance, which is why guns were often referred to as 'pieces'.

Right: John Churchill, Duke of Marlborough, who was Master General of the Ordnance when the Royal Artillery was founded in 1716.

Below: A painting by Joan Wanklyn showing a field train in the Low Countries. Note the drum cart in the background.

New Organization

This was not a satisfactory situation, not least because the Ordnance Office was under constant pressure to save money and reduce its costs. An analysis of these costs showed that a considerable sum was wasted each year on salaries for people who were never employed on any effective service. The Duke of Marlborough, who was Master General of the Ordnance, therefore put forward a plan for reorganizing the establishment.

This plan showed that, with a certain amount of creative accounting – mainly by a mixture of deleting posts as they fell vacant and reducing salaries of certain posts – the savings would make it possible to form two regular companies of artillerymen who would be immediately available when required for operations. The plan was approved and a Royal Warrant to this effect was issued, dated 26 May 1716, creating the Royal Artillery. These two companies were each 98 strong (including four cadets) and, although one of them was disbanded many years later in one or other of the fluctuations in the Regiment's strength, the other is still in the order of battle.

At this point, there already existed two trains of artillery, each at approximately company strength, on active service abroad in Gibraltar and at Port Mahon in Minorca, Britain's new possessions in the Mediterranean. Although they were reorganized as companies in 1717, these two establishments were not included in the new establishment of Royal Artillery until 1 April 1722, when a further reorganization took place. This then introduced the title 'Royal Regiment of Artillery', which now had a headquarters and four companies under Colonel Albert Borgard, appointed the first Colonel of the Regiment.

In addition, there existed – and remained under the plan – a considerable number of master gunners, gunners of garrisons and officers who had served abroad, the latter on half pay. The men in these posts were gradually either absorbed into the newly formed Regiment or the posts were deleted as vacancies occurred.

For the sake of clarity, we should note that the companies at this point were known as 'marching companies', not 'batteries', although their descendants were to become known by the latter title. When a company was deployed in an operational role, whether in a field or siege train, it drew the requisite guns from store or took over the guns of a fortress and 'went into battery'.

Over the years that followed, companies were grouped into larger units (battalions) for administrative purposes, but there was no grouping into operational formations until late in the 19th century. Hence the history of the Royal Artillery is still based on the histories of the individual companies (batteries). They own most of the regimental property and take great pride in maintaining their history and individual traditions.

With the formation of a regular body of artillerymen, ready to go to war as soon as necessary, it became clear that regular training would be important to ensure that these new companies were up to the job. It was particularly important to ensure that there would be a supply of new officers and in 1720 the Board proposed the foundation of an academy bases in the new Tower House.

KAT

The Royal Military Academy (RMA), Woolwich 1741–1806

There was no formal method of training in artillery matters from the time that guns first appeared in Europe until the time of Henry VIII, when 'Gunners in the Tower' had to report every Michaelmas Day (29 September) and then assemble in the Artillery Garden to prove 'their knowledge and cunning in the use of great and small ordnance'. Knowledge lay in the hands of the master gunners, like William Bourne, in 1578, whose treatise *The Arte of Shooting in Great Ordnance* is in the Royal Artillery Museum – the first such book on the subject in English. It is probable that the so-called Gunners in the Tower were those on a register of trained gunners rather than those who were permanently established. To become a registered gunner, they would have attended a school in Spitalfield Gardens (north of the Tower) headed by the Master Gunner of England with a complement of instructors.

However, training in the handling of artillery was treated essentially as a practical exercise and, while there were frequent such exercises, there was no apparent continuity of formal instruction. Little is known of this school, but it may be assumed to have continued in being until the time when the Board of Ordnance began to close down its operations in the City of London and to move them downriver to Woolwich.

Soon after the Board of Ordnance began rebuilding Tower House in 1719, a proposal was made to set up an academy to educate boys starting out on a career in the artillery and engineers, as well as to improve the minds of serving members of those arms. This was to be financed from an investment of £3,000 by the Board of Ordnance in the South Sea Company. A second Great Room was to be built, equal to that already under construction, and a salary of £100 per annum set aside for a mathematical master. Mr Burnett Godfrey, a fireworker

Right: The Academy Room in the Old RMA building in the Royal Arsenal. Note the original wall painting above the door, cut in two by the construction of another floor in 1778.

Below right: The Board Room in the Old RMA building, showing the bow window which used to have a view of the Thames and illustrating the height that was originally the same for the Academy Room, above.

Below: The cadet barracks in the Warren, showing two cadets probably saying farewells to colleagues as they prepare to leave in the coach that is loading luggage.

(specialist in the manufacture of explosives and military fireworks), was duly appointed to the task and recommended for a commission. Pending the completion of Tower House, he was given a room in the Warren barracks for the purpose of teaching mathematics to the cadets on such days and at such times as did not interfere with their service duties.

Sadly, there was a catch – certainly as far as the cadets were concerned! They were notified that they were to be stopped £4 per year from their pay, to go towards 'gratifying the said Mr Godfrey or such other officers who shall instruct them in gunnery, fortification etc.' History does not relate the details of what followed, but it is certain that this early academy was not a success and it fell into disuse. However, the Board of Ordnance clearly felt that there was a need for proper education in the various sciences connected with ordnance because, on 30 April 1741, a Royal Warrant was granted to form a military academy in Woolwich.

The stated aim of this new institution was 'to form good Officers of Artillery and perfect Engineers' – a strange choice of adjectives with which to differentiate the two corps! (It is, of course, possible that it means 'to perfect Engineers', which is quite different.) Moreover, the students for instruction were to be 'all practitioner Engineers, Officers, Sergeants, Corporals and Cadets of the Royal Artillery not upon duty' and 'all such Bombardiers, Miners, Pontoonmen, Mattrosses and others … as have a capacity and inclination to the same'.

In other words, the new academy was to consist of students drawn from across the spectrum of the ordnance corps. One can imagine the difficulty of finding some level from which to begin instructing such a diverse range of students, and it is hardly surprising that a veil is drawn over the early years of this venture. That it had not been a success is evident from the decision in 1744 to form a new company of gentleman cadets (GCs), grouping together the cadets who were part of the establishment of the seven RA companies that had been formed by that time. This new company became a separate unit, with a captain, three lieutenants, a drum major and 40 GCs (shortly afterwards increased to 48).

CADET MEALS IN 1765

Meals were provided by a staff usually headed by the widow of an artillery officer. In addition to her small salary, she received an allowance of nine pence to feed each cadet. To supplement this, the cadet paid one shilling a day out of his pay of 2s 6d per day.

Breakfast: bread and milk, milk porridge or water gruel

Dinner: Sundays – roast veal, fillets or shoulders with potatoes or greens
Mondays – roast leg of mutton and potatoes
Tuesdays – shoulder of mutton and apple pie
Wednesdays – buttocks of beef and greens
Thursdays – roast leg of mutton with salad and pickles
Fridays – boiled mutton and greens
Saturdays – roast beef with greens or potatoes

Supper: bread and cheese (five nights) and bread and butter (two nights), or cold meat when left at dinner

Michaelmas (29 September): roast goose!

A drawing showing Gentleman Cadets in a typical bedroom at the RMA.

They had no barracks at this time and were lodged in the town – a recipe for indiscipline, since they could do as they pleased when off duty. During these early years, it seems that lectures in the Academy continued to be attended by others from the list nominated in the original Warrant: contemporary reports speak of young officers turning classes into a bear garden and their disorderly behaviour setting a bad example to the cadets.

In 1752 the cadet company was moved into barracks especially built for it in the Warren, which made some slight improvement to the discipline, but GCs were still allowed too much liberty and there were too many distractions. Drafts of

cadets could be sent on foreign service with the artillery, and the cadet company's numbers included those in other parts of the country and overseas as well as those in Woolwich – hardly a basis for a properly organized course of instruction.

In addition, there was no set length of time for a GC to be under instruction. This had its roots in the extraordinary range of ages in cadets nominated for the Academy. Nominations could be made only by the Master General of the Ordnance, to whom all applications had to be made. If no vacancies existed at the Academy, a candidate could either study at Woolwich as a 'gentleman attendant' or remain at home until one occurred.

ARTILLERY TRAINING IN THE 16TH CENTURY

Extract from unpublished notes by Adrian Caruana, formerly Curator of Ordnance, Chatham Historic Dockyard

One has to rely upon hints, clues, circumstantial and other evidence, none of which is complete. However, so far as it is possible to tell, the system appears to have been as follows. There was a school of artillery, instituted by Henry VIII, controlled by the Master of the Ordnance, at the Artillery Garden in Spitalfields. This was directly controlled by the Master Gunner of England, but he could be taken away for other duties, so there must have been a small cadre of instructors. To this school were admitted those who wished to become gunners. They must have been literate, and from the continual harping on the need for it in handbooks, they must have had some basic knowledge of mathematics. When they successfully completed their course of instruction they were basically free to pursue other callings, but went on to a register of trained gunners. They were required to report to the Artillery Garden at various times, probably on quarter days, when they received retaining fees and demonstrated that they were still capable of carrying out professional duties. Whenever there was a vacancy in the very small permanent establishment, either on land or sea, or when there was a need to produce the ordnance component of an army, they were either detailed or volunteered for the position: if the latter, a 'sufficient and able' man or men would be chosen from the volunteers.

This system provided Master Gunners, Gunners, and 'servitor gunners' (later, matrosses), for the Trains of Artillery. Initially, the Train was commanded by a Master of the Ordnance — not the main one in London, who increasingly frequently was a 'Great Personage', but the 'Master of the Ordnance for the North Parts [of the Realm]' or the Master of the Artillery', or the 'Master of the Ordnance at Berwick' or some such. According to Sir Thomas Audley's *Treatise on the Art of War*, c.1550, the terms 'Master of the Ordnance' and 'Master of the Artillery' were synonymous (Bodleian Library, Oxford). The Master had under him his Lieutenant, Conductors, Gentlemen Attendant and the Master Gunner, Cannoners and Artificers (ibid). Colonel Cleaveland's 18th-century notes tend to give the impression that the Master of the Ordnance and the Master Gunner were the same person, but this was not the case: the former was the Commander of the Train, and the latter the technical expert on guns, ammunition, shooting and powder.

The Gentlemen Attendant were junior officers, to some extent under training, and not yet sufficiently knowledgeable to be the Lieutenant of the Train, who was very much second in command or commanding officer in waiting. This meant that in fact the Master could be less knowledgeable, but of the necessary social rank to take his place with the nobility and gentry who were expected and, in fact, did command armies. When this was the case, the Master had to learn very fast, since the responsibility was his: but it became increasingly common for him to be a knight, at least.

THE UNIFORM OF THE ROYAL ARTILLERY

A Gunner and Officer in the uniform of c.1750.

When soldiers were quartered in the Warren, it was as follows:

The uniform dress of the officers was a plain blue coat, lined with scarlet, a large scarlet Argyle cuff, double-breasted; and with yellow buttons to the bottom of the skirts; scarlet waistcoat and breeches – the waistcoat trimmed with broad gold lace – and a gold-laced hat. The sergeants' coats were trimmed, the lapels, cuffs and pockets with a broad single gold lace; the corporals' and bombardiers' with a narrow single gold lace; the gunners' and matrosses' plain blue coats; all the non-commissioned officers and men having scarlet half-lapels, scarlet cuffs and slashed sleeves with five buttons, and blue waistcoats and breeches; the sergeants' hats trimmed with a broad, and the other non-commissioned officers' and mens' with a narrow gold lace. White spatterdashes [gaiters] were then worn. The regimental clothing was delivered to the non-commissioned officers and men once a year, with the exception of regimental coats, which they only received every second year; receiving in the intermediate year a coarse blue loose surtout [wide-skirted overcoat] which served for laboratory work, cooking, fatigue duties etc.

Captain Francis Duncan, History of the Royal Regiment of Artillery, Vol. 1 To the Peace of 1783 (London: John Murray, 1872)

Since there were no regulations fixing the age for nominations, these ranged from under ten to as much as 30.

Instruction at the Academy was divided into theory, for which there were two masters, and practical, which came under the military authorities within the Warren. During the early years, the two masters were responsible for teaching on three days of the week, one in the morning from 8 to 11 am, the other in the afternoon from 3 to 6 pm. Although it is not stated in the record, it seems probable that this meant that three hours of theory was complemented by six hours of practical work on any given day, with one hour for lunch.

The theory subjects were mainly mathematics – arithmetic, algebra, geometry, trigonometry, practical geometry and mechanics – but included Latin, French, drawing and fortification. The practical instruction included gunnery, siege work, the mechanics of moving heavy burdens, manufacture of guns and gunpowder, bridging, how to manage stores and practical work in building fortifications.

In 1764 the first Lieutenant Governor was appointed: Lieutenant Colonel James Pattison RA. His 13 years in charge meant important changes to the regime at the RMA, including an entry standard to stop the practice of sending young children and to make it easier to teach cadets. Subjects like chemistry, fencing and dancing were added to the syllabus, but the one improvement that could have made a significant difference – organized recreation to occupy

This plate shows Gentleman Cadets in the uniforms of the RMA at the end of the 18th century.

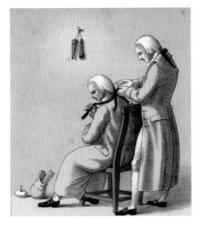

EXPANSION AND LIFE IN THE WARREN IN THE 18TH CENTURY

The Warren was an attractive place in the early 18th century. None of the modern noise of traffic or machinery would have spoiled the peaceful site, where the Ordnance Office had taken pains to plant trees and improve the estate. True, there were days when proof-firing of guns upset the peace, but it was not an everyday occurrence.

There was plenty to do. The newly formed Royal Artillery continued to carry out tasks that had been the lot of their predecessors, working in the Royal Laboratory on fuze-filling, cleaning shot, refining saltpetre, supervising proof. There were also guard duties to do, protecting the site from pilfering as well as tours of duty at the Landguard Fort (Harwich), and at Sheerness, downriver from Woolwich. There was always work to be done in the ordnance stores, which were the largest in England at that time.

The original two companies were probably quite comfortably accommodated in the barracks that were built for them in the Warren, but the increase in numbers that followed the developing need for troops soon led to overcrowding. A fifth company was formed in 1740, with two more in rapid succession, bringing the total to seven companies by 1743.

Three more were added in 1743, with the War of the Austrian Succession, a further two in 1747 and another in 1748, making a total of 13 companies (plus the Cadet Company, formed in 1744). These were not all in the Warren, of course – they were formed for overseas duties – but the general trend of expanding numbers still had its effect on overcrowding.

By the middle of the 18th century, conditions in the barracks had become appalling. The buildings were not well maintained and suffered from dirt and vermin. The bedsteads swarmed with bugs: the soldiers' usual recourse was to put them onto a fire to kill the vermin. It is not surprising that the bedsteads themselves often became unusable. The contractor responsible for clearing the cesspits often failed to do his job properly, so that they overflowed and the Warren acquired a reputation for being an unhealthy place.

As early as 1720, the Board had given some thought to providing for the sick and a simple 'Infirmary' was set up. By 1740, with the increase in numbers and the return of sick men from overseas, it was clear that a larger hospital was needed. One of the older barns was requisitioned for the purpose, but it was another case of 'too little, too late': the one nurse allotted to the task worked under intolerable conditions, reporting on 'the badness of her dwelling place … a dark gloomy hole offensive from the smell of vermin'. In 1756 the RA commander Colonel William Belford reported that the infirmary was unfit for the reception of sick men and urgent plans were produced for a new infirmary, which opened the following year. Shortly afterwards, the infirmary had a cold bath installed – the first bath in the Warren!

In 1774, the Surgeon-General declared that a hot bath would be of great benefit to the officers and men of the Royal Artillery and his proposal was agreed. Curiously, the site for this bath was to be the Surgeon-General's garden.

It was not long after this that, with further improvements and repairs required, the Board decided to put the money into the new hospital being built close to the new barracks. The new bath was removed from the Surgeon-General's garden and placed in the new hospital, erected in 1780 as part of the overall task of building the new RA Barracks. This hospital was later to become part of Connaught Barracks and remained in being as an infirmary until the Herbert Hospital was built after the Crimean War.

The expansion of the Royal Artillery throughout the 18th century was the direct result of the national need for troops to cope with the amount of campaigning overseas. By 1779 there were 32 service companies and 10en invalid companies. Invalid companies were made up of Gunners deemed unfit for overseas service, but fit enough to serve the guns in the fixed fortifications. Of the service companies, 28 were abroad, such was the demand for artillery. Even some of the invalid companies were sent overseas to supplement the effort.

juvenile high spirits – was not included in the RMA's syllabus until almost 100 years later.

The students were divided into two classes, a Lower and an Upper Academy, and cadets were kept in the Lower until they were 15 or were able to prove by examination their ability to enter the Upper Academy. Commissions were granted as vacancies occurred, but again depended on passing an examination. This meant appearing before a board of officers and answering questions orally. Standards varied over the years, usually driven by the need for officers in time of war. Throughout the period up until the end of the Napoleonic Wars in 1815, there were times when the need for officers to fill hastily formed units overcame the need for proper standards. This led to ill-discipline and idleness among GCs who saw little need to make an effort when a commission seemed so easy to obtain.

During the latter part of the 18th century, the continuing expansion of Britain's interests overseas and its involvement in campaigns against its competitors led to an increase in the size of the ordnance corps and the expansion of the manufacturing facilities in The Warren. Space became a problem and, in turn, this led the Board of Ordnance to separate the two sides of its responsibilities, moving the military out of the town centre to the high ground surrounding Woolwich Common. The Royal Artillery moved first, with the RMA following suit in 1806.

KAT

A Gunner stands guard outside the gates at the northern end of the Royal Laboratory. Rows of gun barrels lie on the ground and great pyramids of shells (these are too big to be cannonballs) are stacked awaiting shipment.

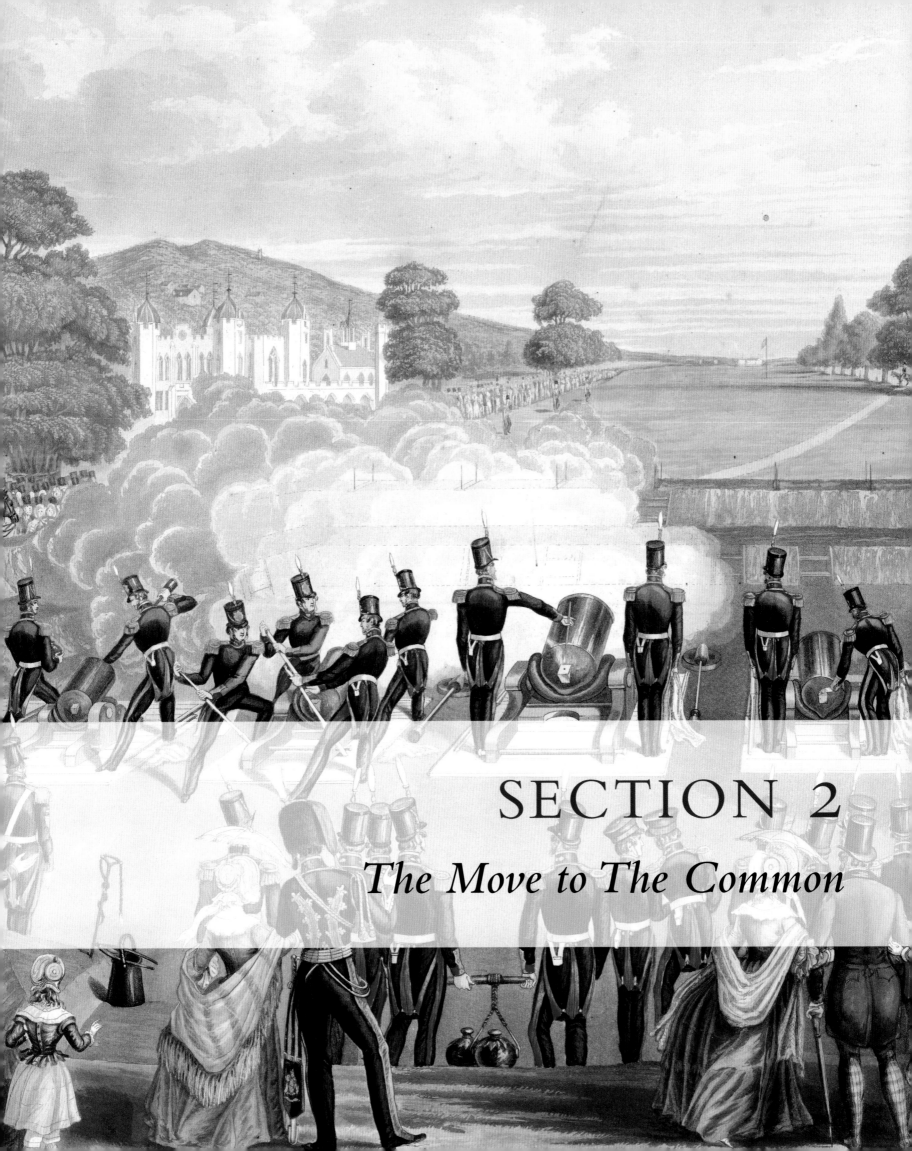

SECTION 2

The Move to The Common

THE ROYAL ARTILLERY BARRACKS 1772–1803

Based on research by The Rev. Dr Michael Gilman

The story of the building of the Royal Artillery (RA) Barracks can be found in considerable detail in the Minutes of the Board of Ordnance, held by the National Archives at Kew, Surrey. These include progress of the various stages of the project, the fitting out, the personnel responsible for different aspects of the work and, by inference, something of the life and working conditions of the soldiers and workmen employed. This article can only provide a flavour of the story, but it may help to give a picture of the events leading to the completion of what was for over 200 years the home of the Regiment. (Quotations in italics throughout this article are from Board of Ordnance Minute Books.)

It was at a meeting of the Board on 28 September 1772 that the Surveyor General was requested to give direction for preparing plans and estimates for building a barracks to contain one battalion of artillery 'without [i.e. outside] the Warren at Woolwich'. Since the Board had already acquired rights to the use of both Charlton and Woolwich commons for artillery practice, it had approached a Mr Edward Bowater, who owned some of the land bordering Woolwich Common. It was agreed that Dr Pollock, the Professor of Fortification at the Royal Military Academy, should carry out the survey.

This survey took in a large tract of land, but concentrated on some 20 acres of fields owned by Bowater north of Woolwich Common and a lease was agreed in March 1773. Planning for the building itself began in July, when the Minutes record:

> *Ordered that the Surveyor General be desired to give the necessary directions for making Plans and Elevations for the intended Barracks at Woolwich … And that the Master Carpenter and Master Bricklayer have notice to prepare materials.*

There appears to have been no special selection of an architect for the barracks, which suggests that they were to be designed to a simple, standard pattern, unlike the New RMA, built a few years later next to Woolwich Common by a well-known architect, James Wyatt.

The bricklayer chosen, John Groves, suggested that the bricks for the new building be made of clay dug on the site,

being a cheaper alternative to bricks brought in from elsewhere. This was agreed and work began immediately: by December, Groves reported that some £10,000 had been spent, which suggests a considerable stockpile of building materials.

However, it was not until the following June (1774) that the Board appointed a Mr Latimer to be the overseer in building the New Barracks, and gave instructions for proceeding as soon as possible. This initial delay may well have been caused by the discovery that the foundations of the first site chosen were unsuitable and building had to be moved 600ft 'further in front'. This must have meant 'to the South', since northwards lay a steep slope down to the Thames. It seems likely that the problem was the Mulgrave Pond, which later became incorporated in the grounds of the Garrison Commander's house. Mr Latimer

EXTRACTS FROM THE MINUTES AND LETTER BOOKS OF THE BOARD OF ORDNANCE (PART 1, 1774–7)

The Minutes record a catalogue of minor decisions connected with the building work, almost always illustrating the Board's concern to save money and therefore to examine any request that would lead to additional cost. They include such things as:

- The appointment of a watchman, armed with a Sea Service musket, to deter thieving from the site. *(August 1774)*

- '*The General and Field Officers at Woolwich suggest that the 12 lower rooms in the Soldiers' Newe Barracks should have chimnies* [sic] – *the rooms are little use without them in the winter.*' They were told to make their suggestion to the Overseer (Mr Latimer), who was to give his opinion and state the cost. The following week it was reported that Mr Latimer approved and that the cost of taking down the walls already built and rebuilding with the proper flues would be £70. This was agreed. *(March 1775)*

- The barracks to be roofed in Westmorland slate instead of clay tiling, at an additional cost of £500. The labour costs for the completion of 20 cesspools are noted. *(May 1775)*

- '*That Mr Latimer be acquainted that a Cupola is to be erected for a Bell and provision made in the pediment for a Clock, and that Mr Thwaites (clockmaker) attend the Board on Wednesday next.*' Mr Thwaites proposed '*a strong 30-hour clock to strike the hours and quarters*', at a cost of £68. This was agreed, and the Board also ordered a 3cwt (152.4kg) bell. *(October 1775)*

- The kitchens to be redesigned, the space behind the soldiers' barracks to be thrown into one yard, the cheapest glass to be used in the windows, there was to be no ornament on the water cisterns and the strongest but cheapest pumps were to be used. *(April 1776)*

- Locks and hinges were discussed and it was agreed that these should be supplied '*as are usual for the Officers' Barracks*' and were to be the same as those used at Chatham. *(June/August 1776)*

- Coal to be provided for the airing of the New Barracks: Mr Cockburn, the Barrack master, requested bedding and utensils for 18 rooms. *(September 1776)*

- Although the New Barracks would not be ready to receive the Troops the following week and the bedding should therefore be held back, the Board agreed to Major Tovey's request for tables and chairs for the Officers' apartments in the Right Wing of the New Barracks. *(11 October 1776)*

- Major Tovey, having requested ten lamps for the Barracks, proposed to dispose of them thus:

  1 at each corner of the Barracks in front

  1 at each of the inner angles of the Officers' Pavillions, to light the front of the Officers' Guard and Mess Room

  1 over each of the barrack doors allotted to the soldiers

  1 at each angle of the Wall in the rear incompassing the Barracks

  1 on the centre of the Wall in the rear of the Barracks

- '*Centinel* [sic] *Boxes were much wanted and also Sheds for in the Soldiers' Barrack Yard for the Men to clean the White Waistcoats … also … Dust Holes in the Yards of the Officers' Pavillion.*' *(January 1777)*

- The theft of 7cwt (355.6kg) of lead from the roofs of the dust holes in the Soldiers' Barrack Yard was reported. *(April 1777)*

A drawing of the RA Barracks c.1840, showing in the centre foreground the earthwork that surrounded the mortar battery position.

appears to have had a free rein to proceed with the work, though anything – no matter how small – that touched on unforeseen cost was brought to the Board's attention.

At this initial stage, the Barracks were to consist of what, today, is the eastern half of the RA Barracks. Nonetheless, the design was symmetrical, which accounts for the double symmetry of the Front Parade as it evolved with the completion of the western half.

Although there is no daily account of the building, the subject arose at almost every Board meeting over the following years until the project was complete. Much of the detail was trivial – surprisingly so for such a high-level body of senior members of the Board – but that reflects the constant pressure to keep costs down at a time when the nation was heavily involved in military expenditure to cope with its growing expansion overseas. The extracts shown with this article are included to provide examples of the kinds of subjects dealt with by the Board.

By January 1777, after pressure from the Board, which demanded 'utmost expedition', the New Barracks were almost ready for occupation, but there continued to be necessary works to be carried out and problems over supplies of furniture

and accessories, not helped by the endless task of replacing items lost or stolen. The bedding that arrived in February had to be stored somewhere, but there was nowhere in the Warren to do so and the Barrack Master was told to hire a room. By the end of the month he had found only one room in Woolwich, in a public house. Since this would cost £20 per annum plus taxes, the Board ordered him to take care of the bedding as best he could, until a room could be found. In March 1777 Lieutenant General William Belford, in command of The Warren, reported that the New Barracks, 'through the inclemency of the weather, continued extremely Damp', but he asked that officers' wives, whose husbands would be entitled to an apartment, be allowed to live there and be given an allowance of coals and candles. The Board was still being careful with money and refused, but gave orders to air the unoccupied rooms. The Board also refused permission for a new stable close to the Adjutant's office to be constructed 'to prevent his horse standing out in all weathers when he has business at the Barracks'. The following month, it did agree to the construction of a chimney in the Orderly Room, but the spirit of parsimony is evident in its decision to make use of old timber stored at the Tower House, 'where salvageable', for work in the Barracks.

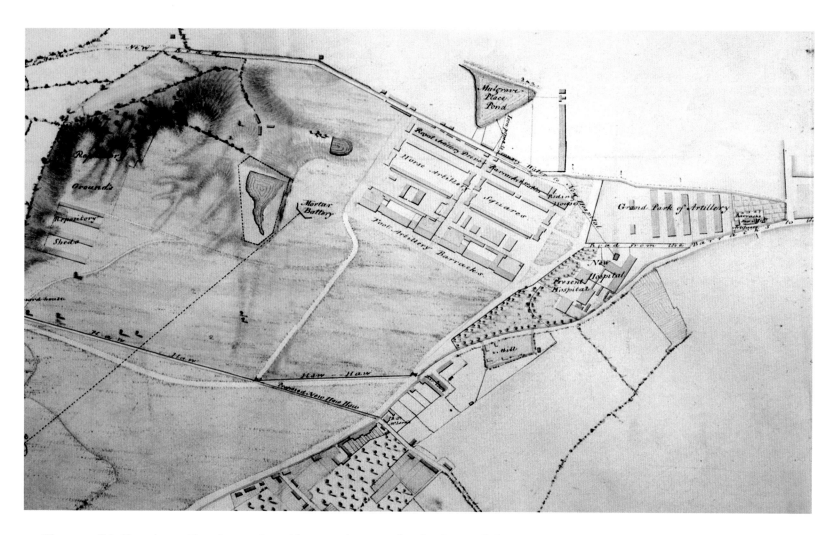

The story of the Barracks would not be complete without reference to what seems to have been an almost continuous problem with the provision of coal for both heating and cooking. Since it mostly came by collier from Newcastle upon Tyne and was vulnerable to losses at sea, deliveries were often late and quality was variable. In view of the amount consumed, it is not surprising that disposal of ashes was a major problem. Disposal was a matter of using the quaintly-named 'dust holes' that appear again and again in the Board's Minutes.

These 'dust holes' equate to modern refuse/garbage areas, where rubbish would collect until it was removed in cartloads by contractors. Much of the 'dust' was cinders and ash from the myriad fireplaces in the Barracks, and it was disposed of at sites like the Great Dust Heap, which was a mountainous heap on the land in London that later became King's Cross Station. (This site was reputed to have existed since the time of the Great Fire of London: after long accumulation, it was eventually exported to Russia for making bricks to rebuild Moscow, following Napoleon's burning of that city.)

In October 1777 the Board ordered Mr Latimer to make a plan and estimate for building a hospital and surgeon's apartment at the New Barracks, though work did not start until the following May.

The ha-ha (ditch with a wall on its inner side below ground level) that gave its name to Ha Ha Road, which runs along the southern boundary of today's sports fields, protected the Barrack fields from incursion by cattle on the Common. It appears to have been built in 1777 although it does not appear on plans for the Barracks until the turn of the century. The ha-ha (in those days

known as a 'haw haw') originally had a dog-leg cutting across where the tennis courts are today (see map), but this was amended to the present line early in the 19th century. It may have been constructed by convicts from the prison hulks on the Thames, who were also employed in the brickfields: the Minutes in July record a request for a shed to give shelter for the workmen and convicts at Woolwich, 'who have been very much exposed to Heavy Rains'.

In the same month, Mr Latimer was ordered to complete the New Barracks by papering the rooms and laying brick floors in the lower rooms. Shortly afterwards, he was instructed to pave the kitchens in Purbeck stone and to put boards – not brick – floors in the soldiers' rooms. All this was to be done while the men were away on duty at the Landguard Fort in Essex, protecting the east coast port of Harwich.

Part of the Board of Ordnance map of 1806, showing the RA Barracks, with the Repository on the left and the barracks to hold the 'Grand Park of Artillery' on the right. Note that the RA Barracks were divided into Foot Artillery, Horse Artillery and RA Drivers.

Rushgrove House lies beside the Mulgrave Pond and was built at the same time as the RA Barracks as the house of the Barracks Master. It later became the official residence of the Garrison Commander: this picture was taken by Brig David Hodge, the last officer to live in it before it was disposed of by the MOD.

In October 1777 alterations included switching the Adjutant's Office and the Corporals' Orderly Room, providing a shed to be built against the boundary wall to shelter guns and stores in inclement weather and to fix an oven in the kitchen belonging to the Mess Rooms. Ground was not to be appropriated for gardens until the likely location of any new buildings was known.

During that autumn there were a lot of other minor alterations, showing that the Board continued to take a keen interest in detailed items such as: *'Each room in the New Barracks has a Coal Tub and a Dust Tub, but the Men use the Coal Tub for Dust, and the Dust Tub to salt their meat, hence this is sometimes called a Beef Tub.'* It is not recorded where they put their coal or why they would be storing their own meat and therefore needing to salt it. In December, it was agreed that 288 earthenware chamber pots be ordered: one wonders how the men had managed until this point.

In addition, the Minutes continue to record the minutiae of expenditure submitted as the Storekeeper's Account, indicating that even these details were scrutinized by the Board on a regular basis. These include such items as:

Dr Pollock's Postage	1777	—£2 2s
Professor Hutton	"	—£2 2s
Mr Killick, taking away ashes etc	"	—£2
Labourer's work at the New Barracks	November '77	—£55 1s 3d
"	December '77	—£21 9s 9d
"	January '78	—£13 9s 2d
Richard Sumpter, for the Clock		—£1 3s

Of particular interest, given the period, is a letter dated 1 April 1778 from the Office of Ordnance at Woolwich, which says:

'Your letter of yesterday by Express did not come to us till half past One, though dispatched from the Post Office at half past Ten, and received by the Express at 11 o'clock: this has often happened and should be complained of.' (How would today's postal system compare?)

In the same month, a letter from the Office of Ordnance acknowledged receipt at the New Barracks of: '*30 pairs of Bellows, 60 Cans, 60 Ladles, 120 Elm Platters, 360 ditto Spoons, 360 Trenchers, 30 Bushel Baskets strong, 30 Coal Boxes, 180 Barrack Bedsteads – New Pattern, 78 Iron Pots with wooden covers, 48 Bails, 60 Trivets, 30 Flesh Forks.*'

An important record in the Board Minutes of 19 June 1778 reads: *'Ordered that Mr Latimer attend on Wednesday with the Plans of the Field Officers' Houses, the proposed situation to be described, with a view to the other Half Barracks being finished.'* The decision had clearly been taken to build the western half of the RA Barracks.

By 1780 the New Hospital had been occupied and a nurse employed. The great increase in the number of sick soon led to the employment of a second nurse. The Surgeon General reported that the water from Mr Latimer's pump was far better than that from any of the springs in the area and he was instructed to continue to supply water to the hospital. The Board of Ordnance map in 1806 shows water being piped from the Mulgrave Pond to the hospital, but it is not recorded whether this was a change of plan. The hospital was the large building at the entrance to what later became Connaught Barracks, immediately to the east of the RA Barracks, and remained in being as a hospital until it was superseded by the Herbert Hospital on Shooters Hill. (It was used for many years after the Second World War for the offices of the RA Charitable Fund, which moved to the RMA when Connaught Barracks were sold for development.)

The work on a house for the Barrack Master was reported as nearly finished, but the lower part was under water: it is not certain, but this was almost certainly Rushgrove House, the house built next to the Mulgrave Pond and which later became the Garrison Commander's tied quarter (see picture).

In due course, the second half of the Barracks was completed, doubling the amount of accommodation available and enabling the Board to complete the move out of the barracks in the Warren. All that remained in the Warren at the turn of the 19th century was the RMA and the Royal Military Repository: these were to move shortly afterwards to their respective positions on the slopes of Shooters Hill and to a site some 400 yards south west of the Barracks.

Information on the building of the second half of the barracks is scant, and it may be that the long period between the completion of the two phases was taken up in the building of the Grand Depot barracks for the Royal Engineers and the military stores, but this is conjecture. It seems that buildings were occupied as they became available, so perhaps there was no need for deadlines. However, there was certainly a considerable spurt in building at the beginning of 1802, when two Clerks of Works and two Overseers were appointed for work on new buildings. This was a substantially larger supervisory body than was employed in 1774 when building work began at the New Barracks and may have been in response to a push for completion.

We can only be sure that the second half was not begun before 1788, the date of a plan that shows the land on the western side of the first set of buildings. This shows Bowater's Farm still on land that would overlap the west wing of the barracks and no sign of building work or preparation for the second phase. The earliest surviving plan to show the completed New Barracks was drawn for the Board of Ordnance in 1806, showing its lands in Woolwich. This shows the Barracks with a front of about 1,000ft, two squares behind, and with accommodation for both Foot and Horse Artillery. This map shows that the accommodation block nearest the Charlton Road was allocated to the Corps of RA Drivers, with a large riding school in the north east corner of the Barracks which housed the Riding Establishment when that was formed in 1803.

The two large 'squares' – an odd name since they were long rectangles – were named after the Master Generals extant at the time of their construction, Charles, 3rd Duke of Richmond and Lennox, and John, 2nd Earl of Chatham, and their respective coats of arms are said to have been shown in cartouches on either side of the South Arch, though they have long since disappeared.

With the Royal Artillery established in new barracks and the development of the Grand Depot, there was little change over the next two decades. Apart from any other consideration, the Board of Ordnance had its hands full with the war against Napoleon. However, with peace coming at last in 1815, there were soon new attractions in Woolwich, not least the rapid developments taking place in the Royal Arsenal, where the new technologies and production methods were becoming the focus of attention from around the world. (The Warren was renamed as the Royal Arsenal following a visit by King George III in 1805.)

As Britain recovered gradually from the aftermath of its long war with France, its confidence returned and, with King William IV on the throne from 1830, there was a new spirit abroad in Woolwich and its garrison began to grow.

The Royal Military Repository (founded 1788)

The original intention of the Royal Military Academy was to provide an artillery education for the whole of the Ordnance Corps. Everyone who was not on duty elsewhere and who had an aptitude for learning was to be given the opportunity to attend the Academy and increase his knowledge. The idea had not been thought through properly: the mix of students was too wide for any viable class and after a few years the Academy became a school for cadets.

Nonetheless, a school for the rest of the Regiment remained an ambition and eventually came to fruition when a brilliant young artillery officer returned from the American War of Independence, wounded in action in 1776. Captain William Congreve was anxious to get back to the campaign, but the Master General found a better use for his talents, setting up a new school of artillery under a Royal Warrant in 1788.

Top left: One of the drawings in a small book containing images of artillery practice. This one shows a gun being hauled up a sheer cliff face after a beach landing, using a pole wedged in a gun carriage to hold a pulley.

Above: A portrait owned by the Congreve family, showing Captain Wm Congreve with his son, William, who was later Superintendent of the Royal Laboratory and inventor of the Congreve Rocket System. In the background of the picture are Gunners at work on 'Repository exercises.'

A drawing from a Congreve notebook illustrating direct fire from a cannon against the walls of a fortress while a mortar is lofting shells over the walls.

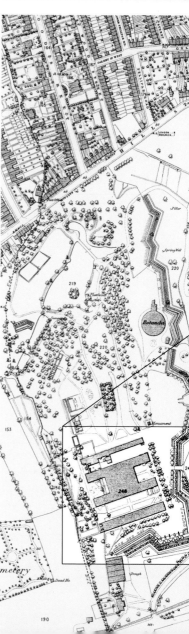

Another Congreve drawing showing how a light battalion gun could be carried for short distances when it was not possible to use horses. Many of his ideas sprang from practical experience in the War of American Independence.

element in developing the Royal Artillery's battlefield skills and flexibility. A glance at some of the drawings on these pages will show his methods. Congreve himself moved on to more important posts, reaching the rank of lieutenant general and being awarded a baronetcy, but his role in setting the Repository on the right course was a significant step along the way.

There is no known record of whereabouts in the Warren Congreve had his Repository, but in addition to classrooms capable of holding up to 100 students, it had facilities for practical work and a collection of guns and models for use in teaching the principles. It is this collection that formed the core of the Board of Ordnance museum, later known as the Museum of Artillery in the Rotunda.

The Repository had a chequered life in the Warren, but its success as a school was such that there was no question of abandoning it when the Regiment moved to new barracks on the Common. Following a disastrous fire in the Warren in May 1802, the Repository was gutted, with the loss of much valuable teaching material. A suitable site was immediately acquired close by the new Barracks and the Royal Military Repository was reopened there in 1803. The site was roughly 700 yards in length and some 250 yards wide. It held a complex of four large 'sheds', each approximately 300 x 50 feet, providing ample space for training. The configuration changed over the years, even growing slightly, and remained a large facility well into the Victorian era.

Congreve was charged with the founding of a teaching establishment in the Warren, to be called the Royal Military Repository. This was to develop the knowledge and understanding of artillery and became, in effect, the first School of Artillery and, coincidentally, the foundation of the RA Museum.

Not only an experienced officer with siege and field campaigning under his belt, Congreve was also an excellent teacher and a man with good ideas. He brought together a deep understanding of the problems faced by artillery in difficult conditions and a sound, practical knowledge of how to overcome them.

Congreve's 'Repository Exercises' became famous and his ingenuity in the handling of artillery was to become a major

Below: A map c.1860 showing the Royal Military Repository. Note the fortification that extends for the entire length of the Repository grounds, used for teaching both construction and destruction in siege warfare.

A portrait of Lt Gen Sir William Congreve, who founded the Royal Military Repository in the Warren, the first purpose-designed School of Artillery.

The school had several acres of rough ground and ponds alongside, part of a wooded area dividing Woolwich from Charlton and known in those days as 'Hanging Woods'. These provided ample opportunity for all types of exercises, including bridging and rafting, and were used both by the serving Regiment and the RMA.

The 1864 Ordnance Survey map shows that the entire length of the eastern side of the Repository, some 600 yards, was fortified with steep banking and gun embrasures. Since the subject of fortification was still being taught, it seems probable that these were the works that were constantly being demolished and rebuilt by students, both from the Barracks and from the RMA. A small part of the fortification remains, close to the Rotunda, but the remainder has long been demolished. For well over 50 years, the Repository flourished as the Regiment's official school of artillery. It had all the necessary space and facilities for teaching the gunnery of that period, though the lack of a safe firing range for the larger guns was always a problem. Shooting on the Common was becoming less and less an option as the century progressed and the population in the area grew.

The need for better ranges for practice led to the development of the firing range at Shoeburyness, on the north shore of the Thames estuary, in the early part of the 19th century, and in 1859 a decision was taken to move the School of Artillery there. The Repository continued to provide a training facility, both for the Garrison and for the 'Shop', but firing no longer took place in Woolwich.

Hanging Woods were used until the end of the 20th century for physical training, providing facilities for assault courses and 'command task' training, but it is now best known for its fishing lake and is no longer in the hands of the military.

The grounds that had for so long held the Repository were used after the Second World War for many years by the drawing offices of the Quality Assurance Directorate, but in turn these gave way to the new garage and office facilities provided for 16th Air Defence Regiment RA when it became the first operational unit to be stationed in the Royal Artillery Barracks after the demise of 17th Training Regiment RA.

At the southern end of the Repository grounds is a gatehouse, now in private hands. This guarded the entrance to Repository Road and the Barrack Field: the road is still Ministry of Defence property. In the days of the RA Drag Hunt the gatehouse was where feral foxes were kept in cages to provide the necessary scent for the hunt.

The Formation of the Royal Horse Artillery in 1793 and the Field Batteries

Major Denis Rollo

Below right: Charles Lennox, 3rd Duke of Richmond and Lennox, by George Romney. The Duke was Master General of the Ordnance at the time of the founding of the Royal Horse Artillery and took a close interest in all aspects of its equipment and organization.

Below: The original uniform of the Royal Horse Artillery, which gave way to the one now more widely known and still worn by The King's Troop RHA.

The early drawings of the Royal Artillery Barracks in Woolwich reflect the thinking of the period in the labels given to them, particularly in the case of 'The Foot Artillery', used to differentiate one part of the buildings from 'The Royal Horse Artillery' part. The Regiment today is structured so differently that it is worth exploring how the change came about.

Prior to 1793 the Royal Artillery was essentially a pool of skilled artillerymen from which groups could be drawn to man the field batteries of an army or to man fortress guns. The very word 'detachment' to describe the men who manned a gun is significant, as these men were detached from the main body of the Regiment. Although companies were known by the name of the current commander (e.g. Pattison's Company), there were no units of artillery with a permanent identity as there were in the cavalry and infantry. This was unsatisfactory in that any artillery required to attend the cavalry and infantry in combat operations, to say nothing of training for such events, had to be put together and equipped from scratch.

Even if there was time to assemble artillery for operations there was no provision for traction for the guns: animals, carts and wagons, with civilian drivers, had to be requisitioned for the purpose. The Gunners simply followed on foot, sometimes assisting the movement over bad ground, until the scene of action was reached. Then the Gunners took over and the civilians, their animals and wagons retired to the rear. Guns were in effect tied to their positions, usually the line of infantry, and it was not possible to move them rapidly to another part of the battlefield. Ammunition supply was also a major problem.

It was against this background that, in 1793, the Master General of the Ordnance, the 3rd Duke of Richmond and Lennox, authorized the formation of two six-gun troops of Royal Horse Artillery. These were regarded as 'the most complete thing in the army', being established with the officers and men to man the troops, together with the guns, the carriages and ammunition limbers, baggage and forge wagons, farriers, wheelwrights, shoeing-smiths, harness makers, saddlers, artificers and a surgeon.

However, the rest of the artillery remained formed into companies, without guns or the means of traction, which were provided from artillery parks when needed. Something had to be done to improve the availability for service of the main body of the Regiment, and in 1794 a Corps of Captain Commissaries and Drivers was formed, attached to the Parks of Artillery serving in England.

In 1801 this became the Corps of RA Drivers, with seven companies each of 3 officers, 75 non-commissioned officers and tradesmen and 380 RA drivers. This was an improvement, but there were still three separate bodies: Companies of Royal Artillery (the gunners), the Corps of RA Drivers (drivers and horses) and the Artillery Parks (the guns and limbers).

It is important to appreciate that, in this period, there was a thriving body of light wagons and coach horses, together with lightweight riders and drivers, operating in a wide variety of civilian roles throughout the country. The horses were smaller than those used by the cavalry and for officers' chargers and were bred as dray-horses. It was these animals and the men to manage them that were recruited for the role of drawing field guns. (Siege guns were usually drawn by large bullock teams.)

In 1822 the Corps of RA Drivers was disbanded for reasons of economy and because the Master General of the Ordnance, the Duke of Wellington, believed it to be in a bad state. He ordered that, in future, every recruit for the Foot Artillery was to be enlisted as a 'gunner and driver', despite the concern of Colonel Sir Alexander Dickson, at that point Master Gunner St James's Park.

The Deputy Adjutant General RA, Major General Sir John Macleod, devised a detailed plan and published it in Regimental Orders. The essence of this was that, since every gunner was then, nominally, also a driver, it was necessary to spread the knowledge of horses and stable management throughout the battalions. For this purpose, the 288 real drivers (of the Corps of RA Drivers) and their 360 horses were dispersed through the 72 companies, with 4 drivers and 5 horses to each RA company at home (185 horses and 148 drivers in all). These companies were grouped at Woolwich and certain outstations as Instructional Field Batteries.

By 1825 it was clear that the Duke's system would not work: according to the recruitment regulations, the men enlisted for the Artillery were to be not less than 5ft 8in in height and such men were too heavy and too long in the leg to be drivers. The opinion of another famous Gunner, General Sir Robert Gardiner, was: 'A man may be enlisted as a Gunner and Driver, but the same man cannot be fit for both duties.'

In 1837 came an order for the formation of three field batteries at Woolwich to each of which was attached a company stationed at Woolwich. This was a first step in the right direction, but it was not until 1847 that the first permanent field batteries were formed. In 1848 there were four field batteries at Woolwich, five in Ireland, three in Canada and half batteries at Weedon (Northamptonshire), Manchester, Leith and Glasgow, all for the training of the companies at those and other stations. The next major step came with the Crimean War (1854–6), when the horses, equipment and men of 13 lettered field batteries were absorbed by 13 RA companies in the Crimea.

The system remained like this until the close of the Indian Mutiny (1857–8), which caused a permanent demand for a large number of field batteries for service in India, with a corresponding number at home to relieve them. From that time the field batteries became permanent although the word field did not appear in the title of the battery until July 1889, when the batteries allotted the field role changed their titles from, for example, N Battery 1 Brigade RA to 1st Field Battery RA.

The Riding Establishment Royal Horse Artillery
Major W.G. Clarke

Since its formation at Woolwich on 1 January 1803 as the 'Riding House Department of His Majesty's Ordnance', the Riding Establishment has held a unique place in the history of the Royal Regiment of Artillery. Housed in stables in the north-east quarter of the RA Barracks, the Riding Establishment was charged with responsibility for the improvement of equestrian standards within the Royal Regiment. The first Riding Master for this new organization was Captain C.A. Quist, an elderly German officer from Hanover, whose appointment came about at the express wish of King George III who was then also Elector of the German principality.

Captain Quist was a student of the Spanish Riding School of Vienna (founded 1735) and brought many of the continental methods of training horses and riders with him. He was particularly well known for working horses between the pillars as practised in Vienna, and the Troop's own crest was created with the figure of a horse between two pillars as used by the Spanish Riding School today. In the early days of its existence the Troop was primarily concerned with the improvement of horsemanship within the Regiment and for the training of officers' chargers. It

was also responsible for the equitation training of the Gentlemen Cadets at the nearby Royal Military Academy.

Initially the 'Riding House Troop' or 'Riding Troop' as the establishment came to be known, was borne on the strength of the Corps of Royal Artillery Drivers and, in addition to Captain Quist, who was both a Riding Master and the first Superintendent, there were 3 lieutenants, just over 20 men and 12 horses. Captain Quist continued to command the Troop until his death in 1821 at the grand age of 91 years. His horse Wonder died at the age of 40 and was buried in the stables area at Woolwich. On the demolition of the Riding Troop stables in 1969, his gravestone and that of other much loved and distinguished chargers were moved to St John's Wood Barracks, north London, where they remain to this day.

In 1857 the Troop along with the rest of the Royal Regiment ceased to be commanded by the Master General of the Ordnance and was brought under control of the War Office. The first Riding Master was posted to the Troop in 1858 and in 1873 a Major Superintendent replaced the rank of Captain Superintendent. For the next 40 years the Troop strength fluctuated wildly. At its height it had more than 144 horses on strength and a staff to match. These were halcyon days for the Troop and, with the creation of the Military Tournament in London in 1880, members of the Troop became a regular and popular feature in the organization and competition for the skill-at-arms champion. Indeed, the Arena Master of the Tournament for many years was Captain and Riding Master George Dann, Royal Horse Artillery (RHA). In 1897 however a dramatic change took place when the Troop was removed from the RHA establishment and reduced to just 77 horses, one superintendent, two riding masters and 85 other ranks. After a period of six years on the RA Establishment the Troop returned to the RHA fold in 1903.

Lieutenant General Robert Lawson, who was the first officer to command a troop of Royal Horse Artillery when it was formed in 1793.

THE REMOUNT DEPARTMENT

In these days of the internal combustion engine it is sometimes forgotten that, in order to maintain a capability for horse-drawn artillery, there was a constant turnover in horses, which had to be replaced by purchase. The Regiment's Remount Department was set up on Woolwich Common, close to the Charlton Road and immediately north of Shrapnel Barracks. Its task was to acquire the necessary replacements and to train them for the task of drawing guns.

Until 1887 the troop horses for the Army were purchased under regimental arrangements: those for the artillery were purchased by an officer specially appointed for the task. In 1882 a Gunner officer, Colonel Frederick Ravenhill, took up this appointment and was almost immediately faced with having to find 2,000 horses for the expedition to Egypt, the usual dealers having failed to produce such a number. Ravenhill got on with the task, going around the breeders and buying directly from them, a system that he then followed throughout the rest of his time in that appointment.

After the campaign in Egypt, there was an inquiry into the procedures for horse requirements for general mobilization. Ravenhill was a member of the inquiry and in 1886 he was sent to Canada to see whether it would be possible to obtain suitable horses there – the first attempt ever made to investigate the advance supply of horses outside the United Kingdom. He sent back 80 horses to the Remount Stables at Woolwich, which brought a host of distinguished visitors to see them, including the Duke of Cambridge.

Ravenhill's acute appreciation of the problems and the lack of an effective system led him to propose the formation of an Army Remount Department. This was agreed and implemented in 1887, with Ravenhill at its head as Inspector General and with the temporary rank of major general.

On the outbreak of war in 1914 the Troop was all but disbanded, with the horses dispersed to various RHA and Royal Field Artillery (RFA) brigades and the other ranks to either 3rd Brigade RHA or 'B' Reserve Brigade RFA. By the middle of September, however, a new Superintendent was appointed, Lieutenant B. Dann, a former Riding Master on the old establishment, and the Troop received 60 horses and 30 civilian grooms. The training of officer cadets restarted almost immediately and continued both at Woolwich and St John's Wood for the remainder of the war.

One of the Troop's other duties at this time was to provide trained chargers for use by senior officers of the Regiment, the Army Council and occasionally foreign attachés and Dominion representatives. Indeed, when His Majesty King George V visited Woolwich in 1918, the Troop also supplied the Sovereign's Escort. It was the performance of this and similar duties that led to the Troop's stables at Woolwich being known colloquially as 'the Cab Yard'.

In 1919 the Riding Troop was split into two branches. One half remained at Woolwich to train the Gentlemen Cadets and the Boys of the Depot Brigade; the other moved to Weedon in Northamptonshire to train the officers and non-commissioned officers of the Regiment. After the great review and reorganization of the Army in 1922, the Weedon branch of the Riding Troop was absorbed into the Army School of Equitation. The Troop at Woolwich, by now titled as the 'Riding Establishment Royal Artillery', remained in existence carrying out much the same duties as before and, by the 1930s, enjoying some spectacular successes in the world of show jumping and skill-at-arms, both at home and abroad. This happy state of affairs continued until 1939 when, on the outbreak of the Second World War, the Riding Troop, under the command of Captain N.H. Kindersley RHA, was disbanded at Woolwich.

After the war, HM King George VI wished to have a battery of the Royal Horse Artillery re-established in London for ceremonial duties, traditionally horsed and provided with the full dress uniform of the Horse Artillery. As all existing RHA batteries were mechanized, the unit was found by reforming the Riding Troop RHA at St John's Wood: it was this unit that was renamed 'The King's Troop RHA' by the King at the close of his first visit there on 24 October 1947. When King George died, HM The Queen wished the title to be retained in perpetuity.

Top: The first Riding Master of the Riding Establishment RHA was Captain C.A. Quist, an elderly German officer from Hannover. He was particularly well known for working horses between the pillars, and the Troop's crest was created with the figure of a horse between two pillars as used by the Spanish Riding School today.

Right: A formal group photograph of members of the Riding Establishment RHA, c.1890.

THE ROYAL ARTILLERY MESS: THE EARLY DAYS

Colonel Martin Cooper

The history of the Royal Artillery Mess is closely interwoven with the history of the Gunners in Woolwich and many key military, political and royal figures played a significant role in its development.

The First Officers' Mess

A mess is defined as a 'place to eat', but an exclusive military establishment providing such a service to officers did not exist until the early 1780s. Before that officers were responsible for their own board and lodgings, usually taking their evening meals at local hostelries. Woolwich inns nicknamed 'Bastion' and 'Ravelin' are mentioned at this period, but specifically it is recorded that officers regularly took meals at the Bull on Shooters Hill. The equivalents of Regimental dinners, accompanied by members of the Royal Artillery Band from its formation in 1762, were held in such inns.

The building of the Royal Artillery Barracks on Woolwich Common presented an opportunity to establish the Army's first exclusive Officers' Mess in the eastern half of what became the Front Parade. The suggestion of a type of mess is first recorded in 1777, when some iron lamps were authorised 'to light the front of the officers' guard and mess room'. Records also show the existence of a Mess Committee from 1783 and the occupation of a Messroom in 1787.

This first mess consisted of a Messroom, or dining room, and entrance hall supported by serving rooms and a kitchen.

Gentlemen Cadets from the Academy, still down at the Warren, were briefly allowed to dine at the Mess until, in 1797, a cadet was found there while absent from duty at the Academy and the privilege was withdrawn. Mess life, even at this early time, was similar to a private club, in that it was a voluntary and social arrangement rather than a military institution.

Twenty years later, a new Messroom was completed in the present location on the west side of the Front Parade. The original Mess was handed over to the Denbigh Militia, who remained in possession until 1808. It was then turned into a thousand-seat chapel until the building of the Garrison Church in 1863, when it became the Royal Artillery Theatre, fondly remembered for its pantomimes by the pre-war generation of Woolwich.

The Early Days

It was in March 1803 that the new Royal Artillery Officers' Mess began to function. It consisted of the Messroom and a small anteroom (where, later, the hall porter would sit), with a committee room on the floor above. What later became the impressive hallway was a court martial room, although the Mess had occasional use of it. The Messroom itself only extended to the line of pillars, then four in number, behind which was a large bow window, with a music gallery above it. The kitchen was on the floor below. The mirrors were included in the original design but not the frieze, chandeliers or sideboards at

Left: The two silver bread baskets in the background were presented to the Mess by Lord Eardley on the formal opening of the Mess. The silver snuff boxes in the foreground were presented to the original Mess by Lord Eardley – the first items of regimental silver.

Right: One of the four smaller Georgian pattern crystal chandeliers owned by the Mess. Note the two panels on the left side of the frieze behind the chandelier: one shows a shield with the face of Thor; the other shows two bees head to head. The bee symbolized artillery, based on the buzzing sound of a shell in flight – hence words like bomb and bombardier from the Greek word for 'bee', bombos.

this early stage, and there were just the two long tables at which 70 officers regularly dined.

A local landowner, Lord Eardley, had presented the original Mess with its first regimental silver, consisting of two snuff boxes, one of which was often placed in front of the President: with the exception of some cutlery they are the only silver from the original Mess. On the opening of the new Mess, Lord Eardley further presented two breadbaskets, which remain in the Regimental silver collection. However, within a year of opening the Mess, a silver fund was established for the purchase of more cutlery. A pastel on silk painting of Lord Eardley was presented to the Mess in 1805 by his son-in-law and was also the first portrait owned by the Mess.

In 1806 a library was formed in the Mess from books donated by the Royal Military Academy and the Repository. Among its first members are recorded Alexander Dickson, Norman Ramsay, Robert Bull and Hew Ross. A century later, when the collection was handed over to the Royal Artillery Institution, there were 34,000 books. The Library also contained a large number of periodicals, the earliest dating back to 1731, which can now be found in the Regimental Museum.

In 1817 the Mess was enlarged when barrack rooms were converted into the two west anterooms. Records show that this was to be a temporary arrangement, but the Mess paid scant regard to this instruction by installing the fine marble fireplaces that set the rooms apart in style from the east anterooms acquired much later.

Fifteen years after the opening of the Mess and following a subscription from all members, two chandeliers were purchased to supplement the candlesticks – hitherto the only lighting in the Messroom – at the considerable cost in those days of £582. (On their move to Larkhill in 2007 the same pair was valued for insurance purposes at £900,000!) In those early days they were hung down the centre of the Messroom. The two tables were widened by a foot to allow officers to stretch out without inconveniencing other diners. The date of the arrival of the top table is unclear, but it is recorded that on occasions up to five tables were used in the Messroom, including one built by the Royal Engineers to fit inside the bow window. In 1827 General the Marquis of Anglesey, the new Master General of the Ordnance, dined with 156 officers using these new arrangements. That said, dinners in the Messroom normally appear to have been limited to about 120 officers, with any extra seated upstairs in the Committee Room. Wine consumption at this time appears to be high, with two and a quarter bottles per officer being recorded at a dinner in 1827.

The Mess was very much like a superior club, and in 1833, after a year's debate, the custom in other gentlemen's clubs of laying a carpet in the dining room was adopted. Arguments against this modernization had included 'the inferior quality of yokel servants and their habits of spilling food and dropping plates, their muddy feet, and the soot flying in from open windows'.

The history of the Royal Artillery Band is closely linked to that of the Officers' Mess, and from the establishment of the Mess the officers were regularly entertained both from the Front Parade and by an orchestra in the Messroom. From 1805, Royal Artillery concerts were a regular feature in the Mess, being weekly events until the Royal Artillery Theatre was opened in 1863, after which mess concerts were reduced to a winter programme. The Band

Above: A portrait of King George III, who was on the throne when the Mess was first opened.

Left: The famous candelabrum presented to the Mess in 1833 by King William IV. It contains over 2,000 ounces of silver and makes a splendid centrepiece at a formal dinner night.

also played at dinners from the gallery above the bow window and, from 1807, at some six balls a year. The acoustics of the Messroom were considered to be ideal. From the very first days of the Mess 'white waiters' were employed, dressed in white livery with silver lace and with blue cuffs and collars. Officers dressed in the uniform of the period or wore evening dress at balls.

BUREAUCRACY IN THE ORDNANCE OFFICE

One of the constant features of the interplay between the civil and military departments of the Ordnance Office is the extraordinary pettiness of the bureaucracy. Throughout the period of the Royal Artillery's service under the Master General of the Ordnance from 1716 to 1856, the minor officials of the Ordnance Office wielded enormous influence simply by controlling the expenditure of every penny, whether in the provision of stores, the maintenance of equipment and property, the settlement of bills or the pay of every single member of the military department, from the newest recruit to the most senior general.

Procrastination was its watchword. If the Brigade Major at Woolwich ran out of paper for correspondence, he could wait months either for resupply or for any recompense for laying out his own money for a stock. If that sounds a minor problem, it might come as a surprise to hear that a company of artillery in the Bahamas, ordered to hold itself in readiness to return to England in 1784, received no clothing that year in expectation of the promised transport. However, no transport was arranged, not only that year but also the following year and the one after – nor did it receive any of the annual clothing issues for those three years.

Operational expenses were even more hotly contended by the clerks. It was frequently necessary during a long overseas campaign to have to borrow money to lay out on horses lost in battle or from sickness, to pay for transport, shelter, food and clothing. This, too, could meet with additional expense in high rates of interest and prices inflated by those taking advantage of the Army's needs. When the officers returned to England, they met the full force of the clerks' demands for complete, documentary proof of all expenditure. Indeed, the initial reaction was simply to ignore the demand, followed by a requirement to refer the claim to someone of higher authority to ascertain the truth of the claimant's demand. The official rule seems to have been to consider anyone demanding money to be an impostor and to be treated accordingly. Once the claim had been verified, the next step was invariably to offer something considerably less than the sum demanded. And so it would go on, sometimes for years before a claimant's legitimate expenses on behalf of the service had been repaid.

The daily duties of those stationed in Woolwich were dogged by the same kind of petty irritations, and it is strange to learn that, at the same time as the lower orders of the Ordnance Office were being such a thorn in the side of the military, the senior members of the Board were diligent in their kindness and care towards the Regiment. There seems to have been a degree of blinkered management that is hard to imagine even in today's era of 'red tape'.

Master General of the Ordnance

Until 1855 the Royal Artillery was under the command of the Master General of the Ordnance rather than under the Commander-in-Chief. With the Master General's direct access to the monarch and political clout as a Privy Councillor and cabinet minister, the Regiment enjoyed a favoured position on which they endeavoured to capitalize. Surprisingly, there is no evidence that the Duke of Wellington actually dined at the Mess during his 20-year tenure as Master General of the Ordnance and Commander-in-Chief, although he visited Woolwich on several occasions. On one occasion Wellington hosted a review attended by the Prince Regent, who adjourned to the Mess for refreshments while Wellington 'who cared for none of these things, returned to London'. Certainly other Master Generals often dined at the Mess and when the Marquis of Anglesey left the appointment he showed his respect for the Mess by asking if he might be made an honorary member, something that many aspired to, such was the social standing of the Mess at this time.

Royal Patronage

Live firing normally took place three times a week on Woolwich Common. There were also frequent reviews that were

Right: A view of part of the Silver Room, showing a small selection of the amazing collection belonging to the Mess. In the foreground is the gold Lonsdale Belt awarded to Bombardier 'Billy' Wells for his successes in holding the British Heavyweight Boxing title for many years.

Far right: King George IV, who was the Prince Regent for the latter part of his father's reign.

occasionally enlarged into Grand Reviews to entertain State guests, often hosted by the Master General of the Ordnance and including visits to the Royal Arsenal and refreshments at the Mess. The first recorded Grand Review was in June 1814, when Tsar Alexander I of Russia, the King of Prussia and the Prince Regent were entertained. This royal patronage was almost certainly promoted by two Gunner equerries of the period: Colonel Sir William Congreve (the younger) was equerry to the Prince Regent (and as George IV) from 1811 until Congreve's death in 1828; Lieutenant General The Lord Bloomfield was an attendant, equerry, aide-de-camp and personal secretary to George IV from his days as Prince of Wales in 1806, largely based on a friendship that arose through their musical interests. Bloomfield, whose portrait hung in the Music Room, finished his career as Garrison Commander at Woolwich from 1838 until 1846 and presented several instruments from the Royal Collection to the Royal Artillery Band.

These links may have led to the presentation of the central chandelier to the Mess in 1829 on the demolition of the Prince Regent's home, Carlton House in Pall Mall. This claim is supported by the royal crown at the top of the chandelier. At this stage the three chandeliers were positioned in line down the centre of the room, where they remained for 50 years. At this time the Duke of Clarence, the brother of George IV, was also a great supporter of the Mess in his roles as Admiral of the Fleet, Lord High Admiral and, from June 1830, as King William IV. He had visited several times as Duke of Clarence and he attended a Grand Review and reception at the Mess a month after his coronation.

In August 1833 the William IV Candelabrum was presented by the King to the Mess at a reception in London. It remains one of the Mess's finest pieces of silver and the first to acknowledge the newly granted Regimental mottoes. The King was said to have been very pleased with the candelabrum

DINNER TO MAJOR-GENERAL SIR W. F. WILLIAMS, AT THE ROYAL ARTILLERY MESS, WOOLWICH—(SEE PRECEDING PAGE)

except that the original design lacked the royal lion, which he instructed should be added at the top. A celebration dinner was held annually for the next three years to celebrate the presentation, and a Candelabrum Ball was subsequently held annually in the Mess for the rest of the century.

Early Mess Etiquette

It is interesting to note some examples of etiquette in the early days of the Mess. The Mess was regarded as a social club where rank was not an issue. On one occasion a Colonel was reprimanded for 'invading the comfort of the Mess' by domineeringly ordering a subaltern to sit down. He was requested to make himself scarce from the Mess until he made a public apology at dinner to both the subaltern concerned and all members present. Rules of the time also show that minor misdemeanours resulted in fines of bottles of wine, but damage had to be repaid at double the cost unless it was deliberate, when the fine was six times the cost. On one occasion a subaltern was written to for repeatedly having ordered his breakfast as early as eight o'clock in the morning and was requested to take his meals elsewhere. We also hear of a subaltern being cautioned for drinking champagne at breakfast and being told to confine himself to claret! It is recorded that one guest was asked to leave the Mess because he was not considered to be a gentleman on account of his table manners, and another for having dirty fingernails.

Letters of the period show that an officer would be responsible for carving the meat at the table for up to one whole side of a table, and that while a dessert for a large dinner might cost £77, the ice would also cost £10, while a bottle of port would cost 3s 2d (16p).

Wine was served under an arrangement known as 'cannons', a term first mentioned in 1784. Officers would indicate whether they intended to partake of the first, second or on some occasions a third cannon and pay accordingly. Each cannon equated to a third or quarter bottle of wine per person. At the end of the consumption of a cannon, a decanter would be passed bearing a silver label to enable diners to regulate their consumption.

Above: A dinner in 1856 to honour Maj Gen Sir William Fenwick Williams, renowned for his victory in the defence of Kars in 1855.

Below left: King William IV, who was a frequent visitor to the RA Mess and presented the famous candelabrum shown on page 42. He also granted the Regiment its mottoes, 'Ubique' and 'Quo fas et gloria ducunt'.

GUNNER COTTAGES

There were few facilities for married soldiers in the early 19th century. It had long been the custom that a small number of married men could bring their wives into barracks, sharing the barrack room with the single men, often merely curtained off to obtain a modicum of privacy. The wives paid for this privilege by performing routine chores like laundry and cleaning.

For some married soldiers this was better than nothing, but in Woolwich it seems that a blind eye was turned to those who helped themselves by building rudimentary hutted accommodation on Charlton Common. On a Board of Ordnance map of its Woolwich land in 1810 there is evidence of these so-called mud huts – almost certainly of wattle and daub construction – along the boundary line between the land owned by Lady Wilson and the Common. Lady Wilson was a major landowner in Charlton and, it seems, a public-spirited person, because she took pity on the poor families living in what she deemed 'hovels'. As a result of her pressure and charity, their lot was much improved in the period shortly after the

Napoleonic Wars by the building of a series of small brick dwellings. Alongside Ha Ha Road, just past the junction with Repository Road in the direction of Charlton and extending in an L-shape layout onto the Common, were over 50 small cottages that were called 'Duke of York Cottages'. These replaced the 'mud huts' and there appear to have been at least two dwellings for Gunner families per cottage, judging from the map scale. The 1864 Ordnance Survey map shows a small school, as well, though this had probably been overtaken by the establishment of the Garrison School in 1854.

When 'Last Post' was sounded in the Garrison, soldiers 'living out' were also required to be at home and the regimental picket would ensure that the 'Lights Out' call was respected in the cottages as well as the barracks.

Rent in the early 19th century was one shilling per week, probably reflecting how little was provided. The cottages were pulled down in 1875 as unsanitary, and the area was redeveloped as the Army Remount Depot.

KAT

This map from 1864 (with enlargement on the right) is the only remaining evidence of the Gunner Cottages, although a map of 1810 shows a line of what could be dwellings along the border of the Common in approximately this area.

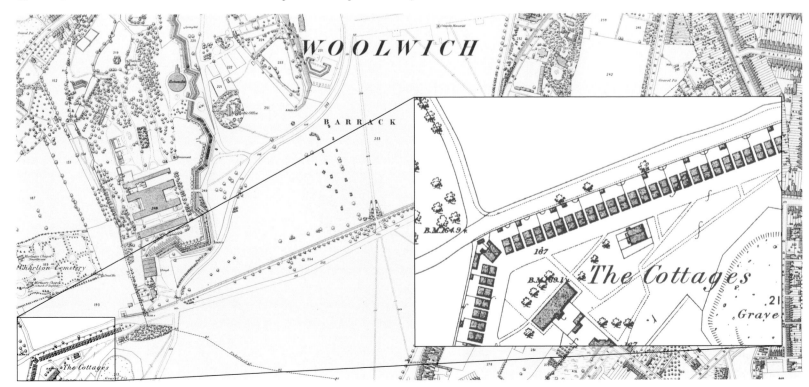

WOOLWICH COMMON

The correct title for the land generally known as 'Woolwich Common' is 'Woolwich and Charlton Commons', because the inter-parish boundary runs across it, with the greater proportion lying in the Charlton parish. Nonetheless, it is owned by the government, having been acquired by purchase, bit by bit, over many years.

From the earliest days of the Garrison until about 1870, it was used not only as a Review and Manoeuvre Ground but also as a practice range. This became increasingly less acceptable to the local population as that expanded, with the occasional ricochet into populated areas and also endangering traffic on the busy Shooters Hill road into London – the 'Dover Road'.

However, the Commons were also used in Victorian times for very different activities – the regimental horse races. At first they were mostly flat races, which began after a change of ministry removed the edict forbidding racing on Woolwich Common in 1841. A local paper report refers to 'one of the prettiest spots for the purpose within 50 miles of London, the officers have set about their revival in earnest. The course, about

a mile and a half round, with a hill in going out, and a fair run in, is in every respect adapted to the sport.'

In 1862 the races were turned into steeplechases and held at Well Hall (about a mile further south, in Eltham). From there they moved to Croydon and eventually to Sandown Park, Esher, Surrey, where they are held to this day.

KAT

THE MORTAR BATTERY

Closely associated with the Common is the famous Mortar Battery, which was built on the southern end of what is, today, the Upper Gun Park, and it was certainly in place by 1806. It was constructed exactly in the form of a siege battery position, complete with gabions (large earth-filled circular baskets) to protect the gun embrasures. In 1820 firing practice used to take place on Mondays, Wednesdays and Fridays at 9.30 am and these were usually attended by spectators from far and wide, as shown in a contemporary print. The print even shows spectators lining the Common, which suggests that the ammunition would not have contained explosives!

Howitzers as well as mortars were fired from here, the target usually being a flagstaff on the Common at a range that varied between 850 and 1,250 yards, and the flagstaff was frequently cut in half – for a mortar, no mean display of accurate gunlaying. Although that seems a short range by today's standards, it was very much in accordance with standards of the day, when practically all engagements were against targets that could be clearly seen from the gun position.

Across the width of the Common lies a banking, approximately 12 feet high and apparently man made. Although there are no references to it in the records, it would seem to have been constructed as a crude 'stop-butt' to limit the number of rounds ricocheting further across the Common.

KAT

Far right: Map showing position of mortar battery on the southern edge of what is today the upper Gun Park.

Below: Mortar battery firing on the Common in 1840, with Shooters Hill and the RMA in the background. This was part of regular weekly practice and was one of the spectacles for visitors to Woolwich.

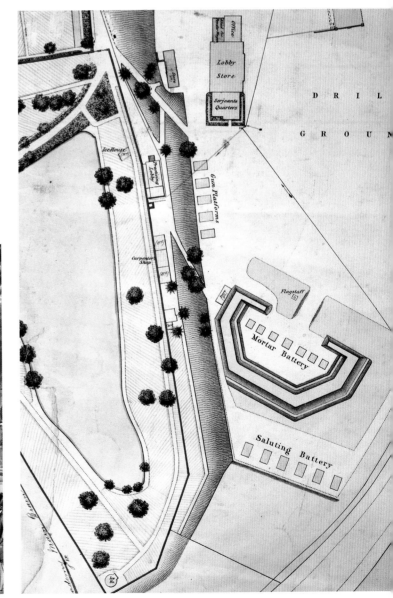

THE ROTUNDA

Based on article by The Rev. Dr Michael Gilman

Perhaps the most important in terms of its architectural and historical interest, and certainly the most visually intriguing building among the complex of barrack buildings on the Common, is the Rotunda. This familiar feature set back from Repository Road, its roof shaped like a Chinese hat, started life as a temporary structure erected by order of the Prince of Wales (Prince Regent and the future King George IV) in the gardens of his home Carlton House, alongside the Mall, in central London.

With King George III increasingly handicapped by his recurring illness, Carlton House became the centre of Court life and the setting for formal royal functions. It was here that the Prince Regent held the grand receptions and sumptuous fêtes that were designed to dazzle the eye of the visitor and to convey a vivid image of the grandeur and wealth, not so much of the proprietor, but of the country of which, from 1811, he was titular head.

However, Carlton House lacked the space to accommodate these functions and additional space was provided in the form of temporary buildings in the grounds. These were designed by John Nash, the architect of Regent's Park and Regent Street, and included a unique building known as the Polygon Room, or Rotunda. It measured 116 feet in diameter and was constructed largely of wood and canvas.

The first occasion on which it was used was for the fête in honour of the Duke of Wellington on 21 July 1814, following the supposed ending of the Napoleonic Wars. The interior was lavishly decorated as always for these grand occasions, with an elaborate ceiling and walls with mirrors, draperies and curtains. In the centre was a floral temple for the orchestra, composed of artificial flowers. The floor was marked out for 12 sets of country dances and the room was lit by 12 glass chandeliers of 24 lights each (on hire).

There was a similar grand event to celebrate the eventual end of the war in 1815, attended by most of the crowned heads of Europe.

In 1815 the Prince Regent decided to reduce the number of temporary rooms, but the Rotunda survived for three more years. When it was clear that the building was redundant, Nash put forward a proposal that it should be converted into a church, but this did not find favour with the Prince. On 7 August 1818 his private secretary, Major General Sir Benjamin Bloomfield (a Gunner officer) informed Colonel Stephenson, the Surveyor General, that the Prince Regent had given instructions that it should be transported to Woolwich. The instructions were that it was 'to be appropriated for the conservation of the trophies obtained in the last war, the Artillery models, and other military curiosities usually preserved in the Repository of the Royal

The earliest known print of the Rotunda after its move from the grounds of Carlton House in the Mall.

THE ROYAL ARTILLERY BOAT CLUB

This began at Woolwich as the 'Rocket Club' (probably named after Congreve's invention), which flourished from 1824 to 1854, winning the Erith Gold Cup in the Thames Regatta of 1844. It is recorded that 'their rate of stroke pulled the old Rocket so clean away from the rest of the competitors that it came in literally alone' – the second boat was Leander.

The Club was raised in 1867 as the Royal Artillery Boat Club and continued in being until 1900, when it fell into abeyance. When it was raised again some years later, it no longer had any direct connection with Woolwich so is not further reported here.

Right: A print showing Gunners training on fortress guns at the embrasures (the gaps in the fortifications on the right of the picture). There is some artistic licence in the portrayal of the Dickson Memorial so close to the Rotunda: it was certainly in the grounds when it was first erected, but some 140 metres away.

Below right: A drawing of the Rotunda in March 1829.

Artillery' – in effect, the Board of Ordnance's museum, although it did not have that name.

The speed with which decisions and actions were taken to secure the Rotunda for Woolwich leads one to suspect that Bloomfield and Colonel Sir William Congreve (the younger) may well have had their eyes on the structure for some time. The fact that the Duke of Wellington had by this time become Master General of the Ordnance might have had an added influence in its acquisition for the Board of Ordnance's

museum, because he had taken a personal interest in the selection and disposal to Woolwich of pieces taken from Paris in reparations. Any discussions with Nash about its possible use as a church may well have been an excuse to ensure the architect's willing cooperation in explaining how to take the building down for the move.

Since the Rotunda was designed as a temporary structure – in effect, a prefabricated timber building – it was perfectly possible to dismantle and reassemble it. It was dispatched to Sir William Congreve at Woolwich in October 1818. Once on its new site, the Rotunda was refurbished with brick walls and its roof was given a new canvas covering. The bricks were taken from a stock already on site, and the canvas was re-used from some already in store. In the event, the dismantling, at least initially, was supervised by William Nixon, the carpenter who had constructed the building. It was not a particularly arduous job – only five men were employed and most of the work was done by a carpenter and a labourer. Members of the Wyatt family were also involved: the carpenter was a Jeffrey Wyatt, and

DISMANTLING THE ROTUNDA

A letter from John Nash to Colonel Stephenson, dated 16 August 1818, advises:

The best course to take in pulling down the polygonal building in Carlton House gardens will be thus. After the boarded casing – the timbers filling in between the posts and the boarded floor – shall be removed and the outside covering taken off, a scaffold of about 8 or 9 feet square should be erected in the centre – the cupola taken down to the main ribs and the hoops taken off which bind the upright timber of the roof together and form the cylinder – then to take out the pushins to steady the other ribs – when the rib is so disengaged raise the foot of it up from the plates by a jack, the rib being suspended by the blocks of a triangle – and then the upper end of the rib being also suspended by the blocks of another triangle on the scaffold – a guide rope at the foot of the rib will pull it over the plate outwards and at the same time disengage the upright timbers at the upper end of the rib from the rest of the uprights which together form the main cylinder – and the rib being thus entirely suspended and disengaged may be easily lowered down by the blocks of the Triangles at each end. The other ribs one by one may be taken down in the same way – after which the Joists of the floor may be taken up and the posts and plates forming the walls taken down.

As the building has been constructed so as to take to pieces and be refixed – I advise that the parts and plates forming the walls be numbered and marked a drawing being previously made of them with the like marks on the drawing – so that the timbers may readily come into their places should the building ever be put up again there or elsewhere – and in like manner the floor, the boarding of which has for that reason been framed in compartments as well as the Joists – the ribs forming the roof should also be drawn marked and numbered and the ribs taken down whole and the pushins marked and numbered.

a William Wyatt is noted as superintending some of the work. The work was completed and the building was ready for occupation by 4 May 1820.

Some part of the collection of guns amassed by the Royal Military Repository for teaching purposes was no doubt housed

BATTLE HONOURS

Like most traditions that had to start somewhere and grow over the years, the practice of awarding battle honours to regiments for outstanding performance in action was slow to take root. It was not until the Napoleonic Wars that the custom caught on in Britain, France and Sweden, though there are a few, rare precursors. Once established, there followed a series of battle honours 'backdated' in time as interest in the system grew.

In the Royal Artillery, there were battle honours for Gibraltar, Egypt (1801), Leipszig (1813) and Waterloo, and in the early 19th century several more were added by the backdating method. For the Regiment, this all came to an end when, on 1 June 1833, a General Order announced that, 'His Majesty has been pleased to grant the following mottoes for the Royal Artillery, viz Ubique [Everywhere] and Quo fas et gloria ducunt [Where Right and Glory Lead]. The word Ubique is to be substituted in lieu of all other terms of distinction hitherto borne on any part of the dress or appointments throughout the whole Regiment.' Given the context in which the mottoes were awarded and the substitution of Ubique for all other terms of distinction, it was clear that Ubique was a battle honour and that the Regiment needed no other.

Meanwhile, the Artilleries of the Honourable East India Company continued to amass battle honours, worn on uniforms and items of equipment because they had no guidons (small flags) or colours, and this continued until they were absorbed into the Royal Artillery in 1861, when they had to follow the rules already in force.

This matter of the Regiment's battle honour should not be confused with Honour Titles, which came about later (see box on page 85).

in one or other of the long storehouses put up in the new Repository's grounds beside the Barracks, but there would probably have been some cannon living outside. Vast quantities of the spoils of war had also arrived in recent years, including much taken from Paris, all of which merited housing in suitable accommodation. Certainly, the question of getting most of the collection under cover was in Congreve's mind when he petitioned the Prince Regent for the use of the Rotunda building.

The Rotunda is the only surviving remnant of the Repository in its original use and, more importantly, it is the only surviving structure of George IV's Carlton House (although decorative elements were re-used widely in subsequent royal buildings). In a strange turn of events, it was the temporary structure that survived, rather than the palace, and it is now an important listed building in its own right.

Below: The central column in the Rotunda records some of the famous names in the Regiment during the first 150 years of its life. The reason why this was not continued is not known.

Below left: The Rotunda c.1995.

Opposite: Work in progress on refurbishing the roof of the Rotunda in 1980, showing something of how it is constructed.

ROYAL REVIEWS

From local newspapers:

July 1830. On Tuesday the town of Woolwich presented the gayest appearance we have ever witnessed, in consequence of his Majesty (William IV) reviewing the Royal Artillery and Engineers. His Majesty was accompanied by his Royal Consort Queen Adelaide, the Princess Augusta, the King of Württemberg, the Duke of Cumberland, Prince George of Cumberland, Prince Leopold, Lord Combermere, Lord Fitzroy Somerset, and others of distinction . The officers of the Artillery had the honour of kissing hands as his

Majesty passed. After the review the Royal party proceeded to the mess-room … In the course of the entertainment his Majesty gave the following toasts: 'The Royal Artillery', 'The Duke of Wellington, and the Army and Navy combined.' Lord Hill [the Commander-in-Chief] then proposed the health of his Majesty.

24 July 1835. The expected visit of their Majesties yesterday to review the troops at Woolwich, and the facility of conveyance afforded by the steamboats (now running for 12 months past) drew an immense number of spectators. The Royal Artillery, 1,600

THE FEAST CELEBRATING THE CORONATION OF QUEEN VICTORIA

A local newspaper reported on 6 July 1838 eight days after the young Queen's coronation:

Yesterday a grand review and sports took place at Woolwich. The coaches which ply between London and Woolwich discharged loads of passengers and from every direction carriages, equestrians, and pedestrians poured in. There could not have been less than 100,000 persons present. Amongst the illustrious visitors were Prince George of Cambridge, the Prince of Saxe-Coburg, the Duke de Nemours, Marshal Soult, the Prince de Ligne, and the Embassies assembled in London to do honour to the Queen's coronation.

The firing commenced on the practice-range in the marshes by a discharge of 30 12-pounder [Congreve] rockets at a target. The company visited the mechanical wonders at the Arsenal, and then proceeded to the Common, where the Artillery went through the manoeuvres of attack and defence, and several rounds of cannon were fired. Sir Hussey Vivian, Master-General of the Ordnance, received the salute, and Lord Bloomfield, the Commandant at Woolwich, had the chief command. Not less than five lines of carriages were drawn outside the line in some places, but all round the square brilliant equipages were thickly congregated. On the side of the line that fronted the barracks, and from the lawn of which the Common-ground is divided by a ditch and a brick wall, the pressure was very great. Several persons were sorely bruised.

A splendid breakfast was afterwards served in the mess-room. About 800 guests sat down. The toast of 'The Queen' was

announced to the multitude by a salute of cannon fired by officers exclusively, the men being all engaged at dinner, which was served to them and their families, in number 4,500, on the barrack-field.

Then followed the old English sports: and at night there was more feasting and a splendid show of fireworks. The affair has caused a great stir at Woolwich, and no accommodation could be obtained at any price.

The celebration of the Coronation of Queen Victoria in 1838. This included a great feast for the soldiers at tables set out on the Barrack Field.

The Duke of Wellington at a 'sham fight' on Woolwich Common, where he was reviewing the Garrison. It is the only known occasion when he visited the Garrison (c.1825).

strong; the Royal Sappers and Miners, 200; the Royal Marines, about 900; were formed in line, having on the right the Royal Horse Artillery with six guns and one battery of four guns, and on the left three batteries of four guns each. The ground was kept by 200 of the Royal Life Guards and a guard of honour consisted of the Grenadier Guards with the band. At 12 their Majesties, escorted by a strong detachment of the 8th Hussars, attended by the Dukes of Cumberland and Cambridge, Prince George of Cambridge, Lord Hill, Sir Hussey Vivian [Master General of the Ordnance], the King's aide-de-camp, etc., arrived on the ground.

The marching was of great excellence, particularly that of the Marines; it was the first time that this distinguished regiment was allowed to be reviewed in conjunction with the other troops of the garrison. His Majesty then proceeded to the howitzer and mortar batteries, where five rounds of six guns from each battery were fired at a flag 1,200 yards distant, the fence building of which was hit several times. Their Majesties then proceeded to the mess-room, where a costly breakfast was served, after which the exercise of the rocket brigade on the [Plumstead] marshes took place. It is computed that there were 100,000 persons present and nearly 300 carriages. The only casualty we have heard of is that of

an artilleryman's leg being taken off by a shell on the marshes, through his own imprudence in getting within its range.

KAT

THE INTRODUCTION OF POLICE IN WOOLWICH

In 1840 the town's petition for the new police force was granted and an eight-man group of Sir Robert Peel's men were introduced to take the place of the single watchman who had had the responsibility to this time. One of its first duties was to deal with an amusing incident:

Mrs Lacey, of the Red Lion, Mulgrave Place, was awakened by loud groans and woke her husband, who found the house full of smoke and the bar strewed with soot. Tracing the cause to the chimney, he poked up an iron bar and found a man stuck fast, but, having taken out the register, the intruder was dragged down. He proved to be an artilleryman, well known at the house, and living a few doors off. He said that he was in the habit of smoking his pipe on Mr Lacey's chimney pot, and slipped down! He was locked up and taken before the court, but his 'little slip' was forgiven.

THE DICKSON MEMORIAL

Designed by Sir Francis Chantrey, the memorial was erected to the memory of Major-General Sir Alexander Dickson (1777–1840), Wellington's Siege Train Commander throughout the Peninsular campaign and for that of Waterloo, and a much-loved Master Gunner. Most of his regimental service was spent abroad and is not strictly relevant to the story of Woolwich, but he spent much of the later period in London and at Woolwich, where his kindly nature made him a great favourite with both officers and men. It is a matter of record that his passing was not only much lamented but was also the scene of an extraordinary funeral in which the entire Garrison took part. A watercolour record of this is in the RA Mess.

The memorial to him was erected initially in the grounds of the Royal Military Repository in 1847, some 140 yards south of the Rotunda, but it was moved to the Front Parade in 1912. In the new location it also commemorates Dickson's son, also Master Gunner, General Sir Collingwood Dickson (1817–1904), who took part in the Crimean War and was the first Gunner officer to win a Victoria Cross.

KAT

The entire Garrison paraded on the Front Parade to march past the funeral carriage of Maj-Gen Sir Alexander Dickson, a much-loved Master Gunner St James's Park.

Left: Maj-Gen Sir Alexander Dickson in a portrait taken towards the end of his illustrious career.

Below: The Memorial under reconstruction following its move from the Repository in 1912.

Bottom: The Dickson Memorial at its re-dedication service after being moved.

General Sir Collingwood Dickson VC, son of Maj-Gen Alexander Dickson. Both served as Master Gunner St James's Park and are commemorated on the Dickson Memorial.

THE ROYAL ARTILLERY CRICKET CLUB

Lieutenant Colonel Peter Salisbury

No one knows exactly when the Royal Artillery Cricket Club (RACC) was founded, but it dates from well before the end of the 18th century, the earliest match of which there is any record being on 8 July 1765. The club was started by officers at Woolwich as a private club and became an official, properly constituted Regimental club only in 1906. Despite this, it was a going concern of some influence by 1818, because on 8 June of that year it was granted a fixture against the Marylebone Cricket Club (MCC) at Lord's. This was the first fixture to be played by MCC against any Service side. For this to have happened, the RACC must, by then, have been a club of some stature.

The RA Barracks at Woolwich was first occupied in 1776–7 and the sports fields on the Barrack Field, on the other side of the Front Parade, were probably laid out about this time. However, the Gunners were playing cricket on Woolwich Common well before the move into the new barracks from the Arsenal. The 1765 match was played there and there is nothing to suggest that the club was not formed much earlier. If, as is possible, it was founded in the earliest days of the Royal Regiment, it predates Hambledon Cricket Club (the 'home of cricket', founded in Hampshire 1750) and MCC (founded 1787), and is one of the oldest clubs in the land.

After the first MCC fixture at Lord's in 1818, there was a return match at Woolwich the following week. This arrangement of home and away fixtures with MCC continued until 1876. Thereafter, the Woolwich match was discontinued, but the one at Lord's went on, with some gaps, for over 50 years. On 8 June 1968 MCC played a one-off match at Woolwich against the Gunners to celebrate the 150th anniversary of the first match at Lord's.

Another interesting match at Woolwich was against the All England XI in 1862. The centenary of this match was celebrated in 1962, when Jack Martin, a wartime battery commander who played for Kent and England, raised an Old England XI to play the Gunners at Woolwich.

Over the years the majority of RACC home fixtures have been played at Woolwich, which until 2003 was regarded as the home of Gunner cricket. The Sappers were first played there in 1864, and thereafter, until 1906, there were two matches against them each year, one at Woolwich and one at

Chatham. From 1907 to 1962, at the invitation of MCC, there was one annual match played at Lord's. After that the game was played alternately at Woolwich and Chatham until 2003, when Larkhill replaced Woolwich as the RACC's official ground. Many of the fixtures in the 19th and 20th centuries were against famous wandering clubs such as I Zingari, Free Foresters and Band of Brothers, to name but three. Matches were of two days' duration, with cricket dinners in the RA Mess on the evening of the first day.

Although the RACC was an officers' club, there were occasions when soldiers of the required standard were included in important matches. It remained an officers' club until after the Second World War when it was agreed that National Service soldiers of the required standard could play 'at match managers' discretion', and they were regularly picked by the selection committee for important matches, including the Gunner/Sapper match. After the end of National Service soldiers continued to appear and the RACC gradually evolved into the club for all ranks that it is today.

A painting by Jocelyn Galsworthy commissioned in 1995 to commemorate Gunner cricket played for so many years on the sports fields of the RA Barracks.

SECTION 3
Woolwich in its Heyday

THE ROYAL ARTILLERY INSTITUTION

Colonel M. J. N. Richards

(Based on an historical note by Brigadier P. W. Mead published in 1972)

Background and Formation

The Royal Artillery Institution was formed in 1838 at the instigation of two subalterns quartered together at Woolwich, although 'The Military Society', which had been established at Woolwich between 1772 and 1775, must have had some part in inspiring Lieutenants John Lefroy (later General Sir John Lefroy) and Lieutenant F. M. Eardley-Wilmot (later Major-General) in their proposal to establish an educational institution principally for the benefit of artillery officers.

The Military Society had been the brainchild of Captain Alexander Jardine RA who in June 1772 wrote to Captain Edward Williams RA to suggest 'a voluntary association might be formed amongst us, on liberal principles, viz. for improvement and amusement, where military, mathematical and philosophical ... knowledge might thus be improved and propagated. The Society might thus communicate and increase their own ideas, preserve themselves from vulgar errors, and ... bear up against pert and presumptive ignorance.' His letter was greeted with enthusiasm, and four months later the Society was established resolving to 'meet every Saturday preceding the full moon'. For the next three years it appears to have thrived, and a list of over 30 papers, all on matters affecting gunnery and ammunition, survives. There is no evidence of the Society continuing after 1775, perhaps because Captains Jardine and Williams and their fellow enthusiasts departed Woolwich for the war in America, although they did leave behind the nucleus of what would become the Regimental Library.

When in 1838 Lefroy and Eardley-Wilmot wanted to improve their knowledge and training in the important artillery subjects of surveying and astronomy, and found they were unable to obtain or borrow the necessary instruments, they not unnaturally considered that more should be done to assist artillery officers with their professional education. This led them to write to their superior at Woolwich with a proposal to raise money by subscription to purchase 'Instruments etc. necessary for the study of military, artillery and general science', to form a committee to administer these funds, to occupy an observatory and library at Woolwich, and to generally further the education of artillery officers. As with the Military Society, Sapper officers were to be included.

As 60 years earlier, the proposal proceeded at a pace that would appal bureaucrats today! Lefroy and Eardley-Wilmot's original letter had been written on 1 February 1838. By the 17th of the

Below left: General Sir John Lefroy, who initiated the RA Institution when a young captain and afterwards served as the Secretary of the Institution before rising to senior rank.

Below far left: Mid 19th-century map showing the Rotunda on the left and, surrounded by trees, the original RAI observatory building.

Below: Air photograph in 1925 shows the RAI building right of centre, on the eastern end of the RA Barracks.

month it had reached, through several intermediaries, the Master General of the Ordnance himself, and had received his approval in principle. By 8 May a special committee, headed by a Lieutenant General, had sat and published its report. This noted the receipt already of £377 10s in donations and subscriptions, an estimated initial expenditure of £814 11s, and included an accommodation plan for the project. On 13 June the Master General approved the report.

Within 18 months of the first letter an observatory and instrument room had been built alongside the Rotunda, where it still stands today, a telescope had been mounted, a small library had been started, a larger room had been provided for lectures and study, and instruction in mathematics and astronomy was actually taking place. However, all these activities were clearly Woolwich-based and, in effect, solely for Woolwich officers. So in 1849 the Committee of the RA Institution issued a 'manifesto' which stated

THE ROYAL ARTILLERY INSTITUTION BUILDING

The RAI building on the eastern side of the RA Barracks was started in 1851 and opened in 1854 by Colonel (later General Sir) Edward Sabine (a Gunner whose scientific standing in the country was recognized when he achieved the distinction of becoming the President of the Royal Society). It seems strange that the only picture known to show the building is an air photograph of the barracks area, taken in 1925. This shows a large, attractive building with an impressive pedimented frontage.

Its principal asset was a lecture theatre in the shape of a banked auditorium like those favoured by other academic institutions. In addition, it had a library, a small regimental museum and offices for the Secretary of the Institution and his staff. It also housed a printing press, used to great effect.

In the early days, French, German, chemistry, mathematics, drawing etc. used to be studied there. In 1863, the first 'Advanced Class' was started and many notable thinkers and scientists came to lecture, among them John Ruskin and Thomas Huxley. It was the precursor to the whole system of higher technical training in the Army.

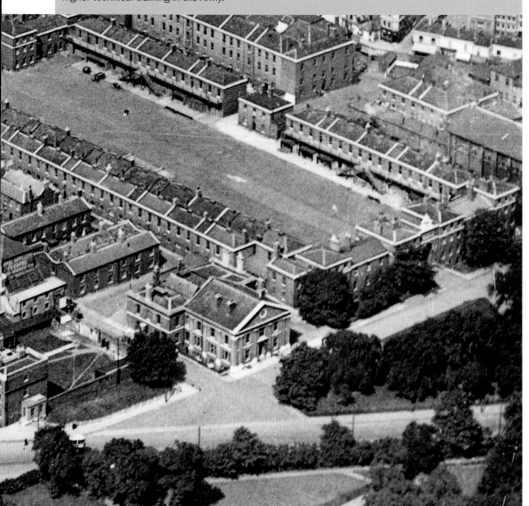

the scope and objectives of the Institution to be: to furnish every officer entering the garrison suitable means of obtaining instruction and information, to make generally known the progress and application of science, and to carry on intercourse with officers retired and abroad.

The Department of Artillery Studies

It was in that same year, 1849, that a Captain William Smythe (who had been the Secretary of the Institution for a year in 1839–40) was appointed at the behest of the Master General of the Ordnance to be the first 'Director of Artillery Studies' and a Department of Artillery Studies was established. Its task was to regularize the studies of young officers joining the Royal Regiment from the Royal Military Academy, and from then on it educated young officers at public expense, while the RA Institution educated the more mature officers, partly at its own expense.

By 1853 when the then Captain Eardley-Wilmot handed over the secretaryship of the Institution to the then Captain Lefroy (for his second term as the Secretary) the appointment had become a full-time one, and in 1854 the Institution itself was housed in new purpose-built accommodation in the RA Barracks at the east end of the Front Parade, which it shared with the Department of Artillery Studies. Over the next 30 years the Department's responsibilities increased to take account of the increasing need for the formal education of artillery officers.

By 1884 the sheer lack of space made inevitable the physical separation of the RA Institution and the Department of Artillery Studies. So on 19 May 1888 the latter moved to Red Barracks, where it was named 'The Artillery College'. Its move was effected, so it is recorded, by a fatigue party of four non-commissioned officers (NCOs) and 20 men, with four duck carts and four pairs of wheels. This is twice the size of the fatigue party of two NCOs and 10 men that moved the RA Institution's property from Woolwich to Larkhill in November 2005, but of course they did not have the two 4-ton trucks that were available in 2005!

In 1898 the Artillery College lost its specific Gunner function with the wider requirement to train officers from all parts of the Army in scientific matters. It became the Ordnance College, and it and the RA Institution finally parted company, although the Department of Artillery Studies had never formally been part of the Institution.

The Development of the RA Institution – 1850–1957

The Committee's publication of the 'manifesto' in 1849 set the course for the development of the Institution over the next century or so into three distinct areas.

The first of these was its educational role, where the formation and subsequent expansion of the Department of Artillery Studies also contributed to the change in the Institution's Woolwich-orientated educational functions. The emphasis soon changed to the Regiment as a whole, with the circulation of the 'Minutes and Proceedings' becoming the principal means of achieving a wider measure of education, and the exchange of knowledge and experience. The first bound volume of the *Minutes and Proceedings of the RA Institution* was published in 1858, containing all the minutes of the meetings and all the papers contributed since 1845. It has to be said that many of those papers would now make very heavy reading indeed for today's members of the Institution! Nevertheless, by 1889 the Minutes and Proceedings had become a regular monthly production, resembling more and

Right: This layout plan is extracted from the only known plan of the RA Barracks to show the RA Institution building.

GREENHILL SCHOOLS AND MALLET'S MORTARS

In Repository Road, opposite the RA Barracks, lay the Greenhill Schools built in 1854 for the children of the Garrison – the first such schools in the country established solely for soldiers' children. Having been superseded by state schooling and lain empty for some years, it was sold by the Ministry of Defence in the early 1990s and converted to private housing.

For a short time during the 1980s, the buildings were under consideration as a possible site for a new Regimental Museum, to work in conjunction with the Rotunda. This idea was discarded on grounds of cost and the continuing problem of location – it was tarred with the same brush as the Rotunda: not being easy for visitors to reach and not therefore likely to attract sufficient numbers to make a commercial museum.

Outside the former Greenhill Schools stands one of the two Mallet's mortars, moved there from the Royal Arsenal in the 1960s (its twin was moved to Fort Nelson, north of Portsmouth harbour, which houses the Royal Armouries' artillery collection). Incidentally, both of Mallet's mortars are owned by the Royal Armouries, having been taken on their books in the 1920s as a means of ensuring their survival as historic pieces. They stood originally side by side in the Royal Arsenal.

They were designed by the engineer Robert Mallet for action in the Crimean War, with a calibre of 36in, a bomb weight of as much as 2,986 pounds, and capable of a range of 1½ miles. They were capable of being completely disassembled for

movement, although this would still have been a difficult and lengthy process. However, they were not delivered until May 1857, more than a year after the war ended. During test firings at the Royal Arsenal, one of the mortars cracked and, with the war over, it was decided not to continue development.

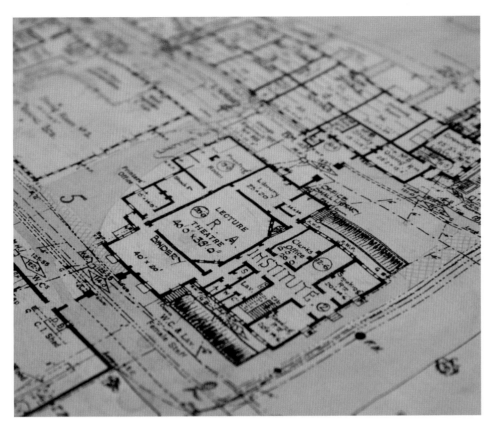

The Institution's second role became that of a publisher, which grew, perhaps more than anything else, from the purchase of a rudimentary printing press in 1847, which remained in place until 1958. Its existence gave the Institution responsibilities for publishing certain books and periodicals in addition to the Minutes and Proceedings and subsequently the RA Journal. The most notable periodicals were the *Royal Artillery Regimental News* – a newsletter for all members of the RA Institution – which appeared monthly from 1904 until it was absorbed into *The Gunner* magazine in 1970, and the *Royal Artillery Seniority List* – The Blue List – which developed in 1904 from a small alphabetical list dating from 1875.

At the same time a continual stream of hardback – and latterly paperback – books and pamphlets was being produced and published, the most notable of which were those relating to the Regiment's history or technical gunnery matters.

The emphasis placed on the publication of Regimental history books was a product of the Institution's third role, which was that of guardian of our history. Responsibility for this had stemmed from the Institution so quickly meeting one of its initial objectives to establish a library. A Regimental museum seems also to have been started at an early stage, presumably partly from trophies brought back to Woolwich by officers returning from overseas, and was certainly an integral part of the new accommodation occupied in 1854. These twin developments led to the gradual acceptance of the Institution being regarded as the principal authority on Regimental history and, in turn, to the War Office transferring custody of the Museum of Artillery in the Rotunda to the RA Institution in 1870. This museum had been in existence since 1778 and housed in the Rotunda since 1820, where much of the reserve collections now belonging to the Royal Artillery Historical Trust remain today, as the Rotunda is still at present an 'annexe' to the new RA Museum now in the Royal Arsenal.

The Regimental library, which had been housed in the RA Mess for all of the 19th century, was incorporated into the RA Institution's library in 1911, the latter having been in place in the RA Institution building since 1854. The Regimental Museum remained in that same building until it was destroyed by a bomb on 2 November 1940. The salvaged collections were moved, first to the Commandant's house and then, in November 1941, into the central block of the Academy buildings where they remained until it was closed in 1999, pending the move to the new museum.

In the aftermath of the Second World War, and when it became clear that the Royal Military Academy would not reopen, the RA Institution itself took up residence in K House on the western front of the RMA buildings. There it remained until the mid-1990s, when it moved again, this time back to the RA Barracks to join the rest of Regimental HQ RA.

The Royal Artillery printing press in action. This did sterling service for the Regiment, printing not only material for the RA Journal and later The Gunner *magazine, but also many of the books that were printed for the RA Institution.*

more a professional 'house magazine' of British artillery. It is therefore not surprising that in April 1905 the title was changed to *The Journal of the Royal Artillery*, which is as it remains today, although through a mixture of a shortage of contributions and the pressure on funds the frequency of publications was slowly reduced, until in 1962 the present biannual publication was set.

THE ROYAL MILITARY ACADEMY, WOOLWICH 1806–1939

'The New RMA', as it was known at first, was designed by Sir James Wyatt and built on the slopes of Shooters Hill alongside Woolwich Common, facing northwards towards the Thames and in sight of the new Royal Artillery Barracks. However, the senior class remained at the Warren, where it was mainly concerned with technical studies and where appropriate facilities were available. The links with the Royal Arsenal's technical resources remained one of the main arguments against amalgamating the RMA with the Royal Military College, Sandhurst, for the next 120 years, despite several such proposals to save money during that period.

For the first 100 years of its existence, Gentlemen Cadets (GCs) at the RMA were required to compile copious notes on all that they were taught, especially in technical matters. Their notebooks were examined as part of assessing their progress, so they were important in their own right, besides providing information of value to the future young officers wherever they might happen to be serving: with no recourse to the telephone or Internet, it took a long time to get help when requests had to go by sailing ship! There are many examples of cadet notebooks in the RA Library and Archives and some of their work is shown on these pages.

The teaching staff at the RMA varied in strength and quality over the years, but some outstanding teachers made their mark. Among them were Paul Sandby, who was one of the country's finest watercolourists and taught drawing at the RMA for nearly 30 years (1768–97), and Professor Michael Faraday, who taught chemistry there for over 20 years (1829–52).

It would take too long to recount the details of changes that took place at the RMA over the years between its move to Shooters Hill and the First World War. The ebb and flow of the

Below: The oral examination of cadets seeking to graduate from the Royal Military Academy.

Far left: An early print of the RMA when it was still known as the New RMA.

Below left: A drawing from a cadet notebook, showing a maquette of a gun being constructed in clay, prior to making a mould from which to cast it.

After three days the casts are drawn out of the pit and the moulds knocked to pieces with heavy hammers, the iron bars and hoops having been rolled apart are again ready for use, the exterior of the cast is found to be in a very rough state which being chizzled and filed and the dead head cut off in a machine, is ready for boring and turning.

re-enacted the humiliations it suffered when, in turn, it was replaced by a new intake.

New cadets were known as 'neuxes' (like 'nukes') during the early years of the RMA, a term that soon became 'snooks' and, eventually, 'snookers'. This name stuck for most of the life of the RMA and – though this is somewhat apocryphal – is even credited with giving the game of snooker its title, based on a version of the game played by junior cadets on the billiard tables that were introduced into the RMA in the late Victorian period. The game's invention is formally credited to Colonel Sir Neville Chamberlain (1856–1944) when serving as a lieutenant with the 11th (Devon) Foot at Jubbulpore (Jabalpur), eastern India, in 1875, although an RA subaltern visiting the Devons' mess gave Chamberlain the word snooker.

The snooker's life was a hard one, intentionally, to ensure that he understood his place in the scheme of things. Conditions were tough: there was little heating, no hot water and baths were taken in the open courtyards where the first ones down had to break the ice. The regime of lessons mixed with constant inspections, drills and physical training, working long hours with little or no recreational facilities, was no picnic. Nonetheless, the snooker quickly learned to cope with all that was thrown at him and by the end of his first term, his parents were often amazed by his growth in confidence and stature.

Food during the first 100 years of the RMA's life was always a source of complaint. There was seldom enough to cope with the appetite of growing boys, and it was frequently of poor

Above: Cadets learning how to dig trenches c.1905.

Below: Cadets at signalling drill c.1905. Semaphore using flags was still a basic skill needed by all officers.

nation's military adventures inevitably affected the way that the RMA had to operate, with fluctuations in the numbers of officers required and changes in the style and pace of cadet life. What stands out from any reading of their history is the nature of the GC himself: youthful high spirits, a natural aversion to any appearance of studiousness and the enjoyment of authority over others. The junior intake took the brunt of this latter trait and

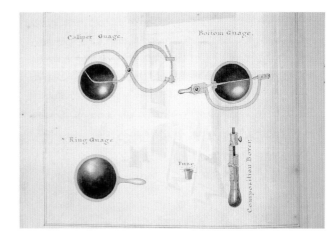

quality. It was the catalyst for a rebellion in 1861, when the entire strength of the cadet body refused to behave properly, throwing food on the floor, dropping rifles on parade, disobeying the order to 'fall in' for drill, breaking bounds to go to the town, and smoking and drinking in their rooms (both of which were against the rules). The affair blew over after a couple of days without serious consequences to the majority of the cadets, though a few of the seniors were 'rusticated' for a while, but it had a useful result in improving the conditions which had led to the 'mutiny'. (It was not strictly a mutiny, of course: parents paid fees for their sons to attend the RMA and cadets were not embodied in the Army.)

Not only did the food improve out of all recognition, but there was a real attempt made to provide recreational facilities and organized sport. The first game of cricket against Sandhurst was played (and won) at Lord's and started a regular series of games against the Royal Military College (RMC). Various clubs were formed (there was even a taxidermy club for a while), not all of which were recognized: the so-called Alpine Club required its members to circumnavigate the entire Academy buildings at roof-top level without touching the ground – no easy feat, considering the number of different heights of building around the circuit. In 1868, smoking was at last permitted and enthusiastically taken up.

In 1867 the social standing of the RMA was enhanced by the enrolment of Prince Arthur, Duke of Connaught. The third son of Queen Victoria, he lived in the Ranger's House at

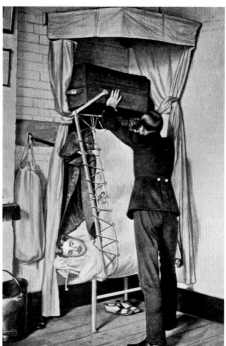

Above: The main dining room of the RMA, a room that later – in the post-Second World War period – became part of a garrison officers' mess for officers of other corps and regiments in Woolwich.

Left: An illustration of 'turning up' – one of the favourite pranks played by cadets on 'snookers' (the new cadets).

Top: A drawing from a cadet notebook, showing calipers and gauges used for measuring ammunition.

Above: A typical informal cadet 'group' photograph as they vied with one another to produce something unusual.

EXCUSES FOR ABSENCE

Many expedients were adopted by cadets to obtain leave of absence, not least the presentation of letters purporting to come from relatives requesting their attendance at some important event. It is said that agencies existed in London for the creation of excuses and that the charge for preparing letters of fiction varied according to the risk of discovery and the probability of success. For personating a parent the writer's charge was five shillings. Aunts and uncles were to be had for a fee ranging from 2s 6d to 3s 6d. In cases of great emergency, cadets were known to prepare these fraudulent epistles themselves, and it is recorded that one young gentleman was in such haste to get away that he forgot to be cautious: 'Sir', said the Governor, with the letter in his hand, 'Ask your grandmother, the next time she writes to say that she is dying, to dry her ink!'

Blackheath, attending the Academy daily in company with his equerry, but he was well liked and completed the course with distinction, retaining an affection for the Royal Artillery and Woolwich throughout his life.

The exile to England of Louis Napoleon, Emperor of France, following the disastrous Franco-Prussian War in 1870, brought his son, the Prince Imperial, to the RMA – the natural place for the son of an artillery officer. He was a pleasant, popular young man who completed the course and duly passed out seventh in the order of merit in 1875. During his time at the RMA there was a disastrous fire in the central tower block that virtually destroyed its contents, including its valuable library. Restocking the library was helped by contributions from many other sources, with a notable contribution from the Prince of a beautifully bound set of books. 'Loulou', as he was known, went to Africa four years later to join the British troops during the Zulu War and was killed by a Zulu war party while on reconnaissance. In memory of him, a statue was erected in the grounds of the RMA, moved in 1955 to Sandhurst. There remains a local reference to him in the name of the married quarters behind the Academy – Prince Imperial Road.

Over the years, the Academy was selected for their sons' education by the scions of many of the ruling castes of other countries, particularly those in the Far East, and it was not unusual to have cadets from Siam (now Thailand), China, Iraq, Egypt, the Sudan and the Dominions, a custom that continues today at Sandhurst.

Practical training continued at the RMA throughout its history, with the emphasis on gun drill and the mechanics of moving heavy loads. There was plenty of equipment for this, and cadets learned to handle all types of guns, including the large-calibre coast guns, of which an example was emplaced in

'THE SHOP'

The RMA was known by everyone as 'The Shop'. No one knows for certain how or when the name came about, but research suggests the following reasons:

The Royal Arsenal itself was often referred to as 'The Shop' by those who worked there, presumably harking back to the days before its formal title, when it was developing as a workshop – or, indeed, many workshops. Interestingly, the nickname survived among some of the older hands well into the 20th century.

Cadets at the RMA presumably used the same expression in those days, so that being at 'The Shop' was just as accurate as being at the RMA, which was sited within the walls of the factory. Simple conservatism seems the most likely reason for the survival of the term 'The Shop' for the RMA when it moved to Woolwich Common, and it remained the same throughout its existence.

Given the Regiment's addiction to the technologies of artillery, perhaps it is also connected with the expression 'to talk shop' – to use jargon that is peculiar to a given community: when an enthusiastic Gunner starts to explain the niceties of ballistic angles, most other soldiers' eyes start to glaze over.

an embrasure especially constructed in the grounds. The Repository provided ample opportunity for rafting and bridging, and the senior term enjoyed a camp at Shoeburyness for live firing. As a result, when they left the RMA, the new officers were already fully trained to take their places in service batteries, whether at war or in peace.

Although the Crimean, Boer (1881) and South African Wars had their effects on the RMA, notably in the fluctuations in numbers required in wartime and the sudden drop in the years

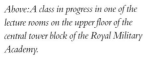

Above: A class in progress in one of the lecture rooms on the upper floor of the central tower block of the Royal Military Academy.

Right; Prince Arthur, son of Queen Victoria, arriving at the RMA on his daily journey from the Ranger's House on Blackheath, where he stayed. He is accompanied here by his equerry.

immediately following the end of hostilities, it was not until 1914 that a war impinged in a significant way.

With the outbreak of the First World War, the course was shortened from 18 to 6 months and the age limits for cadets widened from 17 to 25 years old. During those six months there were no vacations and games were limited to a minimum consistent with keeping fit. Only military subjects were taught and the throughput of cadets was greatly increased, with 860 GCs commissioned by February 1916. In a sad coincidence of numbers, the roll of GCs killed in 1914–18 also reached 860, of whom 578 were Gunners.

In the years that followed the First World War, significant changes began to appear. In 1923 the first cadets were commissioned into the new Royal Tank Corps; the following year saw GCs commissioned into the new Royal Corps of Signals. The new technologies began to make their appearance in the syllabus as mechanization grew in importance.

Nonetheless, the horse remained an important part of the life of a GC, as it had done since the middle of the Victorian era, when cadets were sent to the RA Barracks to be trained by the RA Riding Establishment. Oddly enough, the other important means of transport for GCs was the bicycle, which was provided as a result of its recognition by the Army as a suitable means of moving large numbers of soldiers from place to place on the battlefields of

Europe. Heavy and unwieldy as they were by modern standards, these bicycles provided an endless source of amusement and were used by GCs going on field trips for mapping or sketching exercises as well as to the Barracks or Repository. Long columns of cadets, riding two by two in (fairly) disciplined fashion, would wend their way to Plumstead Common or to Eltham, a familiar sight and no doubt presenting a road hazard to other traffic, but nothing like the hazard they would present on today's over-crowded roads!

An exercise in the Royal Military Repository, where a bridge has collapsed and the students are using sheerlegs to recover the gun before rebuilding the bridge.

Above: A drawing class taking place in the grounds of the Academy. All cadets were required to be able to draw a good representation of the countryside before them, so that they could use it to brief others.

Left: A new intake, not yet in uniform but getting their first taste of foot drill on the square.

Far right: King George V watches the cadets at the Academy's swimming baths during his visit.

Following the First World War, the straitened circumstances in which Britain found herself led inevitably to another round of savings proposals, one of which was a fresh assault on the independence of the RMA. This time, the proposal was agreed and August 1940 was set as the date when the RMA would amalgamate with the RMC. However, the Second World War intervened and the date was brought forward to 1 October 1939. When the order was finally given, the Academy was ready: from the time of its receipt to the time of the last GC leaving was a mere eight hours, with nothing left but a small contingent of staff to close up.

The RMA name lives on, of course. Sandhurst dropped the 'College' from its title and became the RMA Sandhurst from January 1947. Many of the RMA's traditions were adopted, together with other reminders, like the statue of Queen Victoria which stands on the long walk up to the grand entrance to Old College: the statue had originally been erected beside the RMA Woolwich Library in 1904 to commemorate her reign. The Kurnaul mortar (a 27in brass piece brought from a fort near Madras) moved from the Woolwich parade ground to the road junction between Old and New Colleges at Sandhurst, the Prince Imperial Statue to the New College parade ground. There is also the Woolwich Hall and, behind Old College, the administration area is called 'The Warren', recalling the days of the Old RMA in the grounds of Tower Place.

KAT

THE ROYAL MILITARY COLLEGE, SANDHURST

The Royal Military College had been established in 1802 at Great Marlow on the Thames for training officers for the cavalry and infantry, moving to Sandhurst in Surrey ten years later. In 1809 the East India Company took over the training of its own officers at Addiscombe Military Academy (near Croydon in Surrey) until 1861. The RMA remained the sole path to a commission in either the Royal Artillery or the Royal Engineers, neither of which allowed commissions by purchase (abolished 1871), unlike the cavalry and infantry.

Right: A statue of The Prince Imperial, Louis Napoleon, who became a cadet at the RMA when his father, the Emperor of France, was exiled to England after the debacle of the Franco-Prussian War. The statue was removed to the RMA Sandhurst in 1955.

Far right: A parade at the RMA, shown here to point out the statue of Queen Victoria, on the left, outside the Library, and the Kurnaul Mortar on the right, at the edge of the parade ground. Both these items were removed to the RMA Sandhurst where they now help to maintain the historic link with Woolwich.

67

The Royal Artillery Mess
The Victorian Period

Colonel Martin Cooper

The reign of Queen Victoria saw the zenith of Woolwich and the Royal Artillery Mess as well as the beginning of the decline in their status. During the first half of the period 'there was scarcely a crowned sovereign or person of high distinction who had figured in Europe who had not been entertained at the Royal Artillery Mess, which was everywhere renowned for its wealth and grandeur and princely hospitality'. The Mess was considered almost without equal in this country. The Crimean War provided a high point with many royal visitors to Woolwich occasionally hosted by the Queen and Prince Albert who attended Reviews and occasionally took refreshments at the Mess. On one occasion the Queen even visited the Mess library. Balls continued throughout the period with up to 1,000 guests recorded, dancing usually taking place in the Messroom, supper being served in marquees on the Front Parade, and anterooms providing sitting-out areas.

Royal visits reduced significantly after the death of Prince Albert (1861), with Queen Victoria withdrawing from public life. Balls in the Mess were replaced by lunches and dinners and, by the 1880s and 1890s, visitors to the Mess were mainly restricted to distinguished soldiers such as the Commander-in-Chief the Duke of Cambridge, Lord Roberts and Lord Kitchener.

The closure of the Royal Dockyard and subsequent departure from Woolwich of the Royal Navy and Royal Marines followed in the same decade as the death of the Prince Consort. At the same time, there was a gradual move of the centre of gravity of the Army to Aldershot in Hampshire. With improvements in transport increasing the options for State visits, there was a steady decline in the pre-eminence of both Woolwich and the Mess as venues of choice. In the Mess, the atmosphere also changed with the arrival of students from the newly opened Ordnance College.

The Victorian period also saw great change to the structure of the Mess, and 40 years after its opening the Messroom was enlarged by the removal of the bow window and two of the pillars. A breakfast room was created where the current servery is, the frieze added and gas lighting introduced. Finally, the four sideboards were purchased, with the Ordnance Office providing a large grant towards these improvements.

The influence of the Board of Ordnance is also apparent in the crafting of the frieze. It contains three coats of arms and two shields or 'trophies of arms'. The coats of arms are the Royal Coat of Arms in the Victorian form and those of the Board of Ordnance and General Sir George Murray, the Master General of the Ordnance at the time. Of the two shields, one depicts the Norse god Thor, together with a quiver of thunderbolts: this was a pun on *Th'ordnance*, as the words 'the ordnance' had usually been written up till that time. The second shows two bees head to head – a play on *bombus* or *bombos*, the Latin or Greek for a bee, which recalled the humming or buzzing sound

Below: The Messroom laid for dinner, a photograph from the turn of the century.

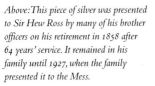

Above: This piece of silver was presented to Sir Hew Ross by many of his brother officers on his retirement in 1858 after 64 years' service. It remained in his family until 1927, when the family presented it to the Mess.

of shells and cannonballs in flight – an experience common to most soldiers on the battlefield. The bee is a well-known symbol for artillerymen throughout Europe: for example, it was Napoleon's chosen symbol. The words 'bomb' and 'bombardier' are derived from this root. A couple of years later, half of what became the east anterooms were taken over as reading rooms.

Twenty years later, during the 1860s, what became the Music Room at the top of the stairs and two adjacent billiard rooms were added to the Mess. The Music Room was initially a smoking room and then a card room. Most of the large paintings which hung in that room were acquired at the same time. Four of them commemorated the earlier link between the Regiment and the appointment of Master General of the Ordnance, namely Wellington, Anglesey and Lord Raglan, together with Field Marshal Sir Hew Ross, who deputized for Raglan while he was in the Crimea and became the Regiment's first field marshal. The Hew Ross silver centrepiece was presented to the Field Marshal on his retirement by the officers of the Regiment in 1858 but presented back to the Mess by his grandson in 1927.

On the abolition of the appointment of Master General of the Ordnance in 1855, command of the Regiment passed to the Commander-in-Chief, an appointment held by Lord Hardinge, a previous Master General. His modestly sized portrait hung on the Tiger landing (so named for the case of stuffed tigers on display there). He was replaced by a key figure in the life of the Regiment, the Duke of Cambridge, grandson of George III, chief aide-de-camp to Queen Victoria and Commander-in-Chief from 1856 until his retirement in 1895. A regular attendee at the Mess as Prince George, he became Colonel of the Regiment in 1862, a post upgraded to Colonel-in-Chief in 1895, and the only holder of that appointment not to be the monarch. He held this appointment until his death in 1904. His portrait joined the Master Generals in the Music Room as part of a set of nine made up by Lord Bloomfield and four officers of the Bengal Artillery. Of the latter the portrait of Field Marshal Viscount Gough by Francis Grant is the finest.

Another artistic addition to the Mess at this time was the marble statue of Armed Science, which was commissioned,

Top: Field Marshal Sir Hew Ross, painted in 1858 when he was about to retire from his post as Lieutenant-General of the Ordnance.

Above: Armed Science.

designed and presented by Colonel R.A. Shafto Adair (later Lord Waveney), Commander of the Suffolk Artillery Militia during the Crimean War and a regular user of the Mess. It was created by John Bell and was exhibited at the Royal Academy in 1855.

In 1861 the Messroom received its first royal portrait with the presentation by Queen Victoria of a copy of her 1859 portrait. The Mess commissioned a matching portrait of the Prince Consort. The year 1877 saw the arrival of the Mess's finest portrait – of General Sabine by George Watts – presented by an unknown benefactor. General Sir Edward Sabine was an officer with a scientific bent who distinguished himself above most others by becoming the President of the Royal Society. In 2000 this portrait was discovered to be missing and after research was located at Pirbright in Surrey where the training batteries had moved on the closure of 17th Training Regiment and Depot Royal Artillery in 1994. (It was replaced by a more suitable painting, *RHA Gun Team* by an unknown artist!)

It was not until the 1870s that the full east anterooms became a part of the Mess, providing four rooms for a variety of uses over the years (reading rooms, quiet room, medal room, morning room, card room, newspaper room and anteroom). The court martial room finally became the official anteroom to the Messroom, with the original anteroom, where the hall porter now sits, becoming the mess office. The Mess purchased a further two matching chandeliers and the final configuration

The gold ram's head, made using the cire-perdue process, was taken as a prize of war in the Ashanti campaign (1873–4). The artillery officers of the battery that supported the attack offered to buy it and presented it to the Mess.

of five chandeliers was adopted. By the time of the Kitchener dinner, photographed in 1898, the candles on the chandeliers, which had been lit only on special occasions, had been replaced by electric light.

THE ROYAL ARTILLERY (WOOLWICH) DRAG HUNT 1866–1939

Lieutenant Colonel A.M. Macfarlane

This pack of scent-hunting dogs was founded in 1866 by Captain A.H.W. Williams RA. The country was originally around Woolwich and Eltham, and the Drag became very popular locally. It suffered a severe setback in 1879, when there was an outbreak of rabies which resulted in the destruction of the pack. Although a new pack was purchased and hunting restarted in 1882–3, a further outbreak in 1884 destroyed the pack again. However, the Drag restarted yet again, and flourished once more.

Because so many officers were away on duty in South Africa, the pack was sold in January 1900, but it was reformed in October of that same year. The pack again completely disappeared soon after the start of the First World War, but was reformed in time for the 1918–19 season. By this time, the country adjacent to Woolwich was increasingly built over and the lines were laid much further afield, towards Sevenoaks and Edenbridge in Kent and around Romford and Upminster in Essex.

The pack continued to be very popular between the wars but, first mechanization and, finally, the Second World War sounded the knell, and the Drag succumbed for the last time in mid-1939.

The final lines in Kent were near Chislehurst, Bromley, Orpington, Farningham, Sevenoaks, Westerham and Penshurst, and in Essex near Upminster, East Horndon, Horngate, Ingatestone, Brentwood, Ongar, Abridge, Havering-atte-Bower and Chigwell Road.

The uniform was a dark blue frock coat with red collar

The Farmers' Dinner

Keepin' The Tambourine a rollin'

The opening Meet & Farmers dinner: Royal Artillery Draghunt

Left: A pastel by Gilbert Holiday showing not only a meet on the Front Parade of the RA Barracks, but also the annual Farmers' Dinner to thank those over whose land the Hunt operated.

Above: The Drag Hunt meets on the parade ground in front of the Royal Military Academy.

Above: This painting of Queen Victoria is a copy of the famous Winterhalter original in the Queen's Collection. The copyist was A. Melville and the painting was presented to the Mess by the Queen herself in November 1861.

Far right: The Goodwood Cup of 1864, a magnificent trophy that shows a scene at the Battle of Namur in 1695, in which Col Borgard commanded the artillery. This piece was presented to the Mess by Sir Desmond Brayley in 1968.

dress in the photograph of the Kitchener dinner, perhaps in deference to his background as Commanding Officer of the 17th Lancers.

The change in style of the period with a move towards entertaining military rather than royal dignitaries was further epitomized at the close of the Victorian era by the dinner given to welcome the return of Field Marshal Earl Roberts from South Africa in 1901 and his assumption of the appointment of Commander-in-Chief, which he held until the formal command of the Regiment passed to the newly formed Army Council in 1904. After a period when the Royal Artillery Band had played at the conclusion of the meal, this dinner marked the return of the band playing during dinner. For this occasion Cavaliere Zavertal wrote two notable pieces of music – the march 'Virtute et Valore', the motto of Earl Roberts, and 'Bless you, Bobs', played with vocal refrain.

The year 1904 was significant in the life of the Regiment and the Mess, as it not only saw the change in the command arrangements of the Army, but also the appointment of King Edward VII as Colonel-in-Chief of the Regiment on the death of the Duke of Cambridge.

THE LIGHTER SIDE OF MESS LIFE

Life in the RA Mess was not all serious! Two stories of this period come to mind:

One features the visit to Woolwich by Buffalo Bill's Wild West Circus, which was immensely popular – so much so that the subalterns of the Regiment invited the 'cowgirls' back to the Mess for dinner. This was held in the small West dining room, which had a superb circular table on which the girls danced after supper! The result was some deep scratches made by the spurs in their boots in the surface of the table, which have never been polished out.

The second story features the suits of armour held in the Rotunda, which excited the imagination of some subalterns. One dark and misty evening after dining in the Mess, they managed to gain access to the museum and, dressed in the armour, they clanked their way to the sentry at the Main Gate. Appearing out of the gloom, they were challenged by a nervous sentry and replied to his challenge with the muffled answer, 'This is the Old Guard.'

Their escapade was rewarded by a large number of extra Orderly Officer duties.

From 1845, following an edict from the Adjutant General that 'the officers of the army shall appear at least once a day in their regular uniform, and that they shall invariably appear in it at the mess', full dress was worn at dinner in the Mess. In 1859 the Duke of Cambridge, as Commander-in-Chief, authorized the wearing of the stable jacket in the Mess, although it took some time to become accepted. Presumably for comfort, it was often worn open until, in 1871, a red waistcoat buttoned to the throat was added. This, with a few modifications, became the Gunners' first mess dress. It continued as such until after the South African War, when it was replaced by the low waistcoat with dress-shirt style of mess dress. Interestingly, the Duke chose not to wear mess dress throughout his 40 years as Colonel/Colonel-in-Chief and he can be seen still wearing full

The Royal Garrison Church

The Rev. Dr Michael Gilman

Woolwich. 14 July 1944. 1855 hours.

Royal Garrison Church of St George, Woolwich, sustained extensive damage. Flying bomb struck West end of Church Hall which was demolished. The church is untenable.

So noted the War Diary for Headquarters, Woolwich Garrison, for the month of July 1944, issued by Brigadier H. A. Young, DSO, Commanding Officer, Woolwich Garrison (PRO WO 166/14584).

Woolwich suffered intermittent damage from what were described variously as 'missiles', during 1944. As well as damage to housing and factories in the town, the War Diary notes, in March and May, 'Nothing of interest'. In June: 'Pilotless aircraft dropped in Garrison area throughout the month; casualties to personnel and damage to barracks and other buildings have been caused.'

The worst month was July. In addition to the loss of the Church – in which there were no casualties – the Diary notes on 1 July, at 0745: 'Accommodation occupied by Woolwich Garrison Group A.T.S. [Auxiliary Territorial Service, the women's service] – 52–57 The Common – hit by flying bomb. One O.R. [other rank] killed and several admitted to hospital. Extensive damage to buildings.'

The Diary for July noted: 'Flying bombs continued to fall in the Garrison Area throughout the month, causing damage to buildings. No fatal casualties other than that reported above. Strength of Garrison – 331 Officers 8,139 Other Ranks.'

Flying bombs continued throughout August, but caused no casualties or damage. September was noted as: 'Nothing of interest', but October saw an 'airborne missile, believed to be rocket bomb, exploded in the air at approximately 5,000 feet over Shrapnel Barracks', but with no casualties and only superficial damage. By November the comment was: 'Nothing of interest'.

For the first few decades after the end of the Second World War – decades of continuing hardship – London was littered with evidence of the bombing raids and attacks by flying bombs – the V1s and V2s – which the city endured. Only a few of these traces now remain, one of which is the skeletal fragment of the building that survives at the eastern end of the Front Parade. The grand Garrison Church of St George, which

Below: The Royal Garrison Church, seen from the Front Parade with the Crimean Memorial in the foreground.

Below left: The nave of the Royal Garrison Church seen from the altar, looking towards the entrance (opposite the Front Parade).

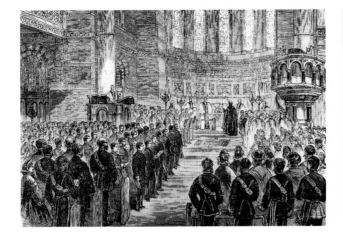

A drawing from the Illustrated London News *of the consecration of the church in 1863.*

had served the soldiers of the Woolwich Garrison for some 80 years, fell victim to a sample of the German advance in artillery which was the VI flying bomb.

Thus ended a distinctive feature of the landscape of the Common and of the complex of buildings of the Woolwich Garrison, together with the end of a well-loved aspect of the link between town and garrison. In the years before the war the church was the scene of the weekly church parades which were a feature of life in Woolwich: people would come from miles around to watch the troops on parade and the church itself would be packed.

The church was designed to replace the existing rather inadequate accommodation, and was built on the initiative of Sidney Herbert, the reforming Secretary of State for War during and after the Crimean War – after whom the Herbert Hospital was named – and was consecrated on 2 November 1863. The architects for the building were two brothers, Thomas Henry Wyatt (1807–80) and Matthew Digby Wyatt, 13 years his junior, members of the distinguished family of architects.

T. H. Wyatt was an extremely successful architect, with a large country house practice. With his brother he submitted the successful competition design for Knightsbridge Barracks (Hyde Park) but, perhaps demonstrating an even closer link with Sidney Herbert, he was also the architect for the parish church of Saints Mary and Nicholas at Wilton, near Salisbury, which was paid for by Sidney Herbert and his mother, Catherine, Countess of Pembroke.

This was built in the 1840s, and is described by John Martin Robinson, in his *The Wyatts: An Architectural Dynasty* as 'the most ambitious Anglican church undertaken for a hundred years and the first of a great series of churches built on their estates by conscientious Victorian landowners'. Wilton church may well

be described as a tour de force. In style it was historicist; the style chosen was Italian Romanesque or Lombardic; a choice that Dr Robinson attributes to Herbert. The interior was inspired by the early basilicas of Rome – particularly San Clemente – and is enriched with works of art imported from Italy. Inevitably, the building was criticized by the Camden Society for being 'unEnglish' – namely not Gothic.

The new Garrison Church at Woolwich was described in the *Illustrated London News*, in an article of 21 February 1863, thus:

> One of the last acts of the late Lord Herbert's official life was to give his sanction to the execution of the designs which had been prepared for the Garrison Chapel, Woolwich, by the well-known architects Messrs. Thomas Henry and Digby Wyatt, who, it may be remembered, had recommended themselves to the authorities of the War Department by obtaining the first premium for the construction of the cavalry barracks.

It continues:

> The structure is very large, and is sufficiently wide and lofty to provide the proper cubical amount of air to 1,500 officers and men forming the garrison at Woolwich. It is situated at the East end of the great Esplanade in front of the Artillery Barracks, and will form a great ornament to the not unpicturesque Common.

The building comprised a nave and two aisles, with balconies in the aisles. These were supported on cast-iron columns with decorative capitals and were continued above the balconies to support the round arches of the nave arcades. The nave itself was raised by a clerestory above the aisles. The walls were of exposed, multi-coloured, patterned brickwork, and the ceiling of the nave was flat and panelled, and supported by cross-arches. There was an apsidal sanctuary and pews of a simple, Gothic pattern. As at Wilton, the same personal choice of style was seen in the Garrison Church at Woolwich and the *Illustrated London News* remarks that:

The style is an adaptation of the general features of Lombardic architecture to the materials and technical processes in use in the nineteenth century … The materials are solid, real and used without any apparent stint. Externally and internally the walls are finished in brick … Without any plastering the effect of the warm red of the internal walls is peculiarly agreeable.

The Garrison Church marked a welcome change from the usual 'official architecture' used for the Church of England as found in many of the chaplaincies abroad. So often in a foreign capital one turns the corner of a street to find a rather uninspired piece of English late-19th century Gothic Revival, faced in Kentish ragstone, which always proclaims, 'this is the Church of England.' The Garrison Church was an interesting example of a blend of historicism with modern materials and technique with the ebullient assurance of the mid-Victorian era that things were only getting better.

The word I would use for it is 'bravura', which the *Oxford English Dictionary* defines as 'brilliant or ambitious execution, forced display', a quality that is expressed even more ambitiously in the parish church at Wilton. This is not far distant from the Regiment's new Wiltshire headquarters at Larkhill, and while it demonstrates the historicism that characterized the Garrison Church, it also demonstrates what that church might have looked like if costs had not been constrained by the War Office.

Above left: A church parade in progress. Until after the Second World War attendance at church parades was a requirement for all members of the Army, and visitors would come to watch them from many miles around Woolwich.

Below and below left: The remains of the Royal Garrison Church, showing the chancel together with an enlargement of the beautiful mosaic Victoria Cross memorial.

OTHER BARRACKS AND MILITARY BUILDINGS IN WOOLWICH

Almost all of the barracks that were erected between the late 18th century and the end of the 19th century have disappeared, the sites now used mainly for residential housing, a hospital and council offices. A time-traveller from that period would certainly recognize the South Front and Front Parade of the Royal Artillery Barracks and the Rotunda, but little else would be familiar.

Grand Depot Barracks. These were constructed in 1787 and were originally the home of the Artillery Park in the days when this organization was defined as a separate part of the Royal Artillery (see map of 1806, page 32). Judging from the state of the buildings in the 1960s, the 'Grand' in the title was something of a misnomer and it is hardly surprising that no part of them was considered worth saving when they were demolished. However, they were certainly extensive, occupying the whole of the north side of the road that runs from the RA Barracks to the town centre. It was clearly not considered to be an attractive posting: a Gunner euphemism for someone dying in those days was, 'He's been ordered to report to the Grand Depot.'

During the first half of the 19th century the Grand Depot Barracks was literally a depot for stores, among which was the Military Clothing Store, which moved in 1868 to Pimlico in the City of Westminster. The Grand Depot barracks were demolished in the major reconstruction that took place in Woolwich during the 1970s and were replaced by council offices.

The Royal Engineers' Barracks were at the town end of Grand Depot Barracks, which lay alongside the road that swept down from the RA Barracks to General Gordon Place. (Major General Charles Gordon was, of course, a famous Sapper.)

When the Sappers left Woolwich after the Crimean War, the whole of the Grand Depot Barracks gradually became used for artillery units.

Army Service Corps. Opposite the Grand Depot Barracks was another complex of barracks occupied by the Army Service Corps as that corps evolved from the Military Train. These barracks were built alongside the old RA hospital (1780), later named Connaught Barracks. A further set of hutted barracks were put up for the Army Service Corps at the town end of New Road, which runs from the Common to join Grand Depot Road near the town centre.

When the Army Service Corps left Woolwich for Aldershot, this latter complex was adapted for rather poor-quality married quarters, but eventually, like the Grand Depot barracks, it was demolished during the 1970s. However, Connaught Barracks remained and, after conversion, is now occupied as private residences.

Below, left and right: Part of the Grand Depot Barracks that lined the road between the RA Barracks and the town. They were demolished in the 1960s. These pictures show the main gate and one of the store buildings that were originally built to contain the ordnance of the Artillery Park.

Red Barracks and Cambridge Barracks were side by side in Frances Street and their use changed frequently during the Victorian and early Edwardian eras. Red Barracks began as the Royal Marine Infirmary in 1859, a substitute for the original hospital built on this site in 1815. The Naval Hospital in Red Barracks was built on lines approved by Florence Nightingale, who was championing the improvement of military hospitals in general. The entrance to the Red Barracks was known as Borgard's Gate – a nice recognition of the important role played by Borgard, the Royal Artillery's first Colonel, in Woolwich.

A fourth 'division' of Royal Marines was established in Woolwich in 1805 to guard the Royal Dockyard and was initially quartered in a converted brewery alongside Frances Street. In 1847 the brewery was demolished and Cambridge Barracks took its place, housing the Royal Marines until 1869 when the

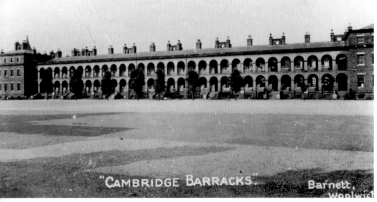

Woolwich Division was broken up, being no longer required for the defence of the Royal Dockyard, which closed that same year.

When the Marines left Woolwich, the Red Barracks were occupied by the Ordnance Corps and used, in conjunction with the storage facilities in the defunct dockyard, for stores. Red Barracks also found rooms for the Artillery College, which gradually expanded to become the main tenant by the end of the Great War.

The Cambridge Barracks side of the complex was also used for a time as the Artificers' training centre. At the end of the 19th century Cambridge Barracks itself was refurbished, and part of it

Above: Part of Connaught Barracks.

Left: Cambridge Barracks, now demolished.

Below: The map shows (highlighted) Red Barracks, Connaught Barracks, Cambridge Barracks and the Grand Depot Barracks, on either side of the RA Barracks. Shrapnel Barracks were on Woolwich Common, half a mile south of the RA Barracks, not shown here.

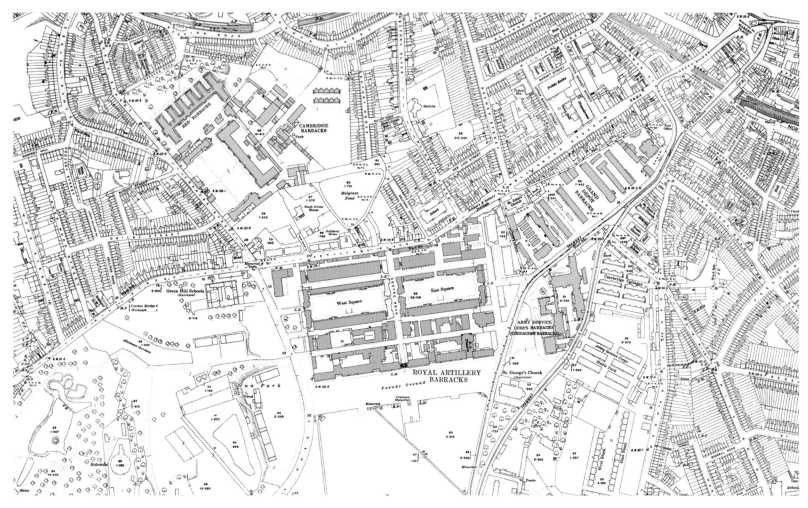

Red Barracks, originally built as a hospital for the Royal Navy in connection with the Royal Dockyard, but later used by the Ordnance Corps and the Artillery College. Demolished in the rebuild of the area and now, like the Cambridge Barracks site, a housing estate.

was used as a normal unit barracks, housing infantry as well as Royal Artillery units during the early part of the 20th century.

Both sets of barracks were pulled down and replaced in the major reconstruction that took place in Woolwich between 1960 and 1975.

A sad story that rings true as typical of the problem of dealing with historical records concerns the huge amounts of ordnance records in the cellars of Red Barracks when the time came for the Ministry of Defence to vacate them. There was nowhere to put them and no organization was interested in taking them, so the cellars were bulldozed with the material still in place and the new housing development was built on top of them.

Shrapnel Barracks. This was a large hutted camp (named after the inventor of the explosive shell in 1785, Lieutenant, later Lieutenant General, Henry Shrapnel RA, whose device was adopted in 1803) on the western side of Woolwich Common and was used as a cavalry barracks for much of the 19th century. It was refurbished towards the end of the century and was then used by the Royal Artillery until the buildings were demolished in the 1960s to make way for the hospital that occupies the site today. (This was for many years a military hospital, but has now become a major National Health hospital serving the Greenwich area.)

While there are no pictures to prove the point, it is probable that the early hutted camp lacked the amenities of a permanent barracks like those of the Royal Artillery, which would explain why the officers of each of the visiting regiments were made honorary members of the RA Mess. In turn, this accounts for the very generous presentations of silver to the Mess – presents that would not have been justified simply as a recognition of occasional hospitality.

In the mid-19th century the maps of the period show well-marked paths between these barracks and a large complex of stables and manèges (riding-school facilities) on the southern border of the Common alongside the Shooters Hill Road, a facility that appears to have been shared with the RA Barracks.

The Artillery College. With the RA Institution's new building as its base, a Department of Artillery Studies was formed in 1850 to supervise the studies of young officers on first joining

the Regiment. However, thanks to the Crimean War, it was not until 1858 that it really got fully under way with a much wider range of subjects and a remit to assist officers of all ranks. Some five years later, following a report on the state of higher instruction in the Royal Artillery, an 'Advanced Class' was established within the Department. In 1885 the Department became the Artillery College and, three years later, moved to its own home in Red Barracks.

In addition to the main courses for officers – the 'Young Officers', the 'Advanced Class' and the 'Firemasters' – the 'Long Course' of the School of Gunnery came for three months every year, and there were constant short courses on electricity, steam, hydraulics and similar subjects.

In January 1899 the name was changed again, this time to the 'Ordnance College', its courses were thrown open to the Army as a whole and it ceased to be a Regimental institution.

After the First World War the College took over the whole of Red Barracks and reverted to its former name, 'Artillery College'. In 1927 the title became the 'Military College of Science' in view of the much wider range of subjects covered. The last Advanced Class was the 57th that graduated in 1940, though that title lived on in the 'Advanced Class Dinner Club' until the 1990s for ex-graduates and, later, for officers who had successfully completed a tour as a Weapons Staff Officer: the dinners were frequently held in the RA Mess.

In view of the risk in being close to London, the College moved to Lydd on the coast of Kent and then to a series of temporary homes until it arrived at Shrivenham, Wiltshire, in 1946, receiving its 'Royal' addition in 1953. It is worth noting that the role of the original founder of the RAI, Captain (later General) Lefroy is remembered at Shrivenham in the name of the Lefroy Lecture Theatre.

Government House, an elegant late Georgian house at the junction of Woolwich Common Road, Ha Ha Road and Nightingale Place was bought by the Board of Ordnance in about 1840 to house Commandants of the Royal Arsenal. Up to this time, they were housed in the Arsenal, but when Lord Bloomfield was appointed Commandant, his wife refused to live there and rented a house in Charlton. When the Board of Ordnance ceased to exist, the building became the Garrison Headquarters. It was in continual use in that role until the late 1990s, when the Garrison HQ moved to the western end of the RA Barracks, occupying the offices vacated by HQ Director RA on its move to Larkhill. In 2007 the building remains unoccupied.

Hospitals. Behind Government House was an Infirmary and the 'Womens' Hospital', later more widely known as the Military Maternity Hospital (or 'milimat') and used as such by the families of military personnel throughout the London area. (The editor of this book was born there, though his father was stationed at that time in Hounslow, attached to a cavalry unit.) This building was also demolished after the Second World War.

The Royal Herbert Hospital was an enormous and important hospital on Shooters Hill Road – the Army's main military hospital built immediately after the Crimean War and surviving in this role until after the Second World War. It has now been converted to attractive private dwellings.

KAT

THE ROYAL ARTILLERY THEATRE

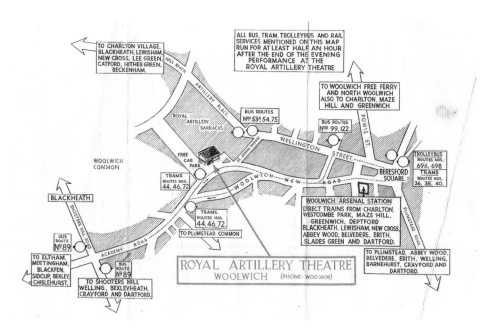

Above: The map on the back of a programme, showing how to find the RA Theatre.

Opposite: The auditorium of the RA Theatre on a typical evening in the early part of the 20th century, showing not only its impressive size but its 'packed house'.

The enjoyment of amateur theatricals extended throughout society in the 18th and 19th centuries and the Army was no exception. Cadets in the Old RMA in the Warren were fond of putting on plays, and this form of entertainment continued to hold a fascination well into the 20th century. This article draws on pieces written for the RA Journal and from newspaper and magazine reports on plays performed at the RA Theatre.

The following is extracted from an article by General Sir Desmond O'Callaghan, a keen amateur actor who was a leading figure in the story of the RA Theatre in the latter half of the 19th century:

NEWSPAPER REPORT ON THE OPENING NIGHT, 22 FEBRUARY 1864

The building is a capacious, comfortable and beautiful theatre, having a lofty and roomy stage and a pretty drop curtain. The seats on the ground floor were occupied by Artillerymen and their female friends; the first tier or dress circle, which is fitted up exclusively with stuffed armchairs, was filled with fashionably dressed ladies and military officers in uniform; and the upper tier, or gallery, was taken possession of by a crowd of persons who, though they gained admission to the place by the payment of one-fourth of a shilling, were perfectly orderly.

My dream as a Cadet in '58–'61, in which I saw prophetically the Garrison Chapel of those days transformed into a Theatre, was realized when the RA Theatre was opened on 22 February 1864. Previous to this, however, the RA Theatrical Club had been formed in 1862 and I had the honour of playing a small part in Theseus and Ariadne, *as a very young officer, in the opening performance under the patronage of General [later Field Marshal]* Sir Richard Dacres, *in November of that year, when a Prologue, written by J. R. Planché, the author of the play, was spoken by Captain Arthur Twiss RA.*

The Club was formed under the Presidency of Colonel, afterwards General 'Charley' du Plat, then ADC and Equerry to the late Queen Victoria. We all had ivory tickets inscribed with our names, and many distinguished play-acting amateurs were numbered among our members. The Canterbury Old Stagers (the founders of the I Zingari [cricket club]) and the Windsor Strollers were frequent performers.

Before the building of the RA Theatre in 1864, we played in the Riding School, and I remember performances being given by the Old Stagers, assisted by members of the Club, in the Town Theatre, which was then close to the Old Mortar Tavern. The RA Theatre was

The entrance to the RA Theatre, c.1925, together with the programme for the theatre's first performance in 1864.

"MURDER ON THE SECOND FLOOR"—BY THE GUNNERS

MRS. F. L. McNAUGHTON (Mrs. Armitage) AND MRS. J. R. BYRNE (Miss Snell)   MR. FEWLASS LLEWELLYN (the producer) AND MAJOR A. J. C. POLLOCK (Hugh Bromilow)   MR. G. E. S. PROES (P.C. Thomson) AND CAPTAIN J. H. LEATHER (Jam Singh)

completed in February of that year, performances (of a play called The Mummy) being given on the 22nd and 23rd, in both of which I had the honour to take part.

Under the able management of Colonel du Plat, the Club throve and performances were frequent. Soldiering was then not quite so strenuous as it is now and there was more time to study one's part and to rehearse.

Burned down in November 1903, the Theatre was not rebuilt until 1905, and was re-opened by Lord Roberts in the afternoon of 21 December. In this performance I also took part, so that I may claim to have assisted at three epoch-making occasions, viz.: the inauguration of the Club in 1862, the opening of the Theatre in 1864 and its re-opening in 1905. I was not present at the fire.

The new theatre was erected at a cost of £11,000 (£850,000 today) of which the War Office paid half, and it continued to be a garrison asset. However, it was leased after the First World War to a commercial company which put on a great many shows with well-known professional actors. Many of the best-known vaudeville acts of the time, Tommy Trinder among them, made a point of accepting invitations to play at the RA Theatre, where they were assured of a rousing reception.

The theatre was patronized by the members of the garrison, but increasingly also by the townspeople of Woolwich and the surrounding area. It was badly damaged during the Second World War, but repaired and re-opened for a short while. However, by this time it was in competition with the cinema and, like many similar theatres in the London area, it was not a viable enterprise and ceased to operate. It was demolished along with other rebuilding of the Front Parade in the 1960s.

KAT

Top left: A cutting from a London paper, reviewing a play at the RA Theatre, together with (above) some examples of the playbills and programmes used.

Above: On stage, the cast of the production of The Pirates of Penzance *by Gilbert and Sullivan.*

FRANKIE HOWERD AND THE RA THEATRE

The father of the comedian, Frankie Howerd, was Sergeant Frank Howard of the Royal Artillery. During the 1930s he was stationed in Woolwich and the family lived in one of the 'hutments' in Eltham, erected for munitions workers at the Royal Arsenal during the First World War – there were hundreds of these still in use at that time.

Frankie Howerd changed the spelling of his name when he became a full-time actor after the Second World War, having served throughout it as a Gunner, rising to Bombardier. In his autobiography*, he recalls as a small boy:

Another crystal clear memory, and one of much greater importance in terms of my later development, is of the first of our regular Boxing Day visits to the pantomime.

My mother took the three of us to the Woolwich Artillery Theatre and queued for eightpenny seats in the gallery. The normal price was sixpence, but Boxing Night was the traditional opening date, so they upped the price, and we had to walk the long distance there and back so as not to make too big a hole in my mother's very tight budget.

The panto's principal boy was Nora Delaney (and was to be in most of the years that followed) and for me, aged six, it was love at first sight ...

So there I sat in what seemed to be this huge theatre ... absolutely hypnotised by the fairyland magic of Cinderella ...

(*On The Way I Lost It – published by W. H. Allen & Co. Ltd, 1976)

SECTION 4
The Depot

THE HOME OF THE ROYAL ARTILLERY 1716–1939

Lieutenant Colonel W.A.H. Townend

From its formation in 1716, Woolwich was the 'home' of the Royal Artillery; the headquarters of the Regiment was in Tower Place in the Warren. This controlled the moves of companies between stations, the allocation of companies to operations and the postings and promotions of officers.

The first two permanent companies – Richards's, long disbanded, and Pattison's, now 19 (Gibraltar 1779–83) Battery – were both based at Woolwich. By 1757 and the start of the Seven Years War the Regiment had expanded to 24 companies and was organized into two battalions, each controlling 12 companies; six of these companies were stationed at Woolwich. By 1771 and the eve of the American War of Independence there were 32 companies in four battalions of which 12 were at Woolwich. The companies in Woolwich were quartered in barracks in the Warren; they trained at the Royal Military Repository and fired their guns on Plumstead Marshes.

The iconic South Arch – in fact the South Gate – of the RA Barracks, which has been in place for over 200 years.

Woolwich remained the home of the Regiment when these activities moved to the new barracks on Woolwich Common. By 1793 and the start of the Napoleonic Wars there were 42 companies of which nine were at Woolwich. Ten years later there were 80 companies in eight battalions, of which eight were at Woolwich as well as nine newly raised companies of the new 8th Battalion. At the height of the war in 1812 the Regiment had expanded to 100 companies (each 142 all ranks) in ten battalions, but only six companies were at Woolwich, reflecting the increasing involvement of British troops in the war. Post-war reductions reduced the size of the Regiment to 72 companies in nine battalions, of which 18 were at Woolwich, the highest proportion ever, with a further 12 having disbanded there during 1819.

These figures remained constant until the 1850s and the eve of the Crimean War, when the Regiment expanded again. Numbers

Previous page: Gunners 'taking post' during gun drill on the Front Parade. The guns are 25-pounders.

Below: A busy scene in the West Square of the RA Barracks, c.1935, as a Royal Horse Artillery Troop assembles for a parade rehearsal, the horse-drawn 13-pounders heading for the West Gate. Note the musicians also getting ready and, among the onlookers, Gunners in the doorway of the barrack-room on the balcony: the stables were at ground level.

rose to 96 companies in 12 battalions in 1853 and 112 companies in 14 battalions by 1856, of which 12 were at Woolwich. In addition, seven field batteries of instruction – the guns, horses, equipment and artificers of a battery – were based at Woolwich. The Riding House Department of His Majesty's Ordnance – later the Riding Establishment RHA and the genesis of the King's Troop RHA – was also there, together with the RA Band.

In addition to the regular companies, eight Invalid companies had been raised in 1770, of which five were based at Woolwich. These companies were made up of older gunners deemed unfit for overseas service, but fit enough to serve the guns in the fixed fortifications. By 1803 there were 12 Invalid companies with eight based at Woolwich. However, the Invalid companies were disbanded in 1819.

Throughout this period, companies rarely spent more than two years, and sometimes as little as six months, at Woolwich before proceeding overseas again. They lived in the Royal Artillery Barracks, expanding into Grand Depot Barracks in the 19th century.

In 1859 the Royal Artillery underwent a major reorganization in which the old system of battalions, companies and troops was replaced by brigades and batteries, the aim being to make permanent the allocation of personnel to equipment, and to decentralize the administration of the Regiment. The intention under the new brigade system was that reliefs were to be carried out by brigades: before a brigade proceeded abroad, it should spend a year at Woolwich, which was not only the headquarters of the Regiment but was where the most advanced instruction was provided. Very nearly a complete field brigade together with some RHA batteries and the whole of a garrison artillery brigade could be accommodated in the, by now, very extensive barracks. The brigades next in line for foreign service were also those most likely to be next for active service and their batteries therefore needed to be the most efficient as, for example, they were in 1860, when 4th Brigade sent batteries to China and New Zealand.

Following their heroic action at Sanna's Post in the South African War, winning four Victoria Crosses, Q Battery RHA returned to a warm welcome in Woolwich. Here, the Battery is on the Front Parade, wearing the uniforms from that war, being addressed by the small lone figure of Field Marshal Earl Roberts of Kandahar - the famous 'Bobs', who was by this time both Chief of the Imperial General Staff and Master Gunner St James's Park. He presented the Battery, on behalf of the Regiment, with a large silver copy of Armed Science, seen on the table in front of him.

With the absorption of the batteries of the Honourable East India Company Armies in 1862, the Regiment increased to 200 batteries in 25 brigades, but by 1877 this had reduced to 120 batteries, still in 25 brigades. There was also a Depot Brigade organized in eight batteries. Its personnel comprised the employed non-commissioned officers and men belonging to the Regiment in the garrison, including the Band, and partly the recruits enlisted for brigades on Indian and Colonial service. Recruits for home service brigades were trained in their units, but by 1889 all the brigade depot batteries were concentrated at Woolwich as the 1st and 2nd Depot Brigades. The Depot Brigade was also responsible for training the Volunteer artillery companies. The RHA had its depot at Woolwich with a similar organization and tasks.

In 1871 there were further changes in the Regiment, and minor changes had already been carried out to the depots including the removal of some of the depot batteries from Woolwich in order to create territorial connections. There was a central depot staff at Woolwich, but the 1st Division of five batteries was at Shoeburyness and the 2nd Division at Woolwich with seven batteries.

Firing practice was carried out on Woolwich Common until the 1860s when the School of Gunnery was set up at Shoeburyness; later, Okehampton (Devon), Trawsfynnyd (north Wales), Glen Imaal (County Wicklow, Ireland), Lydd (Kent) and Larkhill (Wiltshire) were developed as ranges.

The whole period marked the change in the role of Woolwich from being a centre where service batteries were stationed between operational and garrison deployments, to one that concentrated on individual training and administration.

In 1899 the Regiment divided into the Royal Field Artillery – with the Royal Horse Artillery an elite within it – and the Royal Garrison Artillery manning the fixed fortifications and siege trains. Field batteries were reorganized in 18-gun brigades, which were permanent tactical groupings of three batteries commanded by a lieutenant colonel; by the end of the South African War in 1902 there were 50 of them. Six of these were training brigades, of which one, XLIII [43] Brigade, was at Woolwich. In 1913 these were reorganized as

REGIMENTAL ORGANIZATION 1716–1877

DATE	NO. OF COMPANIES/ BATTERIES	NO. OF BATTALIONS/ BRIGADES	NO. OF COYS/ BTYS IN WOOLWICH	NOTES
1716	2		2	Date of formation
1722	4	1	1	Artillery trains abroad incorporated as coys
1757	24	2	6	Start of the Seven Years War
1771	32	4	12	Before the American War of Independence
1793	42	4	9	Start of the Napoleonic Wars
1803	80	8	8 (+ 9 coys newly raised for the new 8th Bn)	The Peace of Amiens
1812	100	10	6	Height of the Napoleonic Wars
1819	72	9	18	Following peace in 1815
1853	96	12		The Crimean War
1856	112	14	12	
1859	Reorganization to include Honourable East India Company's Artillery			
1862	200	25	4 service, 10 Depot	
1877	120	25	9 service 4 Depot	

The changes in organization, training and nomenclature after this period make it difficult to continue this information in tabular form, but the above shows that, throughout the 18th and 19th centuries, Woolwich had a significant role as the Regimental depot. This continued into the 20th century and expanded enormously during the two world wars.

reserve brigades which, together with the six depots, were each affiliated to a division of the British Expeditionary Force; XLIII then became 4 Reserve Brigade.

At the outbreak of the First World War one RHA (X) and three RFA field force brigades (XXXII, XXXV and XXXVII

A group of the headquarters staff at the turn of the century, beside one of the gates within the RA Barracks. They are posed around a 12-pounder Rifled Breech Loader of the type used in the South African War.

trained soldiers for the RHA and RFA and, together with reserve brigades elsewhere in the country, trained over a quarter of a million men for over 400 new batteries. While most of the New (Kitchener) Army field batteries were formed with their divisions at their camps around the country, most of the new Royal Garrison Artillery heavy and siege batteries and brigades were formed from drafts from existing RGA units, many of which mobilized at Woolwich before moving overseas. The School of Instruction for non-commissioned officers, the Heavy Artillery Training Centre and Number 4 Depot RFA were also at Woolwich and the RMA continued to train officers on short six-month courses.

In 1922 the Royal Artillery depots were once again concentrated at Woolwich to become the Depot, Royal Artillery with Depot Headquarters and the Depot Brigade with two training brigades, two boys' batteries and all ranks in transit under command. The Riding Establishment, the Royal Artillery Band and the Royal Military Academy remained at Woolwich, Headquarters RA 44 (Home Counties) Division Territorial Army was in the garrison and a field brigade was stationed in Shrapnel Barracks. This was XIII [13] Brigade from 1921 to 1926, then XVIII [18] Brigade until 1933 followed by XVII [17] Brigade until the outbreak of the Second World War.

[Howitzer]) were stationed at Woolwich, together with the RHA Depot and 4 Reserve Brigade and Number 4 Depot RFA. During the Great War X [10] Brigade RHA acted as the Reserve Brigade RHA and 4 Reserve Brigade RFA split into 4A remaining at Woolwich and 4B at Boyton, Wiltshire; these units

HONOUR TITLES

It is not surprising to learn that, within the Royal Regiment of Artillery, troops, companies and, later, batteries were not entirely happy about losing their treasured distinctions when the order came to remove them all and substitute the one word *Ubique*. They felt that it took away something of their history and traditions, removed something that made them distinguishable one from another and, to make matters worse, used a Latin word that meant nothing to most soldiers: the concept of being distinguished 'Everywhere' took a long time to sink in.

As a consequence, they continued to use unofficial subtitles derived from their history, though these were not, of course, recognized by the Army and varied greatly in worthiness. This loss of individual distinction was a sore point within the Regiment, not helped when the initial attempt in 1902 to regularize some of these 'titles' resulted in the anomaly of the Commander-in-Chief (Field Marshal Lord Roberts) ruling against the proposals, but granting as a title to A Battery RHA the nickname by which it had long been known, but which had not been put forward for official recognition! Nonetheless, from this point it became formally 'A Battery (The Chestnut Troop) Royal Horse Artillery', while other claims were not recognized.

It was not until 1925 that the War Office invited the Regiment to examine claims from batteries for any 'titles or emblems of distinction gained in war or otherwise'. They were to be examined by the Historical Committee of the Regiment and, if approved,

submitted to the Adjutant General. Those which passed muster were to be included in the Regimental List and used within the Regiment. These became Honour Titles and were either original distinctions (like Sphinx), placenames (like Louisburg), the name of a commander at the time of the distinction (like Mercer), or, more rarely, a nickname (like The Broken Wheel). There have been numerous proposals such as these

over the years and many have been granted, though for batteries which have not yet acquired titles, it has become increasingly difficult to find sufficiently strong evidence to convince either the Historical Committee or the Army. However, suffice it to say that there are batteries which are entirely content with their status and happy to remain as they are. As the French might say, *'Vive la différence!'*

The Honour Title of O Battery (The Rocket Troop) RHA stems from the Battle of Leipzig, 18th October 1813, when the Rocket Brigade was in the bodyguard of the Crown Prince of Sweden. Original painting by David Rowlands.

ROYAL VISITS

Although there had been no further royal visits by Queen Victoria after the death of the Prince Consort in 1861, Woolwich was still on the visiting list for the Royal family and frequently visited by Prince Arthur, Duke of Connaught, who had trained at the RMA.

Following his accession to the throne in January 1901, King Edward VII visited the Regiment and reviewed a large body of troops on the Front Parade before moving on to visit the RMA. An interesting feature of the visit was that the royal party travelled to Woolwich by car – the first time motor transport had been used for such a visit.

King George V, accompanied by Queen Mary, visited on 9 April 1913. He, too, reviewed the troops, visited the Royal Garrison Church and the RMA. He was entertained to a luncheon in his honour in the RA Mess, following which he presented a superb silver-gilt cup. The following letter from the Keeper of the Privy Purse to the President of the Mess Committee explains why the presentation was made:

Buckingham Palace
15 April 1913
Dear General Phipps-Hornby,

I have received The King's commands to forward you by messenger a silver-gilt Cup, with its explanatory engraving. His Majesty when at luncheon with the Officers on the 9th instant admired a very beautiful piece of plate presented to the Mess by His late Majesty William IV. The King failed to see that any other of his predecessors had presented

Above: HM King Edward VII with a group of officers standing outside the RA Mess at the RA Barracks

Right and above right: The visit by HM King Edward VII in 1913, showing him in a carriage reviewing the Gentleman Cadets at the Royal Military Academy and taking a salute at a parade in his honour on the Front Parade.

Royal Visit to Woolwich. 9.4.1913.
March past of Cadets. R.M. Academy.

Above: HM King George V arriving at the Royal Military Academy when he visited Woolwich in 1936.

Below: A formal picture of the officers of the garrison on the Front Parade with their Colonel-in-Chief, HM King George V, shown here with Queen Mary, who accompanied him on the visit.

plate to the Mess. Be that, however, as it may, the King remembering that he is a sailor, as King William was, determined to follow King William's excellent example by presenting a cup to your Mess. His Majesty makes this gift not only as your Colonel-in-Chief, but also in remembrance of the most interesting day spent at Woolwich on Wednesday last, the first occasion of the King's visit since the accession. His Majesty also wishes me to assure you and the Officers of his full appreciation of the hospitality that was afforded to The King and The Queen on the above interesting occasion.

> *Yours very truly*
> *William Carrington*

King George VI visited Woolwich in 1950, becoming the first monarch actually to dine in the Mess at what became known as 'The King's Dinner' and during which the decision to change his title to Captain General was discussed. Queen Elizabeth II visited the Mess on five occasions: lunches following reviews in 1958, 1969, and 1993, the latter on the bicentenary of the Royal Horse Artillery; and dinners to celebrate her Silver Jubilee in 1976 and her Golden Jubilee and the 50th anniversary of her father's dinner in 2000. The Queen also visited the *Firepower* museum, in the Royal Arsenal, Woolwich, and unveiled a plaque commemorating the occasion.

KAT

The Royal Artillery Canteen

No one can say when the idea first occurred of providing soldiers with an opportunity to supplement their issued 'rations' with food and drink, but it seems likely to be ages old. It would be surprising if enterprising merchants did not follow the Roman legions on their campaigns, or even the hordes of Genghis Khan as they rampaged across the Asiatic continent. Military provisions have always tended to be spartan and soldiers like their comforts.

Certainly there was money to be made, especially when there was little competition. Cutting out the competition meant getting an exclusive contract and a system grew up whereby a sutler (civilian provisioner) would be appointed by the colonel of a regiment, accompanying the unit on campaign to provide all those items that the Commissariat (the official source of meat, bread and cheese) did not distribute. However, the sutler was a wartime concept and did not operate in peacetime until the late 18th century, when proper barracks started to appear and soldiers began to live together in large numbers, as opposed to being billeted wherever accommodation could be found for them.

At first, these tradesmen set up shops outside the barracks, but it was not long before they were able to arrange contracts for premises inside. A sutler would then pay rent to the Board of Ordnance, which was responsible for all barracks, together with 'privilege money', based on the number of men in the barracks, raking this back in the profits from selling bad liquor at high prices and having a monopoly on the trade.

Among the first of these arrangements was the Royal Artillery Canteen, established in the RA Barracks in 1787, but from the outset, it differed from the normal as regards control. Perhaps because it was the first, or perhaps because the Woolwich sutler made a separate contract to supply the Officers' Mess with food and drink, thereby operating from the back premises of the Mess, but certainly he paid nothing to the Board of Ordnance, contributing both rent and 'privilege money' to the Officers' Mess instead. This questionable system continued well into the 19th century, even when the canteen moved to new premises

in the centre of the Barracks. It was not until 1833 that the Board of Ordnance discovered the anomaly and promptly stopped it, although it did arrange for compensation to be paid from the Treasury – a compensation that continued to be paid every year for well over a century, although the initial scale of 50 per cent was reduced in 1925.

The canteen-keeper, as he was known by this time, continued to operate without any system of regimental control until after the Crimean War, in much the same way as a publican who rents from a brewery. The RA Canteen even had its own system of coinage in operation. Instead of giving normal change, it would hand over tokens stamped with the name of the Canteen. These could only be used in the Canteen, of course, which helped to ensure that the soldier continued to spend his money there, rather than in some other outlet, though there was also the excuse that a system of tokens prevented petty theft by the staff.

The scandals of maladministration that were exposed by the Crimean War led, among other things, to a reappraisal of the canteen system in the Army. New regulations abolished the contractor-cum-canteen-keeper and replaced him with a regimental committee wholly responsible for running the canteen and for the purchase of goods. Records show that in 1878 the RA Canteen's management committee was headed by the Garrison Commander, with two of his principal staff officers and a representative of each of the RHA and RA as members. The Canteen was at this time organized into three departments: a provision department, coffee and refreshment bar, and liquor bar. Under the new regulations, no spirits were sold in the bar, but ale, stout and porter were sold – and only in quarts! The coffee and refreshment bar served cooked meals as well as light refreshments, with a tendency towards the soldiers' traditional fare of sausages, bacon and eggs. The provision department sold virtually everything else a soldier (or his family) might need, rather like a general store in the town.

By the end of the 19th century, the RA Canteen had expanded its reach into the other barracks in Woolwich and was running a delivery service to the married quarters at Brookhill,

One of the tokens used in lieu of coins in the Royal Artillery Canteen. These were partly intended to make it difficult for petty theft, but also served to ensure that soldiers spent their cash in the Canteen, since they always received any change in tokens.

A portrait of Lt Col Freddie Windrum, whose magnificent service in managing the RA Canteen extended from 1910 to 1952, dying 'in harness' at the age of 89. The portrait was commissioned by the Regiment in his honour.

applied to the Canteen to supply them with cooking utensils and small kit, providing generally for their care and comfort. Even when the active units left for France, the Canteen continued to issue 10,000 grocery rations a day to the reserve units formed in their stead. This went on until 1916, when the system was discontinued, by which time the Canteen had issued over nine million grocery rations. The Canteen had made a profit of £10,422 in the process (the equivalent of about £450,000 in 2007), but, feeling it was wrong to make any profit on such a transaction, returned the whole sum to the government – a gesture so generous that it should stand to the glory and credit of the RA Canteen for ever.

As the Regiment expanded, so did the Canteen, extending its activities not only to supply the new units constantly forming in Woolwich, but also to units and establishments all over the south of England, as far afield as Larkhill and the New Forest. A nice gesture was the contribution of a grant to every new battery formed at Woolwich to start the unit funds. At the end of the war, the Canteen had 30 branches outside the RA Barracks in Woolwich. Part of the profits was placed in a trust fund that was intended for the benefit of the Garrison when the war ended.

By 1915 the RA Mess was having difficulty catering for the numbers passing through the garrison and invited Windrum to take over the duties of mess secretary in addition to his role in running the Canteen. He not only did so, but continued to hold both posts for the remainder of his long life. Indeed, so successful was the Canteen in providing good food at low prices that, in 1919, Windrum was asked to cater for all the messes at the Royal Military Academy in Woolwich and did so until it closed in 1939.

During the First World War there was such a need for canteens – administered by 'Regimental Institutes' – throughout the rest of the armed services that, via a series of gradual steps, the Navy Army and Air Force Institutes (NAAFI) was formed and was in operation under that title by January 1921. However, all the developments that took place during 1914–18 passed by the RA Canteen without having any effect on its operation. Neither the Board of Control, the Army Canteen Committee nor the Navy and Army Canteen Board had attempted to take it over or interfere with it in any way. NAAFI was a different proposition.

There followed a two-year battle between Windrum – determined not to relinquish his empire – and NAAFI. He was by this time a well-respected figure, known high and low throughout the Army, and he marshalled his forces with vigour, pulling every string at his disposal. It was a somewhat one-sided battle: NAAFI was not yet strong enough to defeat him and, although the RA Canteen ended up having to pay NAAFI 2 per cent of the turnover on sales, it remained exempt from NAAFI's control, run as a separate institution.

The end of hostilities had brought huge reductions in the size of the Army and the Canteen had to draw in its horns, reducing the number of branches outside the RA Barracks to four, Cambridge Barracks, Grand Depot, RMA and Brookhill. But Windrum soldiered on, despite official retirement and the approach of his 60s. Among other entrepreneurial activities, he arranged for the Canteen to buy a farm at Worplesdon, Surrey, to provide produce at significantly lower prices than could be obtained elsewhere.

well to the east of Woolwich New Road. It was making healthy profits, too, with the money partly reinvested and partly distributed among the units in the Garrison as well as paying for Christmas decorations, bonuses to employees and to families that used its facilities, and making an annual gift in cash to the Families Hospital.

In 1910 the Committee took the step of appointing a serving officer to the new role of Secretary, to be responsible for all matters of finance and the general supervision of administration. It chose Captain Freddie Windrum, a remarkable man, at that time District Officer of the Royal Field Artillery Depot at Woolwich and 47 years of age. He took firm control of the Canteen, gradually ousting all others until he became in effect president, committee, secretary and general manager, all in his own person. He was determined to make the Canteen a successful commercial undertaking, ruthlessly overcoming anyone or anything that stood in the way and, with one short break in 1945–6, he did just that for the next 42 years, literally to his dying day, aged 89.

A typical example of Windrum's extraordinary abilities is that of the Canteen's operations at the outset of the First World War. The War Office had made a contract with the Canteen to supply grocery rations on mobilization to all units in the Garrison. In August 1914, reservists poured into Woolwich – 6,000 to the RA Barracks alone – and the Canteen found itself supplying some 10,000 grocery rations a day. Although the Canteen was able to carry out its contract, the Royal Artillery in Woolwich was quite unable to cope with its 6,000 reservists and

His next target was a completely new facility to replace the now tired old building in the Barracks. The War Office refused to do anything about it, but Windrum turned to the trust fund that was formed during the war. After overcoming hurdles of many kinds, permission was granted and he was able to get started on building: the new Institute was opened in November 1927.

This new building was on three floors: the ground floor held a restaurant with a kitchen, a confectionery and dry goods department, wet-canteen and post office. The whole of the first floor was taken up with a ballroom, which could be used for dances, lectures, whist drives and so on, while the top floor held a billiards room with six tables and a library-cum-reading room with books, periodicals and daily papers. The entire cost had come to a little over £37,000 (worth about £1.5m in 2007). Again, in a magnificent act of generosity, the building was presented to the War Department by deed of gift.

The Canteen continued to operate through the Great Depression and slump of the interwar years, with its farm, bakery and mineral-water factory (both set up in the late 19th century) helping to keep prices down and with a discount to customers running at a steady 10 per cent.

The Second World War brought about change. Fearing immediate air attacks, the garrison dispersed around the south of England to places like Ascot (Berkshire), Sandown Park (Surrey) and Lydd (Kent). The Canteen continued to base its activities in Woolwich, but opened branches at all the new sites to ensure its customers' welfare, with supplies sent daily in the organization's own delivery vans. When it was clear that bombing was not imminent, the RA Depot returned from its country retreats and in early 1940 the barracks were once more full of Gunners. The Canteen now entered the busiest period of its existence, with Woolwich operating as a vast artillery transit camp, crowded with officers and men going to and from the various theatres of war.

However, the provisions department had had to close. The Royal Army Service Corps had taken over the supply of all rations to the Army and, at the same time, the families who had been the other main customers for groceries had been largely evacuated. Furthermore, NAAFI had a monopoly on the supply of rationed goods, which meant that there was insufficient business to keep the department viable.

Despite minor damage from bombing raids, the Canteen continued to serve a vast number of men and women throughout 1939–45, making excellent profits but returning them in rebate to the units for the benefit of the troops. Windrum even managed to provide £100 a month towards garrison entertainments (some £3,000 at 2007 values).

With the end of the war, there was once again a reduction in the number of troops to cater for, but the Canteen continued to sail along, quietly and placidly with Windrum still in control. However, in 1951 there was a fresh attempt to revive the old Canteen Committee, which Windrum had managed to keep at arms' length for virtually the whole of his long tenure of the post of Secretary. Despite his age – he was 88 by this time – he was still visiting Woolwich four times a week from the farm, where he now lived, and he had no intention of handing over control. It was not until March 1952, when the Garrison Commander suggested the formation of a Canteen Committee of himself, Windrum and two lieutenant colonels, that matters came to a head. Sadly, it was all resolved by Windrum dying peacefully the following month, at the age of 89, and the Canteen Committee took up the reins.

One well-remembered legacy of this long saga is the ballroom of the RA Mess, known to most Gunners who have visited Woolwich over the years, whether as a venue for parties, conferences, band concerts or lectures. Few will have been aware of its provenance as part of the RA Canteen, but the name 'Freddie Windrum' echoes down the years. He was a most remarkable Gunner.

KAT

A photograph of the RA Barracks, looking almost due south, taken during the rebuilding of the inner squares during the mid-1960s. Note the large block standing on its own in the left foreground: this is the RA Canteen building mentioned in the text. On its top floor is the large room best known as a conference room and ballroom, linked by a passageway to the Music Room of the RA Mess shortly after this photograph was taken. In the background, on the Barrack Field, an 'At Home' is in full swing.

THE ROYAL ARTILLERY BAND AT WOOLWICH

Colonel Bob Jammes

(With acknowledgement to Majors C.R. Meldrum MBE, D. Rollo and P. Shannon MBE as well as Mr M. J. Sherriff).

Below: The Junior Leaders' Band at the South Arch in Woolwich. The Junior Leaders were the successors to the Boys Battery, which was based in Woolwich until 1948, moving then to Hereford and re-forming under a new name.

Below Right: En route to the town centre, the RA Band accompanies a contingent of Gunners on their way to embarkation for service overseas.

There has been a band in Woolwich since the earliest days of the Royal Regiment's presence in the Borough. While the first formally recognized Royal Artillery Band owes its origins to the Seven Years War, having started in 1762 at Minden in Germany, musical support had been provided, unofficially, in several guises prior to that date. The earliest musical ensemble attributed to the Gunners dated from 1557 and was known as the Trayne of Artillery. The Band was established in 1762 thus reinforcing its claim to be the oldest permanent musical organization in Great Britain, pre-dating the London Philharmonic by half a century. In 1762 there were eight members of the Band recruited from the local population in Germany which accounts for why the articles of agreement establishing it were in both German and English. In 1763 the Band moved to Woolwich where it remains to date. The next major organizational change was the amalgamation in 1801 of the Royal Artillery Band with that of the Royal Irish Artillery, the latter formed in 1756.

The role of military bands has always been to entertain the troops wherever they are posted. During the First World War, half of the Band deployed to France and Flanders to do exactly that, first in the period December 1915 to April 1916 and then again between December 1917 and February 1918. During these deployments, the remainder of the Band remained in Woolwich to give performances to help maintain the morale of those in the garrison as well as raising funds for 'comforts for the men of the Royal Artillery at the Front'. This form of service continued during the Second World War when the Band played at home, but also deployed to operational theatres including North Africa, Italy and northwest Europe.

The Royal Artillery Band has always done more than be just located in Woolwich. It has been part of the Borough's fabric in so many ways. The local concerts that stand out are those undertaken by the Orchestra in the Town Hall and, of course, the monthly and long-standing series of six concerts that run from October to March inclusive in the Ballroom of the Royal Artillery Mess.

Throughout its long history stationed at Woolwich, the Royal Artillery Band has maintained the highest of musical standards and had among its ranks many famous musicians, including Company Sergeant Major (CSM) Andrew Henry, who went on to be awarded the Victoria Cross. CSM Henry began his career as principal keyed-bugler in the Band (1835–41), transferred as a Gunner and won his award on 5 November 1854 surviving a dozen bayonet wounds at the Battle of Inkerman during the Crimean War. There have been some influential and outstanding bandmasters and directors of music of the Band. These included the Italian Ladislao Zavertal MVO (Member of the Royal Victorian Order) – who had been a pupil of the Czech composer Antonin Dvořák – (Bandmaster 1881–1907), Edward Stretton MVO (Bandmaster 1907–36) and Owen Geary MBE (Member of the British Empire) (Bandmaster 1936–50). In their time they brought the Band to international prominence. This high standard of conductor has continued and it is not a coincidence that, of the last six Principal Directors of Music (Army), three have come from the Gunner Band – Lieutenant Colonels F. A. Renton, G. A. Kingston and S. J. Smith.

There have, of course, always been strong links with the royal family. King Edward VII intervened in the selection of the aforementioned Zavertal. At the time the prevailing view was that the previous tradition of employing foreign bandmasters was considered inappropriate, given the high standard of bandmasters being produced by Kneller Hall (the Royal Military School of Music founded at Twickenham, Surrey, by HRH The Duke of Cambridge in 1857). Another link is that the composition of the Royal Artillery Slow March is attributed to HRH The Duchess of Kent, the mother of Queen Victoria, c.1836.

The Royal Artillery Band Today

In 1994 a significant change came about in Army Music when the Corps of Army Music (CAMUS) was formed. All army musicians regardless of which band they were serving in became members of the new Corps but continued to wear the uniform of whichever band they were serving in and could be posted between bands. More parochially, the Royal Artillery (Alanbrooke) Band became the nucleus of the newly formed Band of the Army Air Corps, thus leaving the Royal Artillery Band at Woolwich as the only one left in support of the Royal Regiment. At about this time it also became the first occasion that women musicians were more widely deployed in Regular bands, when previously they had served exclusively in the Women's Royal Army Corps. Many have subsequently served with the Gunner band.

Today there are eight bands that have 'State' status: the bands of the Life Guards, Blues and Royals, the five Foot Guards bands (Grenadier, Coldstream, Scots, Irish and Welsh) and the Royal Artillery Band. The Regiment's band had that status accorded to it in 1994 in acknowledgement of its supporting role to The King's Troop Royal Horse Artillery in its State Ceremonial role. Other than Central Volunteer Headquarters RA, it is the only other tangible service link that the Royal Regiment has maintained with Woolwich now that the Regimental Home has been established at Larkhill.

The Royal Artillery Band is a Type 49 (denoting the size of its establishment) and is capable of fielding – besides its

orchestra – a wide range of musical ensembles including marching, concert (wind band) and pop group. The latter was deployed to Iraq in 2006 for a short tour to boost troop morale. The primary function of the orchestral string capability is to perform in small ensembles at State events, mainly consisting of investitures and banquets at Buckingham Palace. Each of the eight State bands is included in the roster to provide orchestral support to these events.

Above and below: Two formal pictures of the RA Band taken approximately 100 years apart, both on the Front Parade of the RA Barracks. The RA Band is the only band in the British Army to wear gold belts and crossbelts.

Top right: The Royal Artillery Band in its role as an orchestra, ready to play at a formal Dinner in the RA Mess.

In 1904 the establishment for military bands and orchestras was 104 musicians each. In 1926 these had reduced to 75 and 74 musicians respectively. By way of comparison, the RA Band's current instrumental establishment is as follows, although as befits a modern Army band, many of its musicians play more than one instrument:

One Director of Music (normally of Major rank) and one Warrant Officer Class One (Bandmaster) who are the band's conductors.

2 flutes
2 oboes
9 clarinets
4 saxophones
2 bassoons
4 French horns
8 cornets
5 tenor trombones
2 bass trombones
2 euphoniums
4 tubas
3 percussionists

In order to meet the orchestral requirement, some of the musicians playing the above instruments will also be first study players of the following, the minimum number of each being three violins, one viola, one cello, one contrabass and one piano. There will also be a number of musicians whose secondary instrument is one of these, thus increasing the number of players available for orchestral work.

The Band has, like all others, an operational role in support of the Army Medical Services (AMS). Some of its members took part in the First Gulf War (1990–1) serving with Number 205 General Hospital as medical assistants. The role, while still with the AMS, has changed to reflect their new requirements.

The musicians of the Royal Artillery Band continue to carry on the traditions and high standards of their forebears. The Corps of Army Music's motto *Nulli Secundus* (Second to

None) would seem to be an entirely appropriate way to describe their contribution to British Military Music in the 245 years since its formation and the Royal Regiment's departure from Woolwich.

The Junior Musicians' Troop Royal Artillery, 1947–1983

Another musical organization, the Junior Musicians' Troop Royal Artillery, also existed in Woolwich alongside the Royal Artillery Band from 1947 to 1983. It started life as the Bandboys' Troop for the military and musical training of Bandboys of all Royal Artillery Bands. This Troop was affected by the reorganization of Junior Entry training in the 1950s, and in 1958, it separated from the Royal Artillery Band, where training had been centred, and was established as the 'Junior Musicians' Troop Royal Artillery,' with its own regimental musical and military staff.

The original establishment provided for the training of 50 Royal Artillery Bandboys – 20 for the Royal Artillery Band and 10 for each of the three smaller RA Bands, although by 1958, only two of these remained. In 1963 the Royal Engineers sent their first boys to be trained in Woolwich and the Royal Signals followed this example in 1972. As a result of these additions to troop strength, extra staff of one non-commissioned officer was provided from each of these bands.

Throughout its history, the Junior Musicians' Troop produced hundreds of musicians who served their bands with distinction. The high musical standards attained by the 'Boys,' combined in particular with the drive and vision of Warrant Officer Class 1 B. R. Carben (the Troop Sergeant Major, 1967–82), established the Troop's reputation as second to none. On leaving the Army, many of its musicians held principal positions in some of the world's finest bands and orchestras. The Junior Musicians' Troop also produced many bandmasters and directors of music who, captivated by the exceptional musical achievements witnessed throughout their training, inspired future generations of military musicians long after the Troop's disbandment in 1983.

THE WOOLWICH STADIUM

Established as a general sports stadium in the 1920s, the Stadium was a Regimental asset and the brainchild of Major George Hamilton-Jones, a staff officer at the headquarters in Woolwich. His determined project management and drive in achieving his goal earned him the nickname 'Stadium' that lived with him ever afterwards – he even used it to sign his correspondence within the garrison!

Sited on Woolwich Common opposite Shrapnel Barracks, it was a large, banked arena, which was used as a rugby and football sports field, athletics venue and horse trials and show jumping ground. For sporting events, where the terraces were open, the Stadium could accommodate 45,000 spectators. For 'all-seated' events, it could hold 20,000. In the programme for the Searchlight Tattoo of 1955, the description of the Stadium says, 'It is the home ground of both Chelsea and Charlton Football Clubs, who play Metropolitan and Mid-Week League games on the football pitch throughout the season.' However, it is perhaps best remembered by the people of Woolwich as the setting for the famous Searchlight Tattoos.

A visiting band performs in front of the packed stands at a Tattoo in the Woolwich Stadium. This is a pre-War display: the stands were destroyed by bombing and were not re-built after the War.

THE ROYAL ARTILLERY
SEARCHLIGHT TATTOO
AND AT HOME

WOOLWICH
SEPTEMBER TWELVE, 1953.
SOUVENIR PROGRAMME

WOOLWICH
Searchlight
TATTOO
WOOLWICH STADIUM
12TH - 15TH SEPTEMBER · 1956 · 7.30 P.M
1/- SOUVENIR PROGRAMME 1/-

*Souvenir programmes
from 1953 (above) and
1956 (right) for the
Searchlight Tattoo at
Woolwich Stadium.*

*Above: A drill demonstration taking
place under the lights during a
Searchlight Tattoo.*

The first of these took place in 1929. The Tattoos were
colourful, well organized and very well attended, regarded as an
entertainment that matched the similar event at Olympia, in
central London. A programme for the 1930 event had 17
different displays, including bands and pipe and drums, trick
riding, guard mounting, a drill display, a toy soldier display and
ended with an artillery pageant and a grand finale. The 1937
Tattoo, in Coronation year, consisted largely of pageants
illustrating royalty visiting the area, with a Royal Artillery episode
entitled 'Saving the Guns at Maiwand' recalling the 1880 battle in
Afghanistan. It is clear from the programme that this Tattoo was
no longer just a Woolwich Garrison affair and that the Borough
was now playing a large part: indeed, the organizing committee at
this point had only one Gunner officer as a member.

*Below: Show jumping and horse trials
were popular events at the Stadium,
where the huge arena could be put to
good use.*

During the Second World War, when it had part of an anti-
aircraft battery on the site, the Stadium's covered stands were
damaged by bombing and, although it re-opened after the war
and staged many events, there were not sufficient funds available
to rebuild them. Gradually, interest in keeping the Stadium
going faced all the usual funding problems and the pressures of
an ever-decreasing number of troops with ever-increasing duty
commitments. It ceased to operate in the mid-1970s and is,
today, merely a shell of its former glory – an empty stretch of
the Common, its access cut off by ditches and banking, a home
for wild flowers and grasses

KAT

WOOLWICH COMMON

Woolwich Common has long been used for military displays.
History relates that King George III set a fashion for early reviews
when, on 9th July 1788, he ordered the parade to be on
Woolwich Common at twenty minutes past six in the morning,
and completed his review of the Royal Artillery before 11 am.

The Tattoo, close to the site of the original reviews, is still in a
sense a review: the introduction to the civil population of the
military forces of the nation at work and at play. Its main object
is to raise funds for the Charitable Funds of the Regiment.

An impressive amount of work goes into the preparation of a
Tattoo, especially when it is recognized that the performers, for
all their perfection and precision, are in no sense professional
artistes and rehearsals have to be arranged to ensure that their
temporary roles as actors does not interfere with the more
serious art of being a soldier.

(Edited extract from the Official Guide to Woolwich 7th Edition, published
shortly after the Second World War.)

WOOLWICH MEMORIES

Recollections of Shrapnel Barracks

George Goulette

My first recollections of Woolwich come from 1929, when my father, Driver Alfred Goulette, was posted to Shrapnel Barracks. By this time he was approaching the end of his military service, during which he had been a lead driver on an 18-pounder gun team, serving right through the Great War. In this new posting, he worked in the Mobilization Store and was allocated a small flat that was part of the Officers' Mess block, though of course it had its own separate access. I went to school in the town, quite close to the Grand Depot Barracks.

As a small boy, I remember especially the Christmas parties that used to be held at the Ballroom in the RA Barracks for all the children of the garrison, complete with a Father Christmas and some wonderful presents! The two that spring to mind were an air rifle and a splendid cuckoo clock – the latter because I took it apart to see how it worked and couldn't put it back together again.

I used to run around the sports track in the Stadium, just across the road, trying to improve my sprinting, but the Stadium's main attraction for us as children was the Tattoos,

with Musical Drives by the RHA Batteries, like The King's Troop these days. A particular memory was the way that there were always Gunners dressed up as toy soldiers – they used to look after the children very well.

When my father retired in 1934 and went off to work at the War Ministry, we left Shrapnel Barracks. I returned there in 1939 when the Territorial Army Regiment I belonged to – my battery was in Lee Green SE12 – was embodied. We were kitted out for war and, after a month in Woolwich, went off to Dorset for training.

My recollection of Shrapnel Barracks themselves is mainly about the general layout. There were large blocks at the north end, which had stables on the ground floor and barrack rooms above them. Alongside these, on the west side, were the sergeants' mess and the soldiers' mess and cookhouse. The gun sheds were close to this area, right next to the parade ground, with the stores, NAAFI and officers' mess at the south end.

I believe the Barracks were vacated when the Royal Artillery became mechanized in about 1934 and were opened again for units being mobilized when Hitler's war came.

Boys from the Boys Battery dressed as toy soldiers for one of the Searchlight Tattoos.

Bicycles were much in use at the Royal Military Academy for moving Gentleman Cadets to their various places of work, including long rides out to Eltham and Plumstead for field sketching and map-making. However, they moved in a proper military fashion – usually two-by-two in long columns.

'The Shop' in the 1930s
Major Derick Garnier

The first we heard that we had successfully passed into 'The Shop' on leaving school was a letter from the military tailors and outfitters congratulating us on our success and informing us that they were the appointed merchants. This was a welcome relief after the rather awe-inspiring personal interview with the Civil Service Commissions Board at Burlington House, Piccadilly. This consisted of very senior officers of the Services and the tricky questions they asked were legendary. It was believed they were looking for quick intelligence and manners appropriate to become an officer and a gentleman. I recall two stories:

Admiral – 'Name three famous admirals.'
Interviewee – 'Blake, Nelson and – er – I didn't quite catch your name, sir.'

General – 'What was the number of the taxi in which you arrived?'
Interviewee – 'GY 5604.'
After his departure the other members asked the General how could he know if the answer was correct. 'I didn't', he replied, 'but it showed quick-wittedness.'

The outfitters appointed were:
Tailors – J. C. Plumb & Son, Victoria Street (central London).
Bootmakers – Mr Horrocks, Craig & Davies.
Sam Brownes (military belts) – Mr Groves, Groves, Francis Street, Woolwich.

They all had shops at the top end of Francis Street, which was handy for both The Shop and the RA Depot. In those days all military gear for cadets (and officers) had to be paid for by their long-suffering parents, no doubt after years of expensive school fees.

Mr Groves made the excellent Sam Brownes of the finest leather, which polished to a terrific shine, and Mr Horrocks's

military boots, both ankle and riding, were also made to measure of very fine leather. Mr Groves also provided zinc-lined trunks which he advised us would be necessary for tropical service, which proved correct.

I do not suppose the pressure on young cadets with quick changes of kit or uniform has eased since yesteryear, except in style and method. Training, drills, parades, sport were all packed in pretty tightly. Bicycles were an essential for this. They were hired out by Halfords, the cycle dealers, who stored and maintained them within the perimeter. We were issued with a numbered brass disc to identify our individual bikes, the crossbars of which were painted with The Shop colours to establish ownership. One of the joys of the bicycle was to pedal to the orchards and hop-fields of Kent with our plane-tables to carry out surveying and map-making exercises. The other was to cycle down to the RA Riding School for riding instruction.

The staff sergeant riding instructors knew how to handle 'young gentlemen cadets', as did all the senior non-commissioned officer instructors at both The Shop and Sandhurst. GCs were fair game for insults, provided it was done with wit and ended with 'Sir'.

In the Riding School, all the horses knew what was expected of them, having the same instruction, discipline and training as a series of cadets, many of whom had never before seen a horse. Typical of the NCOs' bawdy wit, which of course amused us youngsters was, when taking jumps: 'Mr Garnier, Sir, your legs are wider open than any harlot's in Beresford Street, Sir!'

As cadets at Woolwich, we were dressed in officers' uniform, but without badges of rank. New recruits at the RA Depot often mistakenly saluted us as officers if they met us in the street. This could be embarrassing, but it was advisable to return the salute.

Freedom at The Shop was restricted, not because of specific rules, but because of the intensive programme. At weekends, if not otherwise engaged in sport or other appropriate activities, one could take a train ride up to Aldwych, central London, for the vast expense of £1, or perhaps go to the recently built Odeon Cinema in nearer Lewisham.

Before every event we had to parade and be inspected to see we were properly dressed for the occasion. This even applied to sick parade before being marched to the Cadets' Hospital on Woolwich Common Road, outside the RMA precincts.

Another parade was the Physical Training parade. I remember one occasion when the inspecting officer was Captain Robert Urquhart, Royal Engineers, who later became a general during the 1939–45 war. He had an eagle eye. One item of the PT kit was white socks. It never occurred to me that one white sock could be different from another. 'Your socks have only 15 ribs. The regulation sock has 16 ribs,' he declared. I was awarded a 'hoxter', which was an extra duty parade as a punishment for being improperly dressed. It taught me a trick in later life when I was carrying out kit inspections in barracks, that of a keen eye for detail.

The bedrooms at The Shop, although quite roomy, could be very cold in the winter. Each room had a fireplace and a meagre ration of coal in a scuttle was provided in the winter months. Open fires meant that there was a fire risk and fire drills were practised from time to time.

Gentleman Cadets

by Brigadier Sir Gilbert Heathcote Bt CBE
(An edited version of an article originally published in the RA Journal)

The conventional route to a commission in the Royal Regiment of Artillery was via a cadetship at the Royal Military Academy, Woolwich, known to all as The Shop. Its buildings loom today, fortress-like but largely empty on the slopes of Shooters Hill. The imposing, high railings that provided a serious late night challenge to those of us unable to resist the comparative proximity of Mayfair still surround its silent parade ground.

It is hard now, even with the nostalgic affection of 70 years, separation, not to question the need for the contrived regime thought necessary to toughen us Gentleman Cadets for a military career when, in the Second World War, so many colleagues easily adapted to the task of leading men and rose to dizzy heights, doing so without the rigours of the parade ground, where Drill Sergeants from the Brigade of Guards would emphasize the 'Mister Brown, Sir; that rifle? A bit heavy for them worn elbows today?' One day they would have to defer to us, but not yet. And there were those cheerful torturers in the gym; 'Press *ups* they're called, Sir; nothin' to do with last night'; and there was the Riding School! Ah, that's another story. Most frustrating to some of us, however, were the restrictions to freedom. The encircling railings were a challenge to be overcome, but roll-calls presented a more serious problem to a car-banned group reluctant to refuse invitations to the activities of the London season.

How to attend a debutante dance or take the twinkle-eyed Ursula to Quaglino's restaurant in the West End and not abandon her at an unprofitable hour, yet still reach The Shop before authority was awake enough to spot the blue overcoat covering white tie making for the weaker spots in the defences? The last train from Charing Cross would long since have gone by the time she had been delivered to her doorstep. The milk train next day, known to ensure a dishevelled arrival just as reveille was being sounded, led two of us to discover a tram that left the Embankment for Woolwich and its high-employment Docks and Arsenal in the dogwatch hours.

One night at about two in the morning, George and I boarded what was clearly a working man's means of transport. It was to be an experience that has remained deeply etched in the memory.

'Cor, Charlie, look what we got 'ere'; this from a birdlike figure with a prominent screw-topped bottle poking from the grimy haversack hung round his shoulder.

'Where you bin?', Buckin'am bloody Palace?'

We tucked our patent leather shoes as far as possible under our seats and turned up our collars to hide our stiff shirts and tried to avoid those perky little eyes set in a face aslant with enquiry and determination; all to no avail for all seating faced inwards and our inquisitor could slide along to face us.

'No, er, we've just been to a dance with friends.'

Charlie, the tram conductor, was summoned alongside. 'Hear that, they've been to a bloody dance,' and, leaning forward to place a gnarled hand on my knee, he added, 'Tell us about it, lads, come on.'

We were now the unwilling entertainment of most of the occupants of the tram, some having been hailed down from the top deck. After our audience had enjoyed pouring friendly

Above: Phyical training was both arduous and exacting; high standards were required and expected. The gymnasium stood at the rear of the main building complex, near the church, and was pulled down after the Second World War.

Below: A class of Gentleman Cadets formed up for gun drill on the main parade ground, with an 18-pounder field gun and limber ready for the lesson to begin. For any sort of laborious or dirty work, cadets wore hard-wearing white drill uniforms, possibly still making use at the turn of the century of the enormous amounts of white sailcloth left in Ordnance stores when the Royal Navy turned to steampower.

An old postcard that shows a tram on Academy Road running uphill towards the crossroads at Shooters Hill. On the left can be seen both the RMA and the statue of the Prince Imperial. The tram shown here is approaching the start of a steep uphill climb - the point where cadets were known occasionally to grease the rails.

scorn on the social intricacies of the London season, it was time for the next question.

'So where you bloody goin' to, then?'

Our answer gave Charlie the opportunity to take centre stage, where he clearly intended to stay. 'I know you; you're them bloody cadets. Just as well Cyril' – and he indicated the driver forward on his platform with a sort of one shoulder shrug – 'isn't in 'ere, he'd bloody dump you for sure.'

Our puzzled looks were clearly welcomed by an impatient raconteur: 'Cor, nobody never tell you? That were a night, year or two ago now, o' course. You know that climb up past the Academy, up Shooters Hill to Eltham?' Yes, we certainly did, from struggling up it on heavy, army bicycles loaded with survey equipment as part of an early introduction to drawing maps and panoramas.

'Well, one night, autumn I reckon, it were bloody dark and cold. We was on our last run. We're just beyond them gates near the bottom of the hill when the tram just stopped. Cyril had full power, wheels whizzin' around and we're just hardly movin''.'

There was a theatrical pause as we clanged and swayed our way past the grim terraced houses of Charlton. 'Cyril – mind you, I'll have to tell 'im who he's had on board after you've gone – he turns the current off and gets down to come round to me: "It's them bloody cadets put grease on the lines." And they'd made a proper job of it, too; both lines, trams stuck behind us and, other side, they're skidding down the slope like bloody toboggans; drivers all round us effin' and blindin'; passengers complaining and these damn lads standin' there behind them railings laughing their bloody heads off.'

Another pause to prepare the denouement. 'Well, some of us had to laugh a bit, too, but not Cyril. He goes stormin' through the gates shouting he wants to see an officer.'

What had begun as a sort of gentle inquisition had become, as we lurched through Bermondsey and Deptford and journey's end approached, more like a party in an unstable pub with new arrivals having to be brought up to date with the story while

Bert, our original inquisitor, was not alone in taking surreptitious nips from his bottle. There were demands for the end of the story, but Charlie was not to be rushed. He had a captive audience and he knew it. Friends had to be welcomed and others bidden goodbye before his stage was fully set.

'Well, this officer come out, little red jacket on, and he picks on one of the cadets – had a belt thing on.' George and I exchanged glances. This must have been an Under Officer. 'They come out and look at the rails and listen to Cyril shoutin' the odds. The officer apologizes all round and then he speaks very quiet to this cadet who runs off sharp with the others.

'The officer then says to Cyril somethin' like, "Those young scamps are going to clean every inch of the rails if it takes 'em all night." And they bloody did. Those lads come back in overalls with cotton waste and sand and really got down to it. Before long we was cheering 'em on – even Cyril and remember, he'd been through the [1914–18] war in the Navy.'

By now we were running into Woolwich with the tram nearly full of workmen and their haversacks. George and I received cheerful handshakes and thumps on the back as we got ready to leave the smoke-filled cabin. Charlie was unable to resist leading us to the front to introduce us to the diminutive Cyril standing foursquare on his open platform like the Captain on his bridge and, perhaps, as he drove it bucking through the night, that was how he saw it.

He stared down at us in silence for some time before seizing the great, brass rheostat lever to set his ship in motion. Then, as it began to gather way, he gave us a flat hand naval salute and left us with a shouted, 'Bugger bloody Army'.

Unknown to us, trudging up towards Woolwich Common as the dawn was hinting at its arrival in the northern sky, we would ourselves, only six months later, be facing angry public servants demanding the presence of an officer. It was an April Fools' Day mock fire on the roof of the building in which our younger instructors lived that went dramatically wrong. Failure to picket a public telephone led to our over-ambitious flames being reported in a 999 call with the momentous words, 'Fire at the Royal Military Academy!' Within minutes hard-driven, clanging fire engines, eventually numbering 13, began sweeping on to the great parade ground with their chiefs, now recognizing the dying flames for what they were. As apoplectic as Cyril and in a sort of repetitive chant came, 'So it's an 'oax, is it? Someone's got to pay for this; where's an officer?'

The post of Adjutant of the RMA was given to officers of promise and ours fulfilled it, later becoming a senior general. He showed all his powers of command in quelling what had been, only minutes before as our mentors tumbled out of their home in their pyjamas and a banner announcing the date was hoisted, an uproarious success. The fact that his wife, awakened by the endless clanging of fire bells, was in a late stage of pregnancy, made the thundercloud that seemed to accompany his arrival at the cheerful scene particularly daunting.

Queues for the sole public telephone were not the only unexpected aftermath as we explained the effects of 'Confined to Barracks' on weekend plans and our inability to meet her at Marlow or similar riverine resort. Lolling in the stern of Thames rowing skiffs watching a well-endowed companion bending to her oars had become a much favoured form of gentlemanly voyeurism.

A Woolwich Childhood

Colonel the Rt. Hon. Sir Robin Dunn MC

I spent four happy years from 1926 to 1930 at The Shop, when my father Captain (later Brigadier) Keith Dunn was Adjutant. We lived in a big house on the Front Parade with a garden at the back, and I was fascinated by the life of the Gentlemen Cadets. Every Saturday morning I would hang out of our nursery window and watch Battalion Parade. On Sundays there was church parade after service in the Chapel, which we always attended.

In 1936 I returned to The Shop for 18 months as a GC myself. The routine had hardly changed. It seemed that the main requirement for an officer was the ability to change in 15 minutes from physical training kit into full drill order, including puttees, boots and breeches. Riding was still a compulsory part of the curriculum, and we used to bicycle in half sections to the Depot to ride on the horses of the Riding Troop RHA in the riding schools or outside in the grounds of the Rotunda. Apart from the Saddle Ride the instructors were all non-commissioned officers who had been with the Troop for many years, and managed to conceal kind hearts beneath a flow of invective and biting wit: 'Who told you to dismount, Sir?' if you fell off.

After The Shop my visits to Woolwich were spasmodic. A short driving and maintenance course when we lived in our wonderful mess, undoubtedly the best of any in the Army. And then in 1980 to my great pleasure I was appointed an Honorary Colonel Commandant, having left the Army after the war and gone to the Bar, becoming a Lord Justice of Appeal. So I went every year to the Colonel Commandants' Dinner, sat among my contemporaries and listened to the Post Horn Gallop played by our incomparable trumpeters.

As long ago as 1946 when I was at Anti-Aircraft Command there was talk of the Regimental HQ moving from Woolwich to Larkhill. Now it has happened, no doubt for good reasons. But Woolwich had style with the magnificent façade of the depot, the elegant buildings at The Shop, and the open space of the Common. I can still smell the fog creeping up from the river and, although it had its drawbacks, those of us who lived and served there will miss it.

Woolwich Memories

Brigadier Brian Parritt

My father was stationed in Woolwich in 1927 and was introduced to the daughter of a retired Gunner. They courted, and she followed him to India where I was born in Dagshai, a hill station near Simla. He was serving in 1st Battery ('Blazers').

We returned in 1933 and lived in 4 Green Hill, Woolwich until the beginning of the war. My father, always called 'Polly' Parritt, ran the 'Kick Step', which was a mandatory drill course for the promotion of non-commissioned officers.

My memory of that time is watching the Sunday church parade, which followed the church service, then going to the stables behind the Officers' Mess to look at the horses, followed by the Sergeants' Mess for a 'Tizer' (soft drink).

We had two deliveries to the Married Quarters; first was the Tizer lorry, which took the 'empties' and replaced them with full bottles; the other was the coal delivery. This was when a lorry arrived with Gunners in fatigue dress who shovelled each household a free ration of coal in return for a clandestine bottle of brown ale.

One day in May 1937 I was walking home in front of the Parade Ground when my father was drilling the Gunner contingent who were to march in the Coronation parade for George VI; he was clearly rather upset. In a loud voice he called, 'Boy. Come over here!' I went to the centre of the square and he ordered, 'When I say Quick March I want you to step off and march.' The Gunner band was at the ready.

'Quick March' he ordered and off I stepped left foot first on the beat of the drum. He turned to the soldiers: 'See, even this little boy knows that you start with your left foot and listen to the drum beat.'

'Go home,' he said, 'and tell your Mother to give you sixpence'.

Above and below: Fire drill at the Royal Military Academy, practised regularly in view of previous fires in the buildings and especially in the central tower block.

In 1939 a large circular black construction was built near our new quarter at the top of the hill; it always had a Gunner outside in a tin hat, with a rifle and bayonet. This I was told was a very, very secret building, which to us boys was most mysterious and exciting. It was many years before I learned it was a simulator for anti-aircraft practice.

In 1940 we departed for Shrivenham, Wiltshire, but at the end of Hitler's war my father returned to Woolwich as the Garrison Sergeant Major (GSM). He was subsequently given a Quartermaster's commission, but his first ambition was to be GSM at Woolwich, which he said was the senior non-commissioned appointment in the Royal Artillery.

There was an episode reminiscent of Henry II and St Thomas Becket. One day the Commanding Officer commented to my father that the trees along the Front Parade spoiled the view of the front of the Mess. Next Saturday my father organized a party and cut down all the trees. The CO was devastated, but it was too late.

In February 1952, the Young Officers' Course of which I was a member was welcomed officially into the Regiment at Woolwich. It was a memorable visit.

The Mess was redolent with history and the whole ambience left an overwhelming impression of pride and heritage. One function was the Welcome Dinner; there was also a serious side in that we had all asked to join particular regiments and which friend we would like to go with. Attending the dinner was the Colonel in charge of postings. After dinner there was a series of clandestine meetings similar to the musical *The Fiddler on the Roof* marriage market, where protestations and pleas were submitted to change the published posting list. As far as I was concerned it was successful: instead of going to a much-feared anti-aircraft regiment, I went with my friend, Shaun Jackson, to a field regiment programmed to go to Korea.

In 1955, 20th Field Regiment arrived back from Korea and Hong Kong and we marched from Woolwich Station to

Right: A gun team returning to the West Square via the West Gate of the RA Barracks.

Far left: Greenhill Schools, beside Repository Road and immediately opposite the Western end of the RA Barracks.

SPARTAN ACCOMMODATION

Colonel The Lord Langford OBE, DL

I was a cadet at the Royal Military Academy, The Shop, in 1931 and was commissioned into the Royal Artillery. I attended two courses in Woolwich and I well remember the first, in 1933, when, as a second lieutenant, I got a D on a Barr & Stroud Rangefinder course. I was allotted a very humble and cold single officer's quarter. The baths were in the attic and there was seldom any hot water. The second was after I retired as a regular soldier and was Honorary Colonel of a Territorial Army regiment. This time I was very pleased to be offered what I was told was a Major General's suite – quite a contrast!

Cambridge Barracks. There was great excitement as it was the first time for many years that an active field regiment was to be stationed in Woolwich. I was delighted that my Father was there waiting, now a Major (QM).

In 1975, when filling the appointment of Colonel (Q2) at the Ministry of Defence (MOD) and responsible for all aspects of accommodation in the UK, I received notification that I was to attend a court in Woolwich to defend the MOD case for demolishing the old Greenhill School in Woolwich. The Army had prepared a full brief giving valid reasons: the building was in need of a lot of expensive repairs and, as there was no possible use for the building, it was in the taxpayers' interest that it should be demolished.

In court I stated the case and was then savaged by the conservancy opposition. They had prepared a wonderful brief setting out the history of the building, saying that it was the first army school ever built and was a direct result of Florence

Nightingale putting pressure on Secretary of State Sidney Herbert to look after the families of soldiers, particularly those wounded in the Crimean War. They had commissioned a photographer who had taken photos of the old building glowing in the evening sunset and included a beautiful shot showing the only tree within 100 yards. Witness after witness stated how Woolwich was inordinately proud of its connection with the Army and the Royal Artillery in particular, and they were amazed that we should wish to destroy such an evocative part of our heritage.

I vainly tried to point out the money we had spent on our heritage in Woolwich, including the Front Parade, and that we were trying to save the taxpayers' money, but the mood in the court was quite clear: we were philistines and should be ashamed of ourselves.

A preservation order was therefore placed on the School, and it is still there, albeit no longer in MOD hands, but turned into private residences.

Below: The Royal Military Academy Woolwich, c.1905, clearly showing the different style of the east and west wings, Victorian additions to the front of the Academy.

THE KING'S GUN

State funerals have a protocol all of their own and are very carefully managed. Ever since the funeral of Queen Victoria on 2 February 1901, they have involved moving the royal coffin on a gun carriage and, since the Royal Regiment is the only land-based user of field guns, it has always played an important part in the proceedings.

However, on the day of the funeral, as her coffin was being transferred from its rail journey to a 13-pounder gun carriage, one of the horses – probably excited by the sudden flurry of activity after having stood for a long time in the bitter cold – stepped over the traces. An unnecessarily hasty order was given to unhook the team and to draw the gun by drag-ropes, but the only men immediately available to man the ropes were sailors. A new tradition was born that day, and the task has been shared between the Royal Navy and the Royal Artillery ever since.

The gun used by the Royal Navy for the funeral of King George V on 28 J 1936 was a 13-pounder from F (Sphinx) Battery Royal Horse Artillery, the battery currently doing public duties (these were the days before The King's Troop RHA had been formed). There is no known record of the handover of the gun to the naval detachment, but there was a formal parade at Woolwich for its return, shown in the attached pictures.

The pictures show the parade taking place and, at the march past, the officer taking the salute is Rear Admiral John Tovey DSO, Commodore Royal Naval Barracks Chatham, later famous for sinking the *Bismarck*.

These days the Royal Navy maintains a gun that has been permanently set aside for its use at Royal funerals, so there is no need for parades such as this.

KAT

The parade marking the formal return to the Regiment of the gun used by the Royal Navy to bear the King's coffin at his funeral in 1936. In the upper picture, the gun is marched off parade at the end of the formalities.

Life in a Boys' Battery, Woolwich 1938

Lieutenant Colonel G. W. A. Norton

Arrival

It was May 1937 when I first approached the gates to the Depot at Woolwich as a prospective Boy Trumpeter in the Royal Artillery. I suppose, given the mounting tension in Europe, it was a sensible time to be thinking of military training, but my objectives were more prosaic – I just liked the uniform: the 'breeches, putties and spurs'! There were actually two depots at Woolwich, the Depot Royal Artillery and the Grand Depot, known as the 'Top' and the 'Bottom' depots. They existed quite separately from 1934 until the outbreak of the war in 1939. I was destined for the Grand Depot, which housed the 1st and 2nd Boys' Batteries with a strength of 180 boys split equally between them. These boys were recruited in three intakes of 60 boys each year, and the batteries were tasked with providing them with the same one-year training course aimed at producing the trumpeters required for the Royal Artillery and the Royal Horse Artillery.

On arrival I had been instructed to report to the Guard Room at the lower gate of the Grand Depot. There I was given my regimental number, which was to stay with me for my whole service in the ranks. I had enlisted for the minimum a boy could, which was nine years, with my service actually starting after I reached the age of 18. My parents had to sign a certificate agreeing that their son could receive physical punishment if I was charged with any misdemeanours. I soon discovered that the principal charge levied was one of smoking, which was strictly prohibited!

Each battery had three sections into which the intakes were received and I was allocated to 1st Battery. In this battery the routine was that the January intake was allocated to Ramsey Section, the May intake to Dickson Section and the September intake to Borgard Section, so it was Dickson for me. Our section was then further divided into two so that we could be allocated beds in two adjacent rooms along boarding school lines. The beds and their strange three-piece mattresses were the only fittings apart from a cast-iron coal bunker and a very long-handled floor polisher. I would learn quickly how to manipulate this to keep the wooden boards shining. Finally, there were washbasins and toilets between the rooms with one hot tap to be used by all.

I was allowed a little luggage, which I was told to store in an issued wooden soldier's box, housed under my bed. It was then a short walk to the Quartermaster's store to be issued with the full kit for a boy and which I had to carry in my kitbag. I had

two service dress jackets, one pair of service dress trousers, one pair of riding breeches, two pairs of puttees, one pair of spurs, two service dress hats, one bamboo whip, two pairs of boots (each with 13 studs and a metal toe cap), one pair of gym shoes and three each of shirts, vests, short pants and socks. Finally, although we did not treat it as uniform, we had two canvas suits to do any dirty work in. When we got back to our rooms we were instructed on how to show this kit for the daily inspection, a task that was to become second nature.

Daily Routine

The boys were looked after by excellent officers, warrant officers and non-commissioned officers, all of whom were hand-picked. They had the task of grooming each boy until he had passed his Army 3rd and 2nd Class certificates of education and passed the sounding exams set by the Director of Music, Lieutenant Geary. To achieve this objective a variable programme was issued

This wonderful aerial photograph, taken in 1925, shows not only the Royal Artillery Barracks in the centre, with its two large squares and Front Parade, but also the Royal Garrison Church in the foreground, the gun park top left, Cambridge Barracks and Red Barracks top centre, the Mulgrave Pond top right and, in the only known photograph of it, the Royal Artillery Institution building – the pedimented building on the right of the barracks, standing between dark groups of trees. The Royal Artillery Theatre can also be seen to the right and beyond the Church, with its large flat roof and the tall extension for raising and lowering scenery.

weekly for each section, including foot drill, sounding practice, physical training at the gymnasium and education at the Military School with its NCO instructors. The education included regimental history, map reading, English, mathematics, geography and general subjects such as religious education.

Apart from the training programme, our daily routine was always the same. At 0630 hours, reveille was blasted out by one of the trumpeters and meant an immediate rush to the washroom to get to that single hot tap! Then it was back to make up our beds and kit ready for the inspection. At 0730 came breakfast. The food produced by the regimental cooks was most importantly edible and comprised of porridge, bacon, baked beans and, in addition, twice a week, we had eggs. We were marched to the cookhouse, filed in and sat eight to a table. One boy would then collect eight breakfasts on a metal dish and distribute these to his table. After breakfast it was a rapid march back to the barrack room for inspection at 0830.

The daily programme usually started with foot drill on the main depot square, orchestrated by the dulcet tones of the drill NCO. Then at 1000 came sounding practice under the trumpet major, who wore his badge of rank with pride: four inverted chevrons, a gun above to denote he was a senior sergeant and brass crossed trumpets below, and worn on both arms to denote he was a trumpet major. Our instructor was Trumpet Major Pierce; he was as smart as a pin and used to loosen the metal toe caps on his boots so that when he walked across the cobbles his boots would clink. He was later commissioned and eventually commanded 24th Field Regiment in the British First Army.

We were issued with a trumpet and a bugle, with a mouthpiece for each, and had to take both to practice. The sounding practice started off with just the mouthpiece. The trumpet major would blow the call, each of which had its own accompanying rhyme to remind us how it went. Some of the calls, like reveille, were so long that this was essential. Once we had the call in our minds, using the tongue to control the mouthpiece we would attempt to blow the call to his satisfaction. Only when it was right were we allowed to use the trumpet itself. There were many rhymes and most were very funny, such as Sick Call: 'Come the sick, come the lame, come you buggers you're all the same, you're all swinging the lead.'

Another rhyme I remember, but not the call it was for, went: 'Mary's in the garden sifting cinders cocks up her leg and farts like a man … and the cheeks of her arse went bang, bang, bang.' A last example was the call to the cookhouse: 'Come to the cookhouse door, boys, come to the cookhouse door, jelly, jelly, fill your belly, come to the cookhouse door.' So our practices went, week after week, until we could remember any call and blow it to the Trumpet Major's high standards.

One painful experience was at break time, between 1000 and 1030, when we were marched to the cookhouse for a half pint of milk. First we were formed up and instructed to hold out our hands; then the squad NCO would walk down the ranks with his bamboo whip and, if he spotted any nicotine, he would whack the offending hand and you were placed on a charge. The standard punishment was six whacks for the first offence and ten for the second. This was administered by the squad NCO with his whip in front of the squad in the cookhouse. The guilty party had to bend over a table with his trousers down and receive the punishment on his bare skin. In addition, if cigarettes were found, you were made to eat them – and mighty disgusting they tasted, too!

After the break we had a session at school and then physical training before lunch at 1300 hours. After lunch came more school and physical training before tea at 1700, with a last snack for supper at 1900. On Friday night a meat pie laced with bromide was provided for supper to curb the sexual urges of the young men, given that the following day was the one day we were allowed out of barracks!

After three months, the three best 'Sounders' were appointed as 'Silver Trumpeters' and each issued with a solid silver trumpet engraved with the donor's name, usually an ex-boy who was commissioned in the Great War. My own trumpet was donated by a brevet lieutenant colonel. It is sad to reflect that all these silver trumpets were lost after the outbreak of war.

Sunday mornings we would march up the hill to the beautiful Garrison Church to attend the service. There the RA Band used to play to accompany the congregation. When the service was over the boys were formed up in fours outside on the Front Parade. Each battery would take it in turns to march up and down the parade ground playing their trumpets. This exercise took about one hour before we marched back down the hill to the Grand Depot.

Pay at this time was one shilling a day, and we were allowed to draw two shillings and sixpence a week to spend, the rest being saved as credits. Three times a year we were given three weeks leave and received the remainder of our wages so that we went home with our pockets full!

After a year we were passed out and were allowed to wear the coveted brass crossed trumpets on each arm. We were then sent to our administration block where the vacancies for trumpeters were displayed on a blackboard. The trumpeters were marched in one at a time to select their choice of posting, the order determined by the scores they had attained. I was top of my section and in first, but to my dismay there were no postings to India as all overseas postings had been stopped due to the Munich crisis. There was, however, a posting to 32nd Field Regiment in Preston Barracks, Brighton, and as this was a penny bus ride from my home, I selected that!

One regular event that took place at the Depot had a particular effect on me as a young soldier. This was when, twice a year in the trooping season, in April and September, together with our band we had to escort time-expired soldiers returning from abroad, mainly India. We would go to the goods yard at Woolwich Arsenal Station where the cattle trucks in which the soldiers had been transported from their landing point at Southampton, were waiting. The soldiers made a sad sight, dressed in their greatcoats with their collars turned up against the cold English air. Many of them had served 12 to 18 years overseas, so were not happy in the English climate and were dejected and shivering. In addition I was to learn later they were also coming to terms with their reduced station in life, no longer Sahibs, but forgotten soldiers in cattle trucks in England, and after discharge to what?

I would watch as they were fell in and formed up into fours behind our band before we marched off with the trumpeters playing up the hill to the Grand Depot. There they were dismissed into 'Barrack Room 16' in 1st Battery Lines, where they were isolated: no one was allowed to speak to them and they were confined to their barrack room. They were medically examined, administratively dealt with and then sent on their way, their duty complete, to an uncertain future. I would recall them all too clearly when I returned to the depot from the Italian Front in 1945, with three campaigns behind me, and marched up the hill no longer a boy.

I will never forget that year I spent in Woolwich, when one became accustomed to the life: it was a happy time and Woolwich was like home to all the boys. Thank you Royal Regiment for such a wonderful start to my career.

1st Boys' Battery intake, Dickson Section, in 1937. The author of this article is in the second rank, fourth from the left.

THE WOOLWICH COMMUNITY

The story of Woolwich is only partly the story of the Royal Artillery. The Woolwich community as a whole formed the context and background against which Gunners lived their lives for over 300 years, but Woolwich has its own history, beginning as a Roman crossing-point and later, in medieval times, the site of a ferry port. When Henry VIII moved his court to Greenwich Palace, Woolwich fell within the royal circle of influence, and it became logical for Henry to establish his new Royal Dockyard at Woolwich. From this, as we have seen, a gradual concentration of naval and military enterprise developed, with fortifications in place in the time of Charles II and gun-making in operation by the early 18th century. Thus the Woolwich community encompassed a wide range of artisan crafts, from shipbuilding and rope-making to metal casting and manufacture and the skills needed to handle and transport bulky and massive objects from warships to artillery pieces.

But it was in the 19th century that Woolwich began to grow, with the formal instigation of the Royal Arsenal on what was previously known as the Warren. In 1820 the population of Woolwich was 17,000: 50 years later it had doubled to 35,000 with the Royal Arsenal, now a vast concern covering over 250 acres, as the chief employer. By 1869, when the Royal Dockyard closed, Woolwich had changed from being a port to an

The Woolwich Ferry in operation in the 1920s.

Some of the Royal Arsenal Co-operative workers standing next to their specially chartered train at Woolwich Station, c.1931.

ROADS NAMED AFTER GUNNERS

The Regiment has left its mark on the area in streets and roads named after famous Gunners. We must beware of attributing every possible example to a Gunner: for example, Vincent Road, which lies alongside the Woolwich Arsenal Station, is named after a local historian whose work has featured in this book, not after the distinguished Field Marshal of that name. Nevertheless, although it is unlikely to be definitive, the following list (which does not include all the Master Generals of the Ordnance who also feature in the area) will illustrate the point:

Baker Rd, Everest Rd, Belson Rd, Lord Roberts Terrace, Biddulph St, Mansergh Close, Borgard Rd, Pattison Walk, Brome Rd, Ross Way, Congreve Rd, Shrapnel Rd, Dickson Rd, Whinyates Rd, Downman Rd

It would be patronizing to explain who these great individuals are – or were: any Gunner worth his salt will know! Those who do not may quietly slip away and find a copy of the Regimental history.

industrial manufacturing town, with only the ferry service (steam from 1885) a memory of its maritime past. This process accelerated after the Crimean War of 1854 and Woolwich accumulated the trappings of a Victorian municipality from its own railway stations (Woolwich Arsenal and Woolwich Dockyard) and a tramway (horse-drawn initially, electric from 1908) to a hospital, a Polytechnic, a public library and, shortly after Victoria's death, a new and splendid town hall (but no police station until 1910).

By the First World War Woolwich was flourishing, and at its greatest production, at the end of the war, the Royal Arsenal, now covering 1,285 acres, employed over 80,000 men and women, making it the largest factory in Europe – with all workers paid in cash each week. The Woolwich Building Society, originally founded in 1847, offered financial services to this workforce. In 1868, 20 workers from the Royal Arsenal founded the Royal Arsenal Cooperative Society (RACS), which from small beginnings in a Plumstead food shop developed into huge array of commercial, social and political activities – from food to funerals – catering for its many thousand members in the Woolwich community.

Even after 1918 the Arsenal continued to employ 10,000 workers, turning to manufacture milk churns and railway locomotives as well as armaments until the build-up to the 1938–45 war revived arms manufacturing. During the war years, for obvious reasons, armaments manufacturing was dispersed throughout the country, but as a key target Woolwich suffered badly in the Blitz and continued to suffer bombing raids and subsequent V1 flying bomb incursions up to 1944. While Gunners manned anti-aircraft batteries on Woolwich Common, other Gunners were despatched whenever possible to help the civilian population in the wake of the raids. In the post-war era, the Royal Arsenal once again manufactured armaments (for the Korean War), tanks, military stores and railway locomotives, but was finally closed in 1967, two years after the merger of Woolwich into the Borough of Greenwich.

With the disappearance of the main employer in the area, Woolwich entered a difficult period of isolation, symbolised by the disappearance of the once-mighty RACS in 1975, taken over by Barclays Bank, and the closing of many small

WOOLWICH GENERATIONS

The highly centralized local economy of Woolwich – driven by the Royal Arsenal for more than a century and a half – meant that generations of the same Woolwich families worked there. Writing in the July 2000 edition of Soul Search (a family research site), Diana Kennedy has a typical story,

Three generations of my Sewell family worked at the RA [Royal Arsenal]. My grandfather, Thomas Edward Sewell (1885–1954) worked at the RA for over 50 years retiring in 1952. He was first a machinist, then an overlooker in the laboratory and finally worked in the storeroom. The house that my grandparents lived in at Eltham was one of many built to RA specifications before the First World War. It included a bathroom, range, scullery and garden with a green in the centre of the road between the houses for the children to play.

His father William Thomas Sewell (1858–1920) according to the census of 1871 at the age of 14 years was a Cartridge Maker alongside his two elder brothers. John (Daniel John b.1850) age 20 was a labourer, while Alfred (William Alfred Jones b.1856) at 15 years was a Bullet Maker. William Thomas continued working at the RA as a labourer in the Laboratory until his death in 1920 at the age of 61 years. Their father, Jonathon William (1824–1881) had moved from Suffolk, where he was born, to the East End working as shipbuilder and engineering labourer. When the family moved south to Plumstead in the early 1860s he worked as a labourer at the RA.

engineering works. But the need to regenerate the area known as the Thames Gateway saw early signs of green shoots with the construction of the Thames Barrier, the development of the Arsenal's large proof and experimental acreage into the Thamesmead housing estates and a masterplan to bring 150,000 people into new luxury housing developments on the old Royal Arsenal site alongside small-to-medium business start-ups and service providers. In 2001 Firepower Museum opened as an act of faith by the Gunners in the community they had lived in and with for so long. The year 2009 sees the opening of the DLR link, which will allow easy commuting between Woolwich, Canary Wharf, the City and access to the City Airport. Thus, even though the Royal Regiment has left its Woolwich home (although retaining a presence in the Firepower Museum and on Woolwich Common), it was able to do so with some confidence that Woolwich has a new, brighter future.

TMI

Above: Beresford Square, outside the main gate to the Royal Arsenal, at the end of the 19th century.

Left: A drawing showing part of the town centre's development plans, bringing new hope for the revival of prosperity to Woolwich.

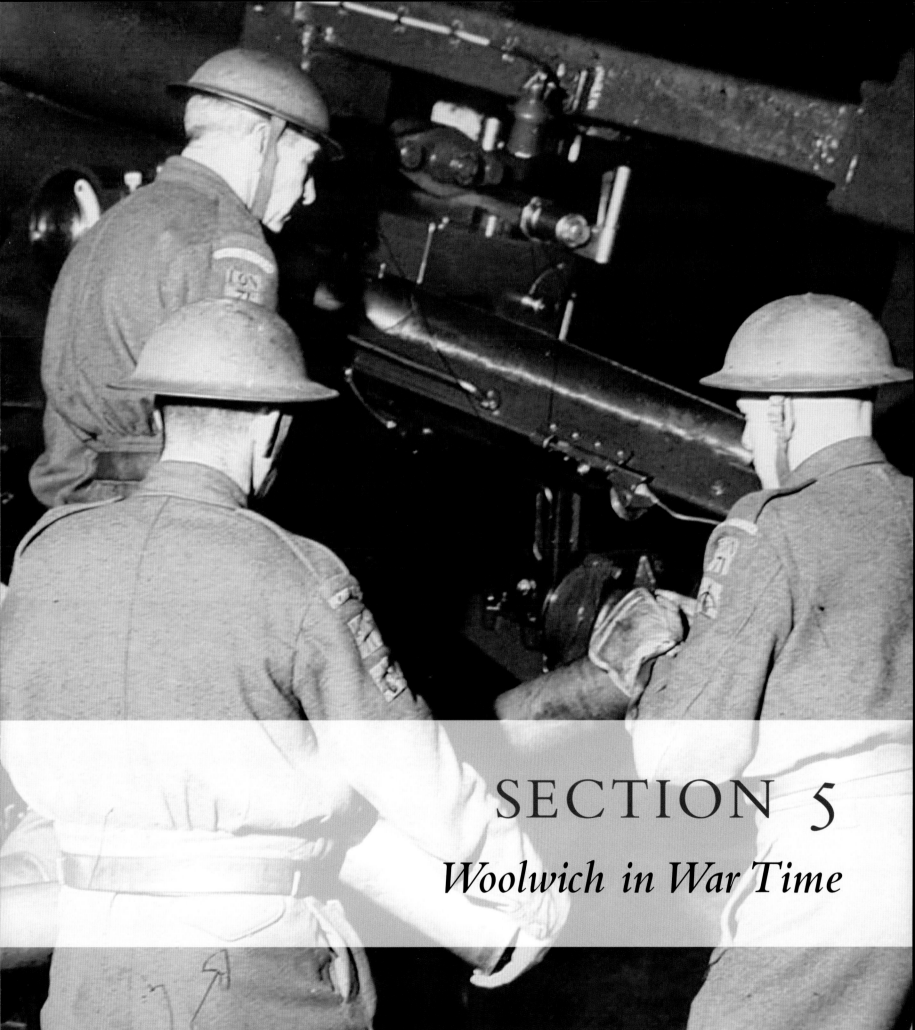

SECTION 5
Woolwich in War Time

Life in the Garrison during the 1939–45 War

Major George Hamilton-Jones MBE

(edited extracts from an article written for a book entitled *The Story of Woolwich* by E. F. E. Jefferson)

George Hamilton-Jones was one of Woolwich's best-known figures, not only for his long service in the Garrison and his building of the stadium, but also for his involvement in maintaining good relations between the military and civilian communities. He remained on the Active List until 1951, when he began a new career in Charlton, working for Harvey's Steel Works.

In normal times the total strength of the garrison was about 4,500 to 5,000. When the final 1939 evacuation was carried out, the numbers were reduced to about 500, including a reduced company of Royal Army Service Corps (RASC) and Royal Army Medical Corps and a small cadre of troops left behind for 'tidying up' purposes.

I had been recalled from the Reserve of Officers and was appointed Garrison Adjutant. To one who had known so well the normal busy whirl of activities that centred around 'The Common' and the Parade Ground, reminiscent of the Sunday Church Parade with the Artillery Band, or with its squads of drilling recruits, the changes brought feelings of nostalgia mixed with a certain depression. Yet, as Thomas Hardy wrote of those who went:

Leaving all that here can win us;
Hence the faith and fire within us,
Men who march away.

Somehow, moreover, the atmosphere seemed to epitomize the 'phoney' war that existed overseas, soldiers 'passively engaged in active service', a stalemate in France which might burst into conflagration any day just as these quiet environs of Woolwich might as suddenly be disturbed from the air. Neither did the fall of darkness disperse this spell of uncanny doubt and depression. Gone was the camaraderie of Mess and Canteen, which was wont to follow the soldier's day duty, and the uncertainty of what might come with the night acted like some counter-charm of memory. To an old Gunner no greater contrast could possibly be imagined. It was as though the whole weird medium was at variance with all the known rules of warfare.

Humour relieves most tense situations: one morning as I left Garrison Headquarters I was dumbfounded to see lining the kerb a party of uniformed girls, apparently very tired and rather dejectedly sitting on kitbags. They were a company of

First Aid Nursing Yeomanry. Their Commanding Officer had temporarily disappeared for advice and information, but it transpired that these girls had come to drive ambulances and the various vehicles used by the depleted RASC company. Was it typical of the Army that we had not the slightest notion of their arrival?

Soon a Territorial Regiment moved in to be kitted up for France; another arrived, destination Singapore, and most of whose members I am afraid were about to become prisoners of war. Matters appeared to be on the move but still the quiet, weird and 'phoney' war continued 'over there'.

One feature we had to preserve was the combined depot cookhouse. Napoleon is credited with the saying that an army

ANTI-AIRCRAFT DEFENCES ON WOOLWICH COMMON

There were no Anti-Aircraft defences on the Common during the First World War, but there certainly were guns there in the Second World War. A battery of 3.7in guns and another of 40mm Bofors were deployed there for most of hostilities and were constantly in action against the raids. In practice, the batteries in busy locations were changed regularly so that batteries in less heavily attacked areas were able to relieve them.

Nearby, on Shooters Hill, there was a large concentration of Z-rocket projectors, 64 in all, each capable of launching two rockets; later versions were multiple launchers. At first, these were manned by the Regular Army, but were soon taken over by the Home Guard.

A 3.7-inch static Heavy Anti-Aircraft gun in position on Woolwich Common during the war, part of a battery of guns that was deployed in the ring of defences around London.

moves on its stomach; likewise a garrison, however static, cannot exist long without food.

Then came the signal that the spell in France had been broken and the town of Dunkirk became famous as the culmination of a tragic if heroic retreat. Evacuees of many units simply poured in by road and rail and it was no time before we found ourselves housing 15,000 troops. With the aid of a few extra men from London District, we began to pile up bedding and food necessary for this surprise influx, overrunning as it did the Academy, the College of Science classrooms, the whole of the RA Depot, Grand Depot, the RE Block, Cambridge Barracks, part of Connaught Barracks and, as a last resort, the stables! Officers crowded into the Mess and non-commissioned officers and men flooded into every available billet and barrack.

We arranged a leave system whereby men were constantly visiting their homes in order to relieve the strain on the garrison. Moreover, anticipating the bombing that must follow this outburst on the continent, we ordered trenches to be dug across the sports fields, cellars to be fitted up for temporary habitation and other retreats earmarked so that troops could move in quickly when bombing began. They were ordered to carry steel helmets and respirators. Soon we were to experience excessive bombing – hostile aircraft appeared in dozens, the first of an attack which was to last for 92 consecutive nights. Evening meals were especially hazardous; no sooner had the troops settled down than the sirens went and we all had to disperse to our allotted posts in the shortest possible time.

Taking the Garrison as a whole the casualties were fortunately extremely light. Our greatest worry was the civilian population of the various boroughs, even allowing for the fact that most of the children were in safer areas. As Garrison Adjutant, I was closely concerned with the issuing of orders to commanders to send aid to borough councils when difficulty or disaster occurred. The civilians, especially the housewives, won our admiration for their cheerfulness and courage, and always the troops were only too willing to render what assistance they could. Morale remained remarkably high.

Gradually the garrison became a clearing house for soldiers of all ranks, proceeding on a variety of tasks in many different directions. Eventually, too, the Allied Air Forces began to gain the upper hand and enemy raids became less and less. Our spirits rose in proportion and gradually unit dances, concerts and other entertainments were arranged to keep troops happy and interested. The Royal Artillery Band was with us and they split into three units to accompany the troops on route marches. At least men were kept occupied until they were required to move out. Gradually the Allied movements widened and our 15,000 troops were slowly but surely equipped to join other theatres of war, but we kept at a steady 10,000 until the end.

In 1945 when demobilization started, it became a matter of complete reorganization so far as the Garrison was concerned. The Academy had gone, the Garrison Church razed to the ground, horses sold – and what more repugnant to an old Artilleryman! – the Drag Hunt discontinued; and a lot of the area destroyed by early air raids and later by V1 and V2 bombs. A Woolwich that was no longer the Woolwich even of the First War.

A Wartime Return Journey

Bernard Skinner

In May 1939 I joined 118th Field Regiment RA at the Drill Hall at Lee Green, a mile southwest of the famous Woolwich Garrison. Towards the end of August, I received a notice of embodiment, ordering me to report to the Drill Hall on 1 September armed with my civilian gas-mask and a haversack ration. Together with many of my colleagues, we were transported on requisitioned lorries to Woolwich and decanted onto the parade ground.

On arrival I recognized a general feeling of extreme urgency. We were quickly kitted out with the basic necessities of army life, which included denim fatigues, but no battledress, which arrived later. Keen to look the part, some of us bought smart side hats and canes from a local outfitters – it helped make us feel like proper Gunners!

War was declared on Sunday, 3 September and, almost as if to give an official seal of approval, the air raid sirens sounded, though no enemy aircraft appeared. Within a week or so, we newly arrived Territorials were settling into barrack life, with daily gun drill and foot drill on the parade ground. There were lectures on discipline, health matters and the history of the Royal Artillery, among others.

After nearly 70 years, my memory is not clear on whether security was included in the lectures, but I do remember being detailed to guard duty on the main entrances to the barracks. I worried that, although I was by now a reasonably qualified gunner and could serve a 25-pounder in action, I had never handled a .303in rifle. Perhaps we were not expected to shoot anyone – any potential intruder, seeing that we were armed, might hesitate and even go away! I need not have worried: we were armed with pick helves.

The inoculations we received suggested that we would soon be serving abroad, perhaps in France, and I prepared myself mentally for active service. It was something of a shock to be told that, along with a few others who had not yet reached the age of 19, I would not be leaving these shores. Classed as immature – a rather inappropriate tag for a keen young soldier – I was transferred to another TA unit at Dover. When I got there, I discovered that I was joining an anti-aircraft unit! Fortunately, my Woolwich training helped me quickly adapt to the new equipment as we settled into life overlooking the white cliffs and the Channel.

Eventually, of course, I got to see a bit of the world and my travels took me to Egypt via Durban, then Iraq, back to the Desert and on to Italy, with lots of journeys around Europe during the military government of the post-war turmoil there. However, I ended my war service of 7 years and 227 days in the Royal Herbert Hospital, back in Woolwich. It was good to be home!

Left: A familiar scene to old soldier – troops cluster round a tea car dispensing 'char and a wads' (tea and buns) at Woolwich Barracks, London, 5 August 1940.

Opposite: The docks and the Royal Arsenal remained key targets for German bombers throughout the Blitz.

The Royal Artillery Mess — Wartime

Major Derick Garnier

During the Second World War the Depot Mess was always full, with officers coming and going. To accommodate them all, the Other Ranks' married quarters in Artillery Place were taken over for the purpose. Two officers might have to share a bedroom.

I was 'repatriated' from the Middle East in 1944 after six years of overseas service and temporarily accommodated there until my next posting. Mr Lund was the Head Porter at that time, a post he had held a long time, and was a most exceptional person. He had an excellent memory for both faces and names, so when you walked into the Mess, he immediately knew who you were or if you were a newcomer. He was the kind of person that Jeeves was to to Bertie Wooster in the famous P. G. Wodehouse stories. Calm and polite, he knew how to help or provide the right answer as the occasion demanded.

The Mess waiters were Auxiliary Territorial Service (ATS) women soldiers. 'Sergeant Connie' (as she was known) was the Mess Sergeant in charge of them, a competent and very capable woman. She selected and groomed her girls, who all looked good and were dressed smartly. Sergeant Connie told me that she gave them lessons in make-up: they were attractive and many of the wartime officers became engaged to and married them later.

Woolwich was in line of fire of one of the sources of the V1 flying bombs targeted on London in 1944–5. One evening a bomb was heard heading directly towards the Mess when it suddenly 'cut out'. This was the danger signal that it was about to drop. Dinner had been prepared and the places laid out. When these bombs cut out, they became erratic in their flight because they had no more control. This particular one changed its course, turned and dropped on the Garrison Chapel, which it destroyed. All the plaster in the Mess ceiling dropped onto the dinner arrangements. Quite unperturbed, Sergeant Connie calmly organized her staff to 'clear the decks' and an hour later had relaid the tables and put out a cold collation.

All round the Common there were barrage balloons, anti-aircraft batteries and searchlights. While I was there, one could hear a few bombs being dropped from enemy aircraft. They always turned out to be incendiary bombs and landed on the Front Parade where they did no damage and were quickly extinguished. It was after the war, years later, that I understood that the Germans had earmarked the barracks as accommodation for its occupying forces when they invaded and so was not to be destroyed. This was only comfort in hindsight!

One of the good things about the Grand Depot was the RA Theatre on the Front near the chapel end. Very good plays were performed there.

The Music Room of the Mess as it was during the first half of the 20th century.

CIVILIAN MEMORIES

John Peters

King George V named the 'Royal' Garrison Church during his visit in 1928.

Factories and nearly every family in Woolwich was connected in some way with the Arsenal, engaged in munitions production and associated activities. When the war ended, jobs became scarce. I remember a street scene in the late 1920s when small groups of men wearing their war medals sang for money. The piano was carried on a handcart.

The first daylight raid on London was made by some 14 aircraft on 13 June 1917 when Central London received attention, but Woolwich was spared on this occasion. There were night raids by Zeppelins and bombs were dropped on Artillery Place, the east end of the Front Parade Ground and Mill Lane. There were casualties, and on 16 February 1918 the Garrison Church lost its stained glass windows. Scars can still be seen on the front pillars of the now-ruined church, a casualty of a V1 flying bomb in July 1944.

In 1928 King George V visited Woolwich Barracks and, after reviewing the troops, agreed to the prefix 'Royal' for the Garrison Church. My grandfather, as choir-master, had the privilege of being introduced to His Majesty.

Treats much enjoyed in the 1930s were the Woolwich Tattoo held in Woolwich Stadium and Army boxing at the TA Drill Hill in Spray Street, off New Road. My sister and I also looked forward to the annual pantomimes in the RA Theatre and, in later years, to the RA Band Concerts.

In 1929 we moved to Shooters Hill and, in 1933, I joined the Garrison Church Choir (some 23 boys and a dozen or so men). Apart from choral duties, we were able to muster a cricket team of some repute which was allowed to play on the Barrack Field.

As church parade was compulsory, it was quite common to have Sunday morning service congregations in excess of 1,500. In the early 1930s, Remembrance Sunday attracted very large congregations. Still alive at that time were those who fought at Mons (the 'Old Contemptibles' of 1914), in the trenches of the Somme, Ypres and the mud of Passchendaele. Their memories of the Great War added to the poignancy and solemnity of the occasion. We sang 'For All the Saints', 'O God Our Help' and, of course, 'O Valiant Hearts'.

The RA Band usually played in the chancel and, for special services, in the West Gallery. The 'Great and Good', some with red tabs, occupied the front pews. Behind, in rank order, were the troops with highly polished boots and buttons and well-

I was born in Woolwich in 1926 and lived in the borough until 1947. My earliest recollections are of the sounds of gunfire, first from the proofing of gun barrels on the marshes of the Royal Arsenal, and second from the One o'Clock Gun, which was synchronized with the descent of the Time Ball at Greenwich Observatory. I didn't like it, neither did the pigeons. Explosions of a more sinister nature would be experienced in later years.

From time to time my parents were allowed access to the grounds of the nearby Royal Military Repository. One severe winter, the lake froze over and I remember being taken to watch them ice skate. On another occasion, the Military put on an impressive firework display in the 'Reppo' as it was called. The three-year old who was allowed to stay up will never forget the noise and excitement.

My parents told me much about the Woolwich of their day; in particular, the General Strike of 1926 which resulted in much unemployment in the area. The First World War had seen a very large increase in numbers employed in Royal Ordnance

wound puttees. Senior boys took the collection. (Strange how buttons and foreign coins found their way into the offertory bags!) After the service the men, who had different priorities, repaired to the Barrack Tavern, while we watched the weekly pageant from a vantage point on the Front Parade. The RA Band played 'Christchurch Bells', 'British Grenadiers' and, of course, the RA Slow March. Later, boy buglers marched and countermarched. A westerly wind always raised much dust – the days before tarmac. My father told me that in 1924, on a moonlit night, he tested his home-made sand yacht on the Front Parade. The sentry was puzzled and turned out the guard. There was much explaining to do.

Wartime Memories

Although I was too young on the outbreak of the Second World War to join the Army, I was active in the Air Training Corps, learning many useful skills. As soon as I could, I enrolled in the Home Guard, joining in February 1941 at the age of 15 and remaining with that body until the end of 1944.

I well remember life in Woolwich during the war, but perhaps the most relevant of those memories concerns my time with the Z rocket battery on Shooters Hill. I had first to qualify by showing proficiency in loading and aiming the projector and to fire five live rounds at the range in Walton-on-the-Naze, Essex.

Each projector was manned by two Gunners. The ready-to-use rounds were mounted on cradles and fuzed by rotating them to a setting received over the headphones. Target bearing and the appropriate elevation to point the rocket also came over the headphones and corrections had to be applied as the target changed direction or altitude. One man was responsible for setting the bearing of the projector, the other for the elevation and operating the firing lever. Once the fuze was set, the 56-pound rocket had to be lifted to shoulder height and slid back

on the rails until the fins engaged the electrical contacts. On receiving the order, the firing lever was depressed to complete the circuit.

It all sounds straightforward, but there was always the one gentleman who got the wrong message over the headphones with the result that 126 rockets went one way and two in a quite different direction!

By 1944 ground radar stations were feeding AA batteries with more accurate target data. Our local command site was manned by Home Guards, whose job was to process range-and-bearing information from the radar so that it could be used by the officer in charge at the plotting table. Our officer in charge was the Head of the Physics Department at Woolwich Polytechnic, assisted by a senior lecturer in the same department: suffice it to say that slide rules were used to cross-check the gunnery fire control data!

I managed to transfer to plotting duties and I shall not forget the sinking feeling whenever the official phone rang and a distant voice announced, 'Operations Commence, DIVER DIVER DIVER.' Grid references of hostile targets began to be read out. Another wave of V1s was on the way.

Far left: The chancel of the Royal Garrison Church.

Below: Z-rocket launchers in action on Shooters Hill during a Second World War bombing raid on London.

'Badgies' – Boys' Battery 1942–48

Lieutenant Colonel Derek Bender

This account covers the period from October/November 1942, when Boys' Battery was reformed at the Grand Depot at Woolwich, until mid-1948, when the Battery moved 'lock, stock and barrel' from Cambridge Barracks, Woolwich, to Kinmel Park Camp, near Rhyl, North Wales.

The training of Boys (Trumpeters – known as 'Badgies'), ceased on the outbreak of the Second World War in 1939. The remaining Boys were moved to Windsor until the youngest pre-war Boys mustered into man's service at $17\frac{1}{2}$ years old in early 1941.

The Battery reformed in 1942 at the Grand Depot and, as numbers grew, it moved into temporary accommodation at the old Royal Military Academy ('The Shop') in mid-1945, prior to moving to Cambridge Barracks, in mid-1946. There it stayed until the latter half of 1948 before moving to Kinmel Park, North Wales, where it remained for many years.

By the time it moved into Cambridge Barracks in 1946, its numbers had swelled to nearly 350 Boys, aged between 14 and $17\frac{1}{2}$ years old. The age of 14 was determined by the fact that at that time, it was the school leaving age. The $17\frac{1}{2}$ stage was the age at which Boys mustered into the ranks and became regular soldiers. Their terms of service were originally nine years with the Colours and three years on the Reserve. This was changed to eight and four in the latter years of the war (by 1945).

The Boys were allocated unique regimental numbers, the last of the seven figure numbers, starting with 1151 and then later 1157. The 1151 numbers were 1151305 to 1151989, and the 1157 numbers were 1157200 to 1157952. These blocks of numbers ceased in July 1947 and the numbers were changed to eight figure numbers, of 2220 sequence.

The Indian Boys (approximately 25 of them) joined Boys' Battery when India and Pakistan gained their independence in August 1947. Over 1,500 Boys were trained or in training from the time Boys' Battery was formed in 1942 until it left Woolwich in 1948.

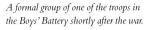

A formal group of one of the troops in the Boys' Battery shortly after the war.

The Battery was commanded by a major, with a battery captain and Battery Sergeant Major (BSM) and supported by adult administrative staff. The first Boy BSM was appointed in September 1944. By 1946, it consisted of seven Troops, A to G Troops each about 45 to 50 strong (G Troop was for the RA Band Boys). Each Troop was commanded by a subaltern, with a troop sergeant and junior NCO. In addition, each Troop had a Boy Sergeant and three or four junior NCOs to assist in the daily discipline and running of the subunit.

As it was wartime (or just post-war), the Boys were basically without their parents to guide them: many fathers away serving their country, some lads coming from broken homes and so on. The permanent staff, especially the troop sergeants, acted as our surrogate fathers. They were pre-war soldiers, ex-Boys themselves who had been through the war and adapted themselves to the task in hand, without any formal training whatsoever. They did a magnificent job.

It is said that some of the Boys joined the Army by 'chance'. It usually meant that the beak on duty when they went before the young offenders court had said, 'I am considering giving you a custodial sentence [Borstal], but I will give you another 'chance' if you join the Army.' (That is a quote from a boy who achieved commissioned rank in later years.)

Basically, the Boys received two sorts of training: first with their education – Army Certificate 1st and 2nd Class – and second military training, both technical and on the guns (25-pounders). They were also taught to play a trumpet and bugle (hence 'Badgies'). There was a thriving band of well over 60, with drums, trumpets and bugles. This used to go on tour annually, together with the Drill Squad and Physical Training Display Team which performed at the Aldershot Tattoo and later at Earls Court Tattoo and around the country.

Pay on entry was ten shillings and sixpence (52.5 pence) of which five shillings per week had to go into credits (savings) so that boys had money for when they were on leave. Incremental amounts, for rank, education and qualification, could increase the pay by a few pence a week (3d, 6d, 9d or a shilling).

The Battery had thriving football, rugby, cricket, hockey and boxing teams that played against other Boys' units (of all services) and civilian agencies and clubs.

The days started with a trumpet call, reveille at 0600 hours daily, parade for breakfast at 0700 and then return to the barrack room to prepare everything for daily inspection before Battery Parade at 0815. They then worked – lessons or training throughout the day, with an hour's break for their midday meal – until 1700 hours, when they had their evening meal. Saturday was best dress inspection, drill/march past on the Main Square (Front Parade) at the Grand Depot, followed by full barrack room inspection, with a full kit layout. The afternoon was Battery Sports. Sunday was a full Battery Church Parade and Church Service at the Garrison Church. Boys were allowed out over the weekend in the evenings if they were free of duties.

When the Boys' Battery was re-formed in 1942, its charter was to train future warrant officers and NCOs for the Gunners. It is interesting to note that, in the case of the Boys who served at Woolwich from 1942 to 1948, not only was this aim achieved, it was surpassed, producing one brigadier, eleven lieutenant colonels (one of whom became a colonel who was a cadet county commandant), numerous commissioned quartermasters and technical instructors in gunnery (too many to count), four bravery awards (one Distinguished Flying Medal and three Military Medals), one lord and one deputy lord lieutenant (DL), one Commander of the British Empire, several members of the same order and holders of British Empire Medals, one with the RA Medal, 1 lord mayor and three justices of the peace.

The last time the 1151/1157 Boys attended Woolwich officially was when they were honoured by being allowed to hold their Annual Dinner in the Royal Artillery Officers' Mess, Woolwich, in the company of their President, Field Marshal The Lord Vincent GBE, KCB, DSO and The Master Gunner, General Sir Alex Harley KBE, CB. It was indeed an honour that none of them, in their wildest dreams, could ever have imagined: the 'Badgies' dining in the RA Officers' Mess Woolwich in such illustrious company.

A lovely comment by one of the wartime Boys when he was asked if he enjoyed the gathering and seeing everyone again after more than 60 years, was 'If the Devil could cast his net?' How true.

ORIGIN OF THE NICKNAME

When he had learned the calls parrot-fashion from the Trumpet Major, the Trumpeter was dubbed a 'Badgie'. Surprisingly, this had nothing to do with the crossed trumpets badge on his sleeve, but was instead derived from the Hindustani 'Baja wallah' (Music Man).

The author of this article (second from the left in the back row) seen with friends in the Boys' Battery in a picture he entitled 'The Scruffs'.

SECTION 6

Gunner Heritage

THE ROYAL ARTILLERY MUSEUM 1778–2008

Mark Smith MA, Curator

The museum as an entity has been open to the public since 4 May 1820, a continuous record we believe to be unrivalled by any other regimental museum in this country. In May 2001, the collection of artillery was moved to the new premises within the gates of the Royal Arsenal and opened under the rebadged name of 'FIREPOWER, the Museum of the Royal Artillery'. The museum had returned to the original home of the Regiment and, indeed, of the collection.

The collection was founded in 1778 at the Royal Arsenal by Captain (later Lieutenant General Sir) William Congreve; King George III required Congreve, through the Board of Ordnance, 'to complete a Repository of Military Machines and to instruct the officers and men of the Royal Regiment of Artillery in the many valuable improvements he has discovered'. The Board of Ordnance added that it wished to 'recommend it in the strongest manner to the officers of Artillery to do everything in their power to promote so useful a plan'.

Captain Congreve, as Superintendent of Military Machines and then Comptroller of the Royal Laboratory, where gunpowder and ammunition were designed and produced, was particularly active in encouraging the acquisition of items from abroad, especially western Europe, primarily to establish a teaching collection. His original objective was: 'to provide practical instruction for the officers, non-commissioned officers and men of the Regiment of Artillery, both in the grand scale and with the aid of drawings and models, and for this purpose to form as extensive a collection as possible of everything tending to improve the science and practice of artillery, and to explain its progress.'

The collection benefited in 1816 by the acquisition of ordnance, arms, models and various articles taken from the Arsenal, central depot, Paris, as part of the British share of stores captured in the city. The British did not take anything from the French Museum of Artillery; however, items were obtained from this museum for the collection through the Prussian Army, which had comprehensively helped itself to items from the museum in retaliation for the looting carried out so effectively by the armies of Napoleon. Some rare items were acquired in this way, and it is both significant and interesting to note that the Duke of Wellington directed that the artefacts should be deposited at the Royal Artillery depository and not in the Tower of London.

Above: The Rotunda Museum in the 1930s, showing something of the huge collection of guns and the generally disorganized state that existed after the First World War.

Left: During the celebrations that took place for the 200th anniversary of the foundation of the Royal Horse Artillery, HM The Queen was briefed by Colonel David Evans and the Master Gunner, General Sir Martin Farndale, on plans for the new museum to be established in the Royal Arsenal.

In 1805 the collection was moved from the Repository in the Royal Arsenal to the new Repository alongside the Royal Artillery barracks on the edge of Woolwich Common. In 1819, it was moved into the Rotunda building, now a listed building in its own right, which was placed in its present position by order of the Prince Regent. The tent had been designed by John Nash

(1752–1832) as the centrepiece of a garden party for the entertainment of the Allied sovereigns in Carlton House Gardens in 1814, and it was also used for the post-Waterloo victory celebrations in 1815. When the Prince Regent agreed to donate the Rotunda to the Board of Ordnance for use as a museum, it was dismantled and dispatched to Woolwich in October 1818. There it was rebuilt, following Nash's instructions, receiving brick walls, a central column and a refurbished roof. By 1820 the collection was established in the now newly-named Rotunda and was based there until 2001. The Rotunda now acts as the reserve collection storage facility, but is still open to the public by appointment. The first catalogue of items held in the collection was produced in 1822.

The collections have continued to grow, first under the direction of Congreve's son and then under other serving officers. A tremendous boost was received in the form of the strong support of General Sir John Lefroy (1817–90), a distinguished Gunner and Fellow of the Royal Society, who, in the course of his extensive service, obtained many new items. It was thanks to Lefroy that the first printed catalogue was published in 1864. This work owed much in format to similar catalogues of the collections of Paris and Madrid and to the

assistance of scholars from the Armouries in the Tower of London and the British Museum. It was during this period that the Rotunda served as a reference collection and repository for models of projects for the Ordnance Select Committee, of which Lefroy was first Secretary and then President. The committee's function was to study and recommend new proposals for the improvement of artillery and the re-equipment of the army. This was as a direct result of experiences learned in the Crimean War and the American Civil War.

In 1870 the Rotunda and its collections were transferred to the Royal Artillery Institution, a professional and charitable organization established in Woolwich in 1838. The collections continued to grow with objects arriving from all over the world thanks to imperial expansion, foreign wars and the travels of individuals. A further boost to the scientific side came when Captain C. Orde Brown deposited the results of his experiments in armour and armour penetration with the museum: his work *Armour and its Attack by Artillery* (1887), a very important work for both the Royal Navy and the Army of the time, is held in the RA Library.

Development of the collection and, indeed, the museum continued until the First World War when the museum was

A view of the Gunnery Hall in the new museum, with the History Gallery on the mezzanine floor. The various pieces of equipment on show are grouped to provide examples of the different roles of artillery and to provide visitors with interactive displays, using computer terminals with touch-screen graphics. The track and wheel marks on the floor are a design feature and not poor house-keeping.

closed 'for the duration'. In its aftermath there was an attempt to rationalize the collections, which by this time included a wide variety of arcana deposited as a result of the Victorian interest in museums. In 1927, 971 important artefacts were loaned to the Armouries in the Tower, as the RAI was encouraged to believe that they would be better displayed there. The Cottesloe Committee formally confirmed the move, subject to an agreement on the collecting policies of the two museums. Sadly, the Royal Armouries did not adhere to the agreed policy and, moreover, unilaterally assimilated the loan into a 'permanent' status within the Royal Armouries' collections.

In November 1940 a German bomb destroyed the offices of the Royal Artillery Institution together with many of the Rotunda's records. Once again the museum was closed during the Second World War and regrettably the Rotunda building was left to deteriorate; lack of funds caused this state of affairs to continue until the 1950s when eventually much needed repairs were carried out. After a period of consolidation the collection once more began to expand with the acquisition of objects from the second half of the 20th century, with visitor figures peaking in 1977.

In the 1960s a separate Regimental Museum was set up to display the history of the Regiment through uniforms, pictures, equipment and memorabilia, some of which had previously been displayed in the RAI building. During the 1970s, the medal collection was formally put on display in the RA Mess to allow access to the growing collection of orders, decorations and medals in a collection of over 10,000 items, including 22 Victoria Crosses. The collection of ordnance, guns, rockets, missiles, ammunition, associated vehicles, equipment, models (834) and small arms remained housed in the Rotunda.

In the 1980s it became clear that the museum could no longer reconcile its remit to collect and record the history and development of British artillery within the space constraints of the Rotunda. The Museum had already experienced a problem at the end of the First World War when lack of facilities for storing

Above: The Phoenix unmanned aerial vehicle (UAV), used to provide real-time imagery from beyond the front line.

Top left: Three early barrels showing manufacture in bronze, cast iron and wrought iron.

Above left: A reproduction of the earliest known picture of artillery from the 13th century, showing a pot de fer loaded with a war arrow.

Left: A model of Colonel Pattison's Light 3 pr of 3 ft, 1775, otherwise known as the Grasshopper.

heavy and siege guns resulted in substantial and irreplaceable gaps in the collection. Furthermore, the pace of technological change meant that even more space would be required to keep up with the introduction of new equipment into current service.

The Regiment therefore began a heritage fund-raising campaign to re-house the collections. A project team was formed under General Sir Martin Farndale, then Master Gunner St James's Park and a keen military historian with a deep interest in the Regiment's collections. Initially all the effort was concentrated on raising funds from Gunners past and present. The team was led first by Colonel Andrew Fowler and then by Colonel David Evans, with Mrs Eileen Noon as the principal office manager. (Mrs Noon remained with the project right through to its completion and in due course became the Chief Executive Officer of the museum, responsible for its day-to-day management.)

On 6 July 1999 all the prerequisites for expansion, including a Heritage Lottery Fund grant, were in place and the Royal Artillery Institution authorized Royal Artillery Museums Ltd to proceed with the construction of the new museum. Progress was boosted in May 2000 by the award to the Museum of 'Designated' status, giving the collections a quasi-national status. *Firepower* opened its doors on 26 May 2001, the 285th anniversary of the founding of the Regiment.

In April 2004 the Museum opened its second phase of development in the buildings that were once the New Laboratories and the Old Royal Military Academy. This was made possible by a generous grant from the European Regional Development Fund, administered via the Government Office for London.

Two new galleries were opened. These are the East Wing Gallery and the Cold War Gallery. In addition, there is now space for temporary exhibitions and for storage, which will gradually be filled by objects from the reserve collection stored at the Rotunda site in Repository Road, continually improving access to the amazing material held by the Royal Artillery Historical Trust. The collections of the Royal Artillery Museum now amount to over 3,500,000 objects, ranging from a wrought iron gun from the *Mary Rose* to a collection of drawings done in secret while the artist was a prisoner of the Japanese during the Second World War.

It is this fascinating diversity that the Museum aims to bring alive with its exhibition programme, providing the visitor with a fascinating insight into the lives and exploits of those who have been connected with the Royal Regiment of Artillery for almost 300 years.

Right: One of the many hundreds of medal groups in the Medal Gallery in the Museum. This one shows the medals of Gen Sir Edward Bruce Hamley KCB KCMG.

Below: The ultimate anti-aircraft gun – a very complex piece of equipment that was designed to cope with aircraft flying ever faster and higher, using such a high rate of fire that it needed a water-cooled barrel. It never saw service because missiles like Thunderbird (see previous page) were more effective at the task.

Below right: A 7.2-inch calibre heavy gun from the Second World War period.

LIBRARY COLLECTIONS OF THE ROYAL ARTILLERY INSTITUTION

Maurice Paul Evans, Librarian

Today the James Clavell Library stands inside the walls of the Royal Arsenal alongside the Royal Artillery Museum. The library opened its Reading Room doors to the public for the first time in October 2001, but the collections had been accessible under different names and in different parts of Woolwich for the previous 200 years.

The Library houses the collections of the Royal Artillery Historical Trust, a charitable trust charged since 9 March 1981 with the protection, maintenance and improvement of collections given over by the Royal Artillery Institution, and for many it is still known as the RAI Library.

The Institution was formed in 1838 on the initiative of the then Lieutenants J. H. Lefroy and F. M. Eardley-Wilmot, who had found educational facilities at Woolwich inadequate, especially for the study of surveying and astronomy. Within 18 months a library had been formed, and a small observatory and instrument room established; the Regimental Museum was started soon afterwards. The Institution's status was that of a 'learned society' concerned with furthering the education of the RA officer. To this end the first bound volume of the *Minutes of the Proceedings of the RAI* was published in 1858, containing papers on artillery matters contributed from 1845 onwards. The Institution soon came to be accepted as the principal authority on the Regiment's history and, in 1870, the

Museum of Artillery in the Rotunda at Woolwich was transferred to its custody, bringing with it a significant book collection first started in 1778.

In 1911 it was agreed that the Officers' Mess Library and staff should transfer to RAI control and, over the next two years, collections dating back to 1806 and earlier moved across the barracks to the RAI building.

The Second World War stopped the growth of the library in its tracks: housed within the RAI building and located within the RA Barracks on Riding School Road, SE18, the building was first struck by an incendiary bomb in October 1940, which caused no damage to the library stock. A week later another incendiary burnt out the attic and destroyed those papers and files stored within. At 8.50 pm on 2 November 1940 an explosive bomb completely destroyed (with the exception of the North Museum and the Committee room) the remainder of the building. Mr Thomas Sullivan, the building caretaker was also killed. Regrettably the recovered materials were moved by DCRE (the District Commander Royal Engineers' works office) salvage party to R House, the adjacent building to the north of the library: this, in turn, was struck by

Below: One of a series of photographs, taken in 1858 after the Indian Mutiny, by Felice Beato, the brilliant photographer who also took pictures in China during the Boxer Rebellion. This picture, taken in Delhi, shows the ruined Secundra Bagh and the bodies of rebels still littering the streets. The album was compiled by Captain Maude VC, who was part of the force that took Delhi.

Left: One of a large set of watercolours painted by Captain John Walford RFA, showing a battery having a break during the First World War. It is full of fascinating detail, like all his paintings of the war, providing information that is hard to find elsewhere.

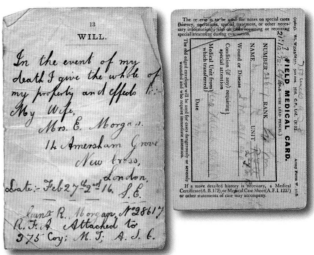

Above: Photographs and letters from the Archives provide the human story of the Regiment. Here, letters and documents are shown alongside the photograph of a Gunner killed in action, together with his gravestone.

Bottom: A photograph of a Gunner killed in action during the First World War, together with a letter of condolence from his Troop Commander to his widow.

bombs on 16 November 1940. Losses included 1,000 books from the libraries of RA Messes Kirkee and Meerut, sent home from India and presented to the RAI library for safekeeping. All were destroyed by fire and bombs; no trace of any of these remain, or any record of the transaction.

DCRE again undertook the salvage work, and all salved property was removed to the RMA Commandant's House, kindly placed at the disposal of the RAI by the Commandant, Woolwich. There the library was re-established with all the rooms furnished with bookshelves, made in part from salvaged material with Depot RA labour and in part new construction by the DCRE. Much of the manuscript collection was stored in the RMA where the academy library was placed at the disposal of the RAI under orders from the War Office.

In November 1941 the Commandant's house was vacated and the RAI Library moved with the permission of the War Office into the Centre Block of the Front Parade of the Old Royal Military Academy Woolwich and into the lecture rooms above the academy library. This move was voluntary as the opportunity of establishing the RAI as a whole in 'The Shop' itself arose and was promptly accepted.

The library situation was precarious: a note from the Secretary of the RAI to the loss assessors, Messrs Harold Brown and Jessop of 62 Pall Mall dated 21 January 1942, concerning the War Damages Insurance claim, states: 'Regret catalogue serial number of books destroyed cannot be supplied owing to destruction of catalogue.' An estimated 16,000 volumes were lost along with dozens of manuscript collections, photographs and drawings. Worse still, the office correspondence, files, lists and catalogues collected over the previous century were consumed by fire.

Many units of the Royal Regiment of Artillery rallied round: in August 1941 36th Signal Training Regiment RA stationed at Mitton Hall, Whalley, Lancashire, sent two crates containing 322 books originally from RA Library Colchester. Seven cases of books originally from the RA Mess Sheerness were sent from the Senior Officers' School, Brasenose College, Oxford, via HQ 158th Infantry Brigade, arriving in January 1944. With furniture and stock supplied by the RA Depot, the RMA and surrounding messes, the library resumed the supply of academic literature to officers for the rest of the Second World War.

On 6 January 1946 the Committee of the RAI agreed the Institutional policy that: 'The RAI exists primarily for the professional education of all officers of the artillery … the library will include sections containing Military Histories, Biographies, books of travel and sport not generally obtainable from lending libraries. It will maintain sufficient copies of books of reference on military subjects to assist officers in their preparation for promotion and other examinations.'

Also in 1946 the books and other property of the RMA were removed to Sandhurst and the books of the Institution moved downstairs and took their place on the academy library shelves. A total of 28 new books were purchased and numerous volumes presented throughout the year. A catalogue of modern books 'suitable for study' was compiled and issued to RAI members in the same year.

In the 1950s a move to simplify RA affairs led to a considerable extension of the role of the Institution. In 1956 it

was made responsible for the financial management of almost all regimental affairs, the production of all regimental publications and the custodianship of regimental history and property, including the Library and Archives. The Institution's duties now encompassed both the domestic and the historical affairs of the Regiment.

A fire on 3 May 1957 started in the roof of the old RMA Middle Tower and, although confined to that portion of the building, did damage the library stock. Practically all the damage was caused by water, but a very small proportion was as a result of the fall of charred embers from the wooden roof beams. Damage was confined to books, documents and papers not in cases; no manuscripts were entirely lost or rendered unreadable, but many were severely water-damaged.

The RAI underwent further change with the new position of Assistant Secretary Historical Section being approved from 1 April 1960. This post was created to work under the general direction of the Secretary and guided by the RA Historical Affairs Committee. The incumbent, assisted by a full-time clerk, was required to:

- Be in executive charge of the maintenance and improvement of the existing collections in the Rotunda museum and the Institution, including the library.
- Be in executive charge of the establishment, and subsequent maintenance, of the new Royal Artillery Museum.
- Supervise all office work connected with historical research, the examination of records, and the answering of historical enquiries.
- Maintain liaison with other service museums and institutions throughout the world.

The advertisement continued: 'ideally he should have some technical knowledge of artillery equipments, qualifications as a historian, and some experience of the techniques of public displays; and the possession of all these qualifications will be considered when the selection is made'. The first incumbent, in 1960, was Major J. P. Kaestlin MBE, RA.

In late 1960 the library closed to under go a complete stock check and cataloguing exercise. Funds were allocated to historical causes in April 1961 from the monies produced by the insurance claim for the 1957 fire and the sale of a rare Dutch 17th century *Blauw's Atlas*.

The 1962 Woolwich Redevelopment Plan recommended Connaught Barracks as 'an appropriate setting for the Royal Artillery Museum and Library … two floors of the Main Block, West Wing, with the main entrance via the existing West entrance … give ample space to provide 12,000 square feet of floor area and for further expansion into the East Wing if required. In addition, storage space for stock is available in the basement.' But the project came to nothing.

In June 1964 the RAI Secretary wrote that: 'The Press is housed in the somewhat inadequate accommodation behind the library in the old RMA buildings at Woolwich and it is hoped that in the not to distant future it may be possible to move and expand it.'

Plans for a new Royal Artillery Museum, Library and RA Information Centre housed in the Greenhill School Woolwich,

to the west of the RA Barracks on the opposite side of Repository Road were drawn up by the Ministry of Public Building and Works in 1969, but the project came to nothing.

In May 1995 the ground floor of the rear rooms in the RMA building was found to be unsafe, and to comply with the Health and Safety at Work Regulations it was found necessary to move the staff out of the Middle Tower into temporary accommodation on site. In the same year floor-loading problems were identified throughout the ground floor of the RMA. The poor condition of the building again caused problems in the 1990s, particularly with leaks in the roof. On one occasion, the guttering failed and a leaking roof became a torrent into the upper floors, where the Regimental Museum was housed, and down the walls into the Library.

The then Historical Secretary, Colonel M. J. Phillips, closed the building on 27 July 1999 following the advice of the health and safety team that the staff were at risk. The library was declared unsafe until the overloading of the floor was relieved by the removal of all free-standing bookcases, packing cases of books, and the ceiling to floor bookcases were secured to the walls and the electrical wiring upgraded. A report on the safety of the ceiling was also to be commissioned.

The books were packed into innumerable packing cases and stored for some months, but by this time the new museum building was nearly ready and that included a purpose-built library. Pickfords, for centuries involved with carrying goods for the military, provided the vehicles and specialist staff for the move into the new facility, properly built, climate controlled and able to look after a unique collection.

Left: One of the treasures of the Royal Artillery Library – a textbook on fortification, bearing the embossed seal of the Board of Ordnance. This leather-bound copy was found in the pocket of General Wolfe, who died in the attack and capture of Quebec. It has his signature inside and praise for its contents.

Below: A Christmas card sent home by Major 'Jock' Campbell ('Grump') from the Western Desert in 1939. He went on to win the Victoria Cross as an acting Brigadier at Sidi Rezegh and was killed shortly afterward in a tragic accident.

Below left: The cover sheet of a document written by Sir William Congreve, setting out the detail of the arrangements made by him for the fireworks in London celebrating the end of the war in 1814.

Above: The flyleaf of a book presented by Florence Nightingale, bearing her signature.

THE ROYAL ARTILLERY MESS IN THE 20TH CENTURY

Colonel Martin Cooper

The Mess, photographed in 1900.

In the Royal Artillery Mess the 20th century was notable for the effects of the two world wars, a continuing debate about Woolwich as the home of the Regiment and a return to more regular royal patronage with the appointment of King Edward VII, and successive monarchs, as Colonel-in-Chief.

At the beginning of the century and with Gunner representation at Woolwich consisting of only the Riding School, two RHA batteries and three field batteries, the argument over the status of Woolwich versus Aldershot continued. The idea of moving the home of the Regiment to Aldershot was diverted by the use of the barracks as a mobilization centre during the First World War, but the establishment of training camps at Tidworth (Wiltshire) and Catterick (North Yorkshire) and subsequently at Larkhill created continuing pressure for a move. Apart from during the world wars the Mess settled into its role as a regimental headquarters mess with a programme of events, including a return of the lavish balls, and occasional visits by the Colonel-in-Chief and other dignitaries.

The War Years

A point of note during the First World War was that, illogically, the call-up of the mess staff led to soldiers being employed in the Mess for the first time; after the war, most of the surviving staff were re-employed. The same thing happened in the Second World War, when the Barracks was used by home defence and training units, with women from the ATS (Auxiliary Territorial Service) employed as mess staff. Such was their success that the ATS were retained after the war, subsequently being replaced by the WRAC (Women's Royal Army Corps) until the running of the Mess returned to contractors in the 1980s.

Much of the mess property was removed from the Mess during the 1939–45 war – the first time that air power presented a significant threat – with the result that only minor structural damage was caused when a bomb passed through the Messroom and exploded in the cellar. The repair of one of the mirrors in two parts remains a reminder of the event. In 1944, at the peak, 650 officers were being fed daily in the Mess.

Royal Visits

On taking up his role as Colonel-in-Chief in 1901 King Edward VII attended a review at Woolwich, including luncheon in the Mess. The splendid piece of music 'Hail the King' composed by Zavertal, as Director of Music of the Royal Artillery Band, was first played publicly on this occasion. The same visit saw the start of the tradition of recording such events with a signed copy of the menu card.

King George V lunched in the Mess following visits to the Regiment in 1913 and 1928 and, possibly as a result of an inspection of the Mess silver collection on the first occasion, he presented a magnificent silver gilt cup.

In 1950 King George VI became the first monarch actually to dine in the Mess at what became known as 'The King's Dinner' and during which the decision to change his title to Captain General was discussed.

Queen Elizabeth II visited the Mess on five occasions: lunches following reviews in 1958, 1969, and 1993, the latter on the bicentenary of the Royal Horse Artillery; and dinners to celebrate her Silver Jubilee in 1976 and her Golden Jubilee and the 50th anniversary of her father's Dinner in 2000. This latter occasion was similarly named 'The Queen's Dinner' – a wonderfully relaxed occasion during which Her Majesty paid tribute to Field Marshal The Lord Vincent on his retirement as Master Gunner. Lieutenant Colonel Harry Langstaff attended the Queen's Dinner as one of only two survivors from those who had been at the King's Dinner.

The use of the Mess as a venue for dinners to entertain State visitors continued, but on an infrequent basis. Prince Fushimi of Japan, a general and uncle of the reigning emperor, visited in 1907 and the Emperor Haile Selassie of Ethiopia in 1936; the final occasions were visits by the President of Ghana, in 2000, and the President of Slovenia, in 2001, both of whom dined as guests of the Mayor of Greenwich, continuing the theme of the use of the Royal Artillery Mess as a venue of choice for such occasions.

The Drawdown of Woolwich

During the 1950s, the debate continued as to the future home of the Regiment, with a poll of all officers resulting in an equal split between Woolwich and Larkhill. The situation was resolved this time by a War Office decision to rebuild the barracks for the Royal Artillery Depot and Training Regiment. Throughout the 1960s, the extensive Georgian barracks that had stretched from the Thames up to Shooters Hill were almost entirely demolished. In their place came the new internal structure of the Royal Artillery Barracks and the various high and low rise blocks of flats which now surround it. Apart from one or two buildings, the Front Parade, including the Royal Artillery Mess, was the only survivor of the original barracks. The dispersal of the armaments industry also continued with the Royal Ordnance Factory in the Royal Arsenal finally closing in 1967 after almost 300 years of activity.

Changes to the Mess

Significant changes to the structure of the Mess occurred on three occasions.

In 1921 the portico in front of the dining room was extended by several feet to allow for what became the Palm Court, at the cost of the symmetry of the Front Parade (a listed building from 1964). At the same time the library over the east anterooms was handed over to the Royal Artillery Institution and the space turned into the idiosyncratically named 'Cubicles' – marginally superior bedrooms for senior officers.

Second, in 1927, central heating was installed and the Music Room was linked by a bridge to the Ballroom, built above the Soldiers' Club in one of very few remaining original buildings (see article on the RA Canteen, Section 4, pages 88–90). This allowed for a revival of the Royal Artillery Band concerts that had been a regular feature since the opening of the Mess until 1939. In the Messroom in 1961, a centre table was built from 'seasoned wood' from the Royal Arsenal to match the outer ones, which were reduced back to their original size plus a half inch, possibly in commemoration of the changes. Hitherto narrow trestle tables had been brought into the Messroom for large dinners, as depicted in the King's Dinner painting.

A third, significant change occurred in 1965, when for the first time the Mess was evacuated to allow it to be extensively modernized. Thanks to a very generous gesture by the Garrison Sergeant Major and his colleagues, the officers took over the newly completed Warrant Officers' and Sergeants' Headquarters' Mess, delaying their occupation for a year. The

Above: 'The King's Dinner', painted by Terence Cuneo. This was the dinner attended by King George VI in 1950, when the decision to change his title to Captain General was discussed. Note that most officers were in white tie and tails: it was soon after the austerities of the War and many officers did not possess the uniform Mess kit.

Left: The main entrance hall of the Mess, showing the entrance to the Silver Room and, at the top of the staircase, the entrance to the Music Room.

Silver Room, Ladies' Room and walled garden were created. The basement was radically changed by bringing the kitchen up to the Messroom floor while a back entrance, cloakroom, bar and billiard room were created on the lower ground floor. The East Anteroom was panelled and the main bar and Mess offices created. One of the first-floor billiard rooms was turned into a dining room with a lift (dumb waiter) to the new kitchen below and the other into a television room. This small dining room became known as the Harrison Room and accommodated a selection of the possessions of Major General E.G.W.W. Harrison CB, CBE, MC (1893–198?), including furniture, athletics medals and African hunting trophies, which he had bequeathed to the Mess.

The Cubicles were further extended and the link-way put in to connect the Tiger landing to the west accommodation. The only significant changes since that time have been the inclusion of ladies' bathrooms and, on the lower ground floor, the development of the cellar bar and function room for the officers of the collocated regiment. The television room was also moved to the attic, with the Medal Room taking its place. When the medals moved to the Firepower RA Museum, that space became the Heritage Room.

DINING IN TO THE REGIMENT

Brigadier Ken Timbers

Like all Gunner officers, the night I was 'dined in' is engraved on my memory. After all the trials and tribulations of officer training, these occasions, welcoming new officers into the Mess, set the seal on being commissioned into the Royal Regiment, and very impressive and glamorous events they are, too.

On a mild autumn evening in 1956, we 'Young Officers' were all carefully briefed on the procedures and traditions of the Mess. I remember in particular being told about the after-dinner drill for passing the snuff. Snuff-taking was still a habit for many in those early post-war years and, of course, had been even more popular in the earlier years of the Mess's history. Indeed, some of the earliest pieces of silver in the Mess had been snuff boxes in various shapes and forms. Those of us who did not take snuff were warned that, when the box was passed to us, we should simply tap the cover (helping to keep the snuff loose) and pass it on.

As the senior subaltern on my course, I made my way into the famous Messroom lit by candles and glittering with silver, and found myself sitting between the Director Royal Artillery (DRA) and the Representative Colonel Commandant on the top table. Dressed in my new dark blue Number One dress uniform sporting a single pip on each shoulder and feeling highly privileged, I sat chatting politely between the two most senior officers at the table, listening to the RA Band and thoroughly enjoying a wonderful evening. However, the gin and tonics in the anteroom, followed by sherry with the soup course, white wine with the fish, red wine with the roast beef and followed by port and brandy were having a strange effect on my vision and I found that I could see at least five of everything in the room.

I had managed to stand up straight for the Loyal Toast, but I was not at all sure that I wanted to experiment with snuff, and tapped the box when the DRA offered it to me. 'Don't you take snuff, my boy?' he asked, kindly.

'No, sir', I replied.

'Then it's about time you did! Follow me!' He took a liberal pinch of snuff, placed it on the hollow formed by his thumb and forefinger, and sniffed lustily. Unable to dodge the issue, I followed suit. It was magic – instant 20/20 vision!

I must admit that I did not take up the habit, despite the advice, but I recommend it to anyone whose head needs clearing after having one over the eight –and, unlike some other substances people sniff – it's still legal!

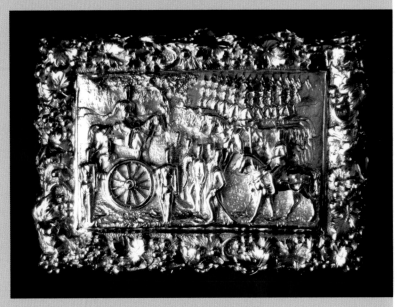

The lid of the splendid silver snuff box presented by the officers of the 9th Lancers, stationed at Shrapnel Barracks but invited to use the Mess as Honorary Members during their time in Woolwich.

The year 1968 saw the arrival of 17th Training Regiment and Depot Royal Artillery. This combined unit shared the Mess with the staff of Headquarters Director Royal Artillery until 1984, Regimental Headquarters Royal Artillery until 2005 and Central Volunteer Headquarters Royal Artillery. In 1995 16th Regiment Royal Artillery replaced 17th Regiment on the reorganization of Army recruit training and in 1999 the Commanding Officer of Central Volunteer Headquarters Royal Artillery took over as Station Commander from the Regimental Colonel and President of the Mess Committee from the Commanding Officer of 16th Regiment, on the reduction in status of Woolwich from a Garrison.

Mess Staff

There is no doubt that the senior Mess staff have been a particular feature of the Mess, from its earliest times until the departure of Mr Russell in 1988 after 43 years of service. An earlier Hall Porter, Mr Lund, provided the collection of royal pens used to sign the menu cards since the visit by King Edward VII, and Lieutenant Colonel Freddie Windrum distinguished himself by serving the Regiment for the longest period by any member since Lieutenant General Borgard, the first Colonel of the Regiment. When Colonel Windrum died at the age of 89 in 1952 he was still serving as Mess Secretary, an appointment he had held for 37 years. The history of the Mess has many such stories of service to the Regiment.

Mess Pictures

Of the 135 pictures belonging to the Mess, the oldest painting is a portrait of Albert Borgard (copied from the original in 1785 and still in the family's hands), and the newest are the 'Queen's Dinner' and General Sir Alex Harley, the Master Gunner, completing the set of Master Gunners since the Second World War, which were hung in the East Anteroom.

The portrait of Queen Victoria was the Mess's first royal portrait, hung in the Messroom in 1861. This was joined by

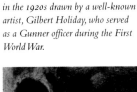

A pastel drawing of a dinner night in the 1920s drawn by a well-known artist, Gilbert Holiday, who served as a Gunner officer during the First World War.

Edward VII in 1905, a portrait purchased by Mess subscription and originally larger than that of Victoria. From this period, Queen Victoria and Prince Albert hung at the north end of the Messroom. The portraits of George III, George IV (as Prince of Wales) and William IV were copied from originals in Windsor Castle in 1933, with that of George V commissioned by the Mess in the same year. The picture of George VI was commissioned by the Mess in 1951. A legacy from Lieutenant Colonel Windrum in 1952 paid for the portrait of Queen Elizabeth, with the Mess paying for a matching portrait of Prince Philip and a portrait of Colonel Windrum, latterly hung in the Heritage Room.

To accommodate these final portraits, that of Edward VII was reduced in size by folding to enable it to fit above a door. Prince Albert now faced Queen Victoria across the Messroom and Queen Elizabeth and Prince Philip took their places on the northern wall. It would be remiss not to draw attention to the lovely portrait of Queen Elizabeth by David Poole, hung in the

East Anteroom since its commissioning by the Mess in 1975, and depicting the Monarch in a Royal Artillery cloak without tiara or Garter sash as if dining informally with the officers of her Regiment.

Above: HM The Queen attending a dinner in her honour to celebrate her Golden Jubilee.

Left: HM The Queen saying her farewells after the dinner. Here she is taking leave of Field Marshal Lord Vincent, Master Gunner St James's Park, to whom she paid a moving tribute in her speech at the dinner.

Above: The Coptic Cross taken from Magdala as part of the reparations following the Abyssinian campaign in 1868, and presented by Sir Robert Napier to the artillerymen who took part.

Above right: The magnificent silver gilt cup presented by King George V in 1913.

Far right: a superb replica of a Carolean tankard originally made for the Sadlers Company and presented to the Regiment.

Mess Silver

The Silver Collection contained more than 250 separate pieces, falling into several categories: that purchased by the Mess or its members consisted mainly of cutlery and plate; that recognizing the service of individual officers of the Regiment included the Huthwaite and Schuler Columns, the Willoughby Memorial and the Hew Ross Centrepiece; and presentations by visiting dignitaries and units. These included the William IV Candelabrum and the George V Gold Cup; and from visiting units the best known are probably the 17th Lancers' 'Peace' Centrepiece (1868) and the Royal Scots Greys' Vase (1876), presented following short tours of duty at Woolwich by these cavalry regiments, when they were invited to become honorary members of the Mess – the lack of suitable mess accommodation in Shrapnel Barracks was a feature of the hutted camp.

Right: The Willoughby Memorial, commemorating the bravery of Lieut G.D. Willoughby during the Indian Mutiny in blowing up the magazine at Delhi. His fellow officers survived and were awarded the Victoria Cross, but he was killed and VCs were not awarded posthumously in those days.

It should be noted, however, that only Royal Artillery officers were usually accorded the status of full mess membership. The final category is silver acquired through operational service – the trophies of war or in lieu of reparation, such as the Gold Ram's Head (1873) and the Abyssinian Cross (acquired in 1868 but from the 4th or 5th century AD), which, due to its religious significance, was never placed on a dining table. The Cross was finally presented to the Regiment by Emperor Haile Selassie in 1936 after he had reclaimed it during a visit.

Interesting Property

Lastly, among the interesting items displayed in the Mess were the drum banners (RA Historical Trust property), received from the Royal Arsenal in 1924, previously kept in a glass case in the hall of the Ordnance Office and probably dating from the time of George I or even earlier; and the bronze statuette of St Barbara taken from Hitler's residence in Munich. There was also the Empress Eugénie Shield presented to the Mess in honour of her son the Prince Imperial, Louis Napoleon, who was an honorary member of the Mess during his time at The Shop and who was killed in Zululand in 1879; and Bombardier 'Billy' Wells's Lonsdale Belt for boxing (1911–19).

Regimental Affairs

The start of the 20th century had seen officers wearing their first low waistcoat and dress shirt style of Mess Dress, introduced in 1902 and worn throughout the Regiment from 1906, similar to the current Warrant Officers' and Sergeants' Mess Dress. This was replaced in 1913 by the current Mess Dress, worn at first with a white waistcoat and, from 1920, as we know it now. As an austerity measure, Mess Dress was not worn for several years after the Second World War, illustrated by the King's Dinner being in Evening Dress. During the early part of this period the waiters continued to wear their Georgian coats, breeches and wigs, latterly only worn on the occasion of the principal dinners.

The Music Room of the RA Mess, showing five of the nine splendid portraits that hung on three sides of the room, often used for receptions and important committees.

The pattern of dinners in the Mess over the last 50 years has remained fairly constant although titles have altered. The annual programme has included the Spring and Autumn (Alamein from 1992) Dinners instigated in 1952 and, since the late 1950s, the dining-in of Young Officers, ladies' guest nights, Colonels-Commandant dinners and reunion dinners, the latter usually restricted to Friday evenings. Regimental dinners and monthly guest nights gave way to 'Hail and Farewell' dinners in the 1970s.

While the pattern of dinners may have remained similar, the atmosphere in the Mess changed. Before the 1970s, the Mess retained its club-like atmosphere and ladies were restricted to the West Anteroom, except on special occasions. Hiring the Mess out for weddings, other private functions and conferences has been a relatively recent innovation requiring careful balancing between fund raising, the maintenance of standards and respect for those living in the Mess. The West Anteroom, with its attached small dining room, and the downstairs (cellar) bar and function room have provided facilities for resident Mess members when the public rooms were being used for functions. Interestingly, statistics for 1979 and 2005 indicate the same level of special lunches (91), an increase in dinners (46 to 61) and a similar number of special events (14–18).

During the summer of 2002 and as a part of our Captain General's Golden Jubilee celebrations the Mess was opened to the public on six days, probably for the first time. A total of 3,000 visitors took the hour's guided tour. On 20 March 2003 the Spring Dinner celebrated the 200th anniversary of the Mess.

The Royal Artillery's move from Woolwich in 2007 saw the end of the Mess as the Royal Artillery Headquarters Mess, a distinction passed to the Royal Artillery Mess at Larkhill along with much of the movable fabric of the Mess including chandeliers, pictures, silver, dining tables and chairs. However,

the Mess remains under Gunner control in the person of the Commanding Officer of the Central Volunteer Headquarters Royal Artillery, until the arrival of a full infantry battalion planned for 2009.

The last 20 years have seen major improvements at Larkhill as what has became known as the Artillery Centre has striven to achieve its claim as a centre of excellence in all areas, including the Officers' Mess. For many officers, however, the RA Mess at Woolwich will conjure up memories of one of the most elegant messes and the preferred venue for Regimental occasions such as reunions and celebratory dinners. Over its 204-year history it adapted to military, political and social changes while remaining a place of civilized standards of behaviour, dress and traditions – perhaps a touch too formal for everyday use, but always a cause for Regimental pride. As a setting for dining-in officers on commissioning or dining-out those retiring, it will remain a treasured memory for many Gunner officers.

SECTION 7
The Gunner Family

GUNNER WELFARE CHARITIES

Lieutenant Colonel I. A. Vere Nicoll MBE

Largely unknown, the Gunner welfare charities have been helping those in need for over 165 years. A jewel in the crown of the regimental family they have been doing work, often unsung, in helping a large number of Gunners, whether serving or retired, and their dependants over nearly three centuries. The earliest Gunner welfare charity for non-commissioned officers (NCOs) and men was a Friendly Society formed in 1839 in Woolwich. It was formed by a group of Gunner officers concerned at the plight of soldiers' wives left behind when their husbands went on foreign service. Its objects were 'to provide relief and employment for the wives and children of NCOs and privates of the RA embarked on foreign service'. Officers contributed a proportion of a day's pay.

The oldest Gunner charity is the *Royal Artillery Charities*, which was started in 1840 by subscriptions from officers for the welfare of soldiers and their families. Officers could not benefit but they recognized the plight of those below the rank of commissioned officer. In later years it also helped Gunner orphans at school. In 1904 four houses were built and presented to the *RA Charities* by the next of kin of officers killed in the South African War: these were for the benefit of other ranks who were unable to work. Two are in Colchester and two are in Bath, and they are in full use today by retired Gunners.

However, the *RA Charities* is not the oldest of the Gunner funds set up to help in times of crisis. The oldest recorded is the *Royal Artillery Marriage Society*, which was established in 1752. In practice, this was and still is an insurance society: officers subscribe an annual sum that accords his widow an annuity depending on the size of his contributions. Its terms were considerably better than commercially available at the time and did not incur the expenses of an agent. It later became the *Society for the Benefit of the Widows of the Officers and Warrant Officers of the Royal Regiment of Artillery*, but it closed for new business in 1993, as there had been no new business written since the First Gulf War and the cost of promoting the Society was thought to outweigh the possible benefits. In 2007 the Society still looks after 65 annuitants and has 43 members paying subscriptions.

After the First World War, funds were sought from donations to raise a memorial to all those killed in the war, to help Gunners in need and to establish a headquarters in London for all the Gunner Charities. This fund was called the *Royal Artillery War Commemoration Fund* (RAWC). Donations raised £185,000 and, at a cost of £27,000, provided the monument at Hyde Park Corner. The remaining funds were invested to help those in need. The aim of housing the charities together was not achieved until the mid-1990s.

Part of the RAWC Fund was the *Ladies Work Guild*, working through over 60 branches across the country. This aimed to collect new and second-hand garments and money to buy footwear and garments for retired Gunners in need. It also contained an education scheme to help those children born before 31 December 1919 to fathers killed or unable to work due to war injuries: this scheme was wound up in 1935, having allocated about £65,000 in the 16 years since the war ended.

The *Kelly Holdsworth Artillery Trust* (KAHT) was formed in 1914 from a bequest by Colonel Kelly Holdsworth. This provides assistance through grants and annuities to Gunner officers, their wives or widows, unmarried daughters and children under 21 who are in need. It also helps with educational costs for the children of Gunner officers or widows in need.

In 1920 the Royal Artillery Employment Bureau was started to assist retiring Gunners to find employment. All ranks were eligible for registration but it mainly concentrated on the London area, whereas outside of London local Royal Artillery Association (RAA) branches or 'Gunner Friends' tried to help. In the first nine months of 1946 it interviewed 5,152 officers and soldiers for jobs and secured permanent employment for 1,423. The RA uniformed servicemen supplied by the bureau copied the cap-badged Corps of Commissionaires who have acted in a security role since 1859. Its aims are now part of the Royal Artillery Charitable Fund's objects.

In 1927 the *Royal Artillery Benevolent Fund* (RABF) was established and the *Royal Artillery War Commemoration Fund* was subsumed into it. The RABF had two objects; first, to increase the income to the *RA Charities* and, second, to make grants on behalf of the Regiment to outside benevolent societies and institutions which helped Gunners, thus relieving units of the necessity of meeting charitable appeals. It only dealt with and received subscriptions from the serving regiment, but this was the first time serving soldiers could subscribe regularly to their charities. The officers who subscribed to the *RA Charities* were

Previous page: In-pensioner, Jim Townsend, who was born on 20 Feb 1915, pictured at the Royal visit to Larkhill.

asked to switch their subscriptions to the new RABF. However, in 1943 the RAA agreed to abolish the RABF and liquidate the funds and the RA Association Trust in order to start the *RA Association Benevolent Fund*. This recognized the nature of the RAA and its key role in welfare to those Gunners in need.

In 1951 a new fund, the *Royal Artillery Charitable Fund* (RACF), was formed. The driving force for this was connected to relief from tax. This meant that the RAA, hitherto the driving force behind Gunner welfare and benevolence, no longer had specific benevolence funds to distribute. All the Gunner welfare charities, less the KHAT, came under the RACF and funds in total amounted to about £500,000. The welfare funds moved from Artillery House in Earls Court to 58 The Common, Woolwich in the 1960s. The RACF was formed as a company limited by guarantee without a share capital with some members from whom the trustees are elected. In 1955 the

A recent group photograph taken during a visit to the Royal Hospital to visit Gunner In-Pensioners Alan Rice, Bill Kent and Joseph Allen. The visitors include the Director Royal Artillery, Brigadier Colin Tadier and the Controller of the RAI, Major General Michael Shellard. The others present are the Lieutenant Governor, Major General Peter Currie and the Adjutant, Brigadier David Radcliffe.

RACF appointed the first professional investment managers to manage the funds, in place of the committee of senior officers who previously had done it themselves. They had invested mostly in gilt-edged stocks, but now began to look towards growth of the funds by investing in equities.

Towards the end of the Second World War a regimental consensus was sought on how best to commemorate those who had died during the war. It was decided to raise money from those serving and to add three bronze panels to the Hyde Park Memorial, using the remainder to buy or build houses for those in need. In all, 164 houses were built and five in Scotland acquired, but in 1949 an agreement was reached with the Earl Haig Fund that the stock of housing would be run for their use with the proviso that Gunners should have first call on the RA houses. The 'Gunner' Haig houses around the country are often recognizable by the Gunner badge on the front of the house.

The *Royal Artillery Charitable Fund* is recognized as our main Gunner welfare charity, but in reality, though the biggest, it is one of two welfare charities dealing with all ranks. The other is the old *RA Charities* and each contains many smaller trusts and funds, all there for specific purpose to help various Gunners and their dependants in need.

Other funds exist for specific purposes, such as the *RA Prisoners of War Charity*, which started in the First World War and was added to in the Second World War, designed to help the families of those captured. The *RA Memorial Society* is there to help fund new memorials and maintain those requiring maintenance. It first appeared in 1909 and became a Trust in 1932. Interestingly it does not seem to have been a driving force for the building of the RA Memorial at Hyde Park or its extension in 1945 and, though still a separate Trust, it is now run by the RACF.

Since the 1950s the RACF has been the major benevolence charity for the Gunners, providing over £1m a year. Its income is from investments together with subscriptions from serving and retired members of the Regiment. Cases now come mainly from the Soldiers, Sailors and Air Force Association (SSAFA), the Royal British Legion, the Officers Association and the Royal Commonwealth Ex-Services League. All these have trained staff who can assess needs and requirements and can arrange for our benevolence to be spent appropriately. RAA members can and do still identify those in need, but the RACF then tasks one of the agencies to interview the potential beneficiary and assess the need.

What of the future? Although the number of cases has reduced in the last 55 years, the amount required to assist those in need has risen. For instance, in the 17 years from the end of the Second World War to 1962, the RACF disbursed a total of £1.2m on individual cases. In comparison, the RACF and RA Charities spent nearly £1.1m in 2006 alone. The requirement for funds – whether in donations or legacies –remains vital.

In summary, the RACF is a key part of our Gunner family. It helps all those in need and it helps the serving regiments and soldiers. In the requirement to continue to support and reinforce the notion of a Gunner family, the Gunner welfare charities do not just support Gunners from enlistment to death; they help from enlistment to after death because the RACF will help those dependants left behind. That is why the Gunners are called a regimental family!

THE GUNNER MAGAZINE

Major John Timbers with the help of Major John Braisby

The Gunner Magazine has a long and distinguished history and for at least a decade has been one of only two regimental magazines that appear monthly – the other being that of the Royal Electrical and Mechanical Engineers, whose origins owe much to the old Artificers Royal Artillery – so it is in good company.

The Gunner was started in the aftermath of the First World War, with the stated intention of maintaining the camaraderie that had grown up in the trenches between officers and men of the Regiment to a degree that had never before been known. Prior to that early nod in the direction of interpersonal relationships there had never been much effort to keep soldiers in touch with what was going on outside their own particular brigade (regiment) or even battery. Officers had had the professional *Journal of the Royal Artillery* since the mid-1800s, intended to keep them in touch with the technicalities of gunnery and military tactics as they developed, but little thought had been given to any form of morale-boosting publication for other ranks.

The first issues of *The Gunner* came out in early 1919, but it did not flourish and all went quiet for a while. There was an attempt to resurrect the near-stillborn magazine in 1920, but that had no more success. In 1921 a third attempt was made when the Royal Artillery Association was founded, adopting the magazine as its mouthpiece or 'organ', as it was known until quite recently. In those early days no editor was named.

The first named editor was Captain J. F. Martin, a wartime-commissioned officer. He ran the magazine from home, promising not to take any salary unless or until it became a viable proposition (which eventually it did). He did this for some 13 years with the help of his immediate family, organizing distribution by a runner system set up with the Gordon Boys School. Sadly, Captain Martin died of a heart attack in 1934, and his daughter kept things going for a while until the publishers, Messrs Barrell of Portsmouth, undertook to continue the project in her place. There was a glowing tribute to Captain Martin and his work on the magazine at the time of his death, but, sadly, there was no follow-up on the dedication of his daughter, and we hear no more of her.

There have been several distinguished editors, but few served for more than the average army officer's tour of duty lasting two or three years. The first to equal or surpass Captain

Martin's endurance record was Lieutenant Colonel A. H. Burne RA who had two DSOs from the First World War, and who was able to reminisce about his experiences with the British Expeditionary Force as he watched the new generation of Gunners depart for France in 1939/40. Alfred Burne was a historian to boot, and wrote some fascinating articles and books on famous Gunner battles, illustrating them with his own sketch maps derived from personal research, conducted both in libraries and on the ground.

One article that brought in a fair amount of correspondence at the time was begun in response to articles in the press of the day pooh-poohing the Gunner tradition that the first use of cannon on the battlefield had been at the Battle of Crécy in 1346. Burne proved beyond much doubt that the Crécy bombards (as those 'cannon' are known) had indeed existed, and produced photographs of himself alongside the farmers holding both stone and iron 'cannonballs', which they claimed to have found while tilling the fields at the battlefield site. He backed up the finds with his own reckoning of the range of the bombards and their likely position on the field in relation to the place where the balls were found.

At some time during the post-war years the post of editor became once more a job for a serving staff officer, a member of Headquarters Director Royal Artillery who was responsible for looking after the domestic affairs of the Royal Regiment. Then the appointment of editor went to another famous member of the Regiment, Brigadier Frank Siggers CBE, MC. In 1970 he handed over the post to Lieutenant Colonel (later Brigadier) Paddy Ryan,

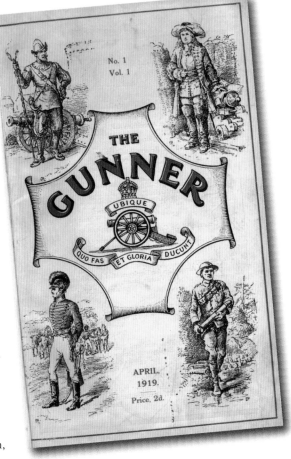

The first edition of The Gunner, *issued in April 1919. Opposite are covers from 1944 and 1970, showing the magazine's evolution in style and ending with one of the ultra-modern and highly attractive covers from the 21st Century.*

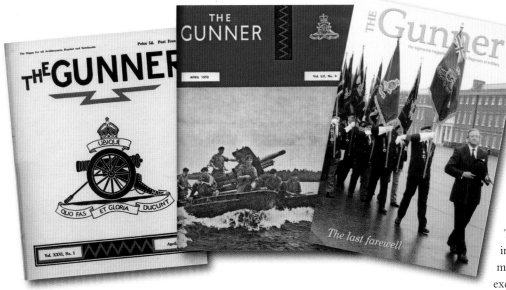

who was tasked to produce a magazine for the whole Regiment. The magazine now took on a completely new format. Away went the buff covers with the red and blue zigzag Gunner border and badge motif to be replaced by colourful glossy pictures and a new (and, for some, shocking) title – *The Gunner* became *Gunner*. This was not the arbitrary decision of the editor alone. A Board of Management, made up from Gunners then working in the publishing world, was now superimposed on the RA Publications organization to act as helpful advisers. The board continued to function as such through the 1970s and 1980s.

Change was brought on by a variety of both commercial and pragmatic necessities. However, the driving force was that the Regiment had no desire to be left behind by the move into glorious technicolour of the magazine world at large, and other regimental magazines in particular. The change of format heralded a significant increase in the profile of the magazine, which, if the truth be told, had not been very widely available to the Regiment at large.

The magazine now came under the control of HQ Training Brigade RA at Woolwich and, in due course, Regimental HQ RA. The RA Printing Press, then established in premises on the Plumstead Trading Estate as a commercial enterprise, took over the printing of the magazine. The print run increased from some 2,000 to 8,300 copies. From then on every officer of the Regiment received a copy of the magazine, paid for out of his subscription to the Royal Artillery Institution. Every Regular Gunner Regiment received 40 copies of the magazine for distribution to its respective batteries. The magazine also included the data from a publication that, up until that time, had been called the *RA Regimental News*. This had covered mainly sports results, notices and officer promotions.

The RA Printing Press did not survive the financial pressures of the 1970s and in 1976 the Press was sold to Instance Printers. The latter published *Gunner* during 1977, but the following year the printing contract was moved to Buxton Press, located in Buxton, Derbyshire. The colour on the covers did not (except on very special occasions) extend into the body of the magazine, but the glossy format did and the quality and quantity of photographs made for a much more interesting and entertaining publication. The focus changed somewhat, too, and became far less formal and stilted.

Other editors included Majors Murray Franklin, John Braisby and Malcolm Lochhead. Major John Braisby returned to the chair after these changes had been implemented, first as a serving officer and then as a retired officer. He carried the magazine forward, developing its content from a somewhat stuffy formality towards the much more relaxed style of modern media. John's experience in Public Relations staff jobs was a critical factor in its success. He was something of a stickler for standards in terms of grammar, spelling and content – many will say 'good for him'!

When John Braisby retired in 1995, Major John Timbers, who had retired in 1978 to take up a second career in the defence industry, took up the challenge of taking the magazine into the computer era. This was done with the excellent support of the magazine's (by now) long-term printers, Messrs Buxton Press, who lent him a superannuated Macintosh computer and a copy of the industry standard publishing software, Quark Express. With their active help and encouragement the magazine changed format again, adopting mainly superficial changes to begin with, but as time went on moving towards a more all-ranks oriented style.

With the passage of time, more was to change than mere typeface and layouts. At the turn of the millennium, *Gunner* became *The Gunner* once more, and the magazine grew slightly from a long-forgotten quarto measurement to the modern A4 printing paper standard, saving money and giving marginally more space for news and pictures. The editor's personal style began to develop, too. His beloved Boxer dog began to appear regularly, to the annoyance of some and delight of many who looked for him first before even turning to the obituaries to find out if they were still alive. It was a way of getting across the odd caustic comment without too much of a barb. That could not be said for one or two of his editorials, which raised eyebrows from time to time, and not a few hackles.

After eight and a half years, John Timbers retired, handing over to a female retired officer, Captain Jess Bate – and what a good move that was! Jess, using her feminine powers of persuasion and interpersonal skills, was able to talk Buxton Press into a new contract for an all-colour glossy magazine. A new, much more soldier-friendly style was launched as Jess put her journalism degree and her Display Troop recruiting experience into practice. Sadly for *The Gunner*, but happily for her, along came Bate junior rather earlier than expected, putting paid to Jess's short reign, but bringing in another feminine influence in the person of Catherine Redpath, now Brumwell. Catherine's timely arrival as the fiancée of an Regimental HQ RA staff officer and ex-reporter for the British Forces newspaper in Cyprus was just one of those serendipitous coincidences that so enrich life.

And so we come up to date. With the move of Regimental Headquarters to Larkhill, Major Mike Shaw took over the reins and continues the action with his talented assistant, Kate Knowles, and the continuing cooperation with Buxton Press. The extant Editors all wish him luck and an enjoyable tenure of office. It is a super job and one that we all left behind with some reluctance. May *The Gunner* continue to flourish as the biggest and best Regimental Magazine in the British Army bar none!

THE ROYAL ARTILLERY ASSOCIATION

Lieutenant Colonel I.A. Vere Nicoll MBE

Following the First World War, the Regiment was well aware of the impact of their shared experiences on the huge number of Gunners who had served together through those terrible years. It had amassed from donations a considerable sum, known as the RA War Commemoration Fund and, in 1920, used part of this to create the Royal Artillery Association. Its aim was to form branches in every part of the United Kingdom, Empire and Commonwealth, fostering a bond of comradeship irrespective of rank between all who had served or were serving as artillerymen, helping those in need or distress and maintaining contact with old comrades.

The RAA was organized into regions, each with its own districts based on county boundaries; each district contained several branches. A small staff at Artillery House administered the Association on a day to day basis, helping branches as required and organizing national events for the members.

For many years, this staff was based in Artillery House in Earls Court, west London, but eventually it moved to Woolwich – Connaught Barracks, the old Academy and the Front Parade – before moving to Larkhill in late 2005 to collocate with the Director Royal Artillery's staff. Branches meet wherever they can find suitable rooms; some in public houses, some in Royal British Legion or other military clubs and some in village and church halls. Comradeship is fostered through regular meetings, normally once a month, when members get together to plan activities and have a quiet drink or two to discuss life and to watch over fellow members and their dependants who are in need.

The standards of the Royal Artillery Association outside the Garrison Church at Larkhill.

Above: The RAA standards lowered in salute.

Below right: RAA members at the Annual General Meeting at Blackpool.

Many branches started their own Gunner Clubs for socializing, and local members and the RAA helped purchase them. There are four left, of which one is still owned by the RAA. Branches vary in size and composition, but sadly membership is on the decline as later generations seem less eager to seek comradeship with old friends. In 1946, there were 378 local branches; in 2007, they numbered 135 branches and ladies' sections. Initially, ladies formed their own sections, but increasingly branches encouraged ladies to join them where ladies' sections did not exist or had had to close due to the shortage of numbers.

In order to encourage links between serving soldiers and retired Gunners, each branch is affiliated to a regular or Territorial Army battery which is either local or recruits in its area. Recently all batteries became branches in their own right as all soldiers who contribute to the 'One Day's Pay' scheme are automatically members.

Through its quarterly newsletters and its website, Artillery House promotes various central activities of the RAA. These include the Annual General Meeting – normally held at Blackpool where there is a weekend of parties and fun combined with the business meeting – and the annual Remembrance Services at the Hyde Park Memorial, London, and at the National Memorial Arboretum near Lichfield in Staffordshire. A St Barbara's Day Service is held each year at Larkhill to celebrate our Patron Saint on the Sunday nearest to her feast day of 4 December.

In April 1919 *The Gunner* magazine was started by General Sir William Furze to help inaugurate the RAA. *The Gunner* was and is the official organ of the RAA and publicizes branch

activities and future events. The RAA's income is derived from investments, annual and life membership fees, and from a proportion of the day's pay scheme paid by serving officers and soldiers; it also carries out fund-raising activities.

Branches play a key role in welfare and most branches still have welfare officers. It was always the branches who sought out those in need and informed the Gunner Welfare Charities which provided the benevolence, but the net is now spread much wider to ensure need is recognized in all our communities. The RAA is at the heart of the retired regiment and very supportive of the serving Regiment.

Nothing is more apt than music to raise man to great deeds and chiefly inspire him with the degree of courage necessary to brave the dangers of war. Plutarch.

Royal Artillery Record Office

Major Denis Rollo

The Regiment had always kept records of personnel if for no other than that it was necessary to prove to the Board of Ordnance that disbursements to officers and soldiers were properly accounted for: these records consisted of muster rolls and pay lists for all RA companies and other detachments. At the beginning of each month the company paraded for a check by a neutral person: in the United Kingdom it was often a magistrate, and this person attested the accounts and the muster rolls. Up to 1862 the office was known as the Record Branch of the Deputy Adjutant General's Department, Horse Guards, London, but was accommodated in the east rear range of the RA Barracks at Woolwich. The Officer-in-Charge was Captain R. Oldfield until 1871 when Captain, later Brevet Lieutenant Colonel, Francis Duncan CB, was appointed Superintendent.

In 1872 the Office moved out of the barracks to the Clock Tower, just inside the gate of the Woolwich Naval Dockyard at the bottom of Francis Street. The building still exists. During his time at the Records Office Duncan wrote the two-volume history of the Artillery service from the earliest times until 1815. His work included tables of service for each Company of the Regiment, but sadly this was marred by the fact that Duncan allotted numbers to all the companies. The muster rolls and pay lists, which were in the Records Office when Duncan was in charge, would have clearly shown that the companies did not have numbers and were known by the names of their Captains, for example Captain D. Scott's Company 1st Battalion. At some time, that date is not known, the muster rolls and pay lists were handed over to the Public Record Office and now reside in the National Archives at Kew.

In 1905 it became the Royal Horse and Royal Field Artillery Records, a Royal Garrison Artillery Records having been formed at Dover. In September 1938 the Office moved to a new building at Foots Cray, near Sidcup (Kent), south-east of Woolwich probably because the Clock Tower was not large enough. In the Second World War the strength of the Royal Artillery rose to nearly 800,000 men and women – at one stage it was bigger than the Royal Navy – and there were separate records offices for the Field Branch, which remained at Foots Cray, Anti-Aircraft records at Rugby (Warwickshire) and London, while Coast Artillery and Searchlights records were at Bournemouth (Hampshire). After the war these offices were all merged into one, at Foots Cray. The Record Office remained there until late in 1979 when it moved to York. All the record offices are now merged into the Army Record Office at Glasgow.

The Clock Tower building in the Royal Dockyard, Woolwich.

SECTION 8

The Later Years

Woolwich Post Second World War

Major Denis Rollo

After the 1939–45 war, the maintenance of the Gunner presence at Woolwich was not supported by the whole of the Regiment. There were those who preferred that it should move to Larkhill, Wiltshire, the home of the School of Artillery since 1920 and in the centre of a great training area with facilities for live practice. Many of the officers lived in the area and many who had retired had chosen to settle in Hampshire, Wiltshire and Dorset. There were undoubtedly heated arguments – for many the thought of giving up the magnificent RA Mess was just not acceptable – but there was no clear majority for the one course or the other. Eventually, after the Regiment failed to reach a decision, Headquarters Eastern Command, which had the responsibility for the Barracks, announced that the Headquarters would remain in Woolwich.

With a large Army due to worldwide commitments, the Woolwich Depot was a busy transit camp. The main barracks housed the Anti-Aircraft and Coast Artillery Branch in the East Square and the Field Artillery Branch in the West Square. The soldiers' accommodation in the two squares consisted of old stables at ground level (there were no horses, following mechanization in the late 1930s), with double-tier bunks, and sergeants and above on the upper floor in large barrack rooms with only a small coal fire-grate for heat. The coal was delivered by an immaculate horse-drawn General Service wagon and a

following of fatigue men to carry the coal bins. The coal ration never lasted for the period intended and many raids were made on disused buildings within the barracks to find wood.

There were hundreds of transitees and the great problem of the staff was to keep them all occupied. The Depot seemed to be responsible for guarding almost everything in Woolwich and guard mounting on the Front Parade was a large affair. On the conclusion of the parade the various detachments departed for their guard duty. One of these was the detention ward at the Royal Herbert Hospital and the guard marched up the main road and back again in the morning. An annual function for the guard was to ring the Common for 24 hours once a year to protect the right of way. On the given day, sentries were posted at about every 100 yards to warn those wishing to pass that the Common was War Office property. (Fortunately for the author his post was right opposite the pub on the main road.)

Other uses for the transitees were to go to various service guard rooms across the UK to collect those Gunners who had

Below left: The entrance hall of the WOs' and Sergeants' Mess at the RA Barracks.

A dinner at the WOs' and Sergeants' Mess in Woolwich in 2004, the culmination of that year's Warrant Officer Class I Convention.

Below: The magnificent Georgian frontage of the East Wing of the RA Barracks – built before the West Wing – showing the entrance to the WOs' and Sergeants' Mess, its white pillars almost mirroring the Officers' Mess in the West Wing.

Below right: A recent piece commissioned for the Mess, showing the gun carriage bearing the coffin of Princess Diana at her funeral in 1997.

decided not to report for duty, but had been picked up by the civil or military police. A more interesting task was the journey by rail and ship to Rhine Army to deliver the special British Army currency then in use in Germany. Another job for non-commissioned officers was tasks connected with courts martial, which seemed to be in permanent session.

The RA Barracks then looked rather different from what they became after the rebuild. Entering the barracks through the South Arch from the Front Parade, there was the RA

Canteen on the left. The Regiment was still allowed to run this facility in place of a NAAFI and it was a going concern with much business and its own coinage.

Further down the road and on the right was the Sergeants' Mess. It was rather small for the purpose and there were queues for meals. There was a television set with a 14 inch screen (one needed to hold at least Warrant Officer Class 2 rank even to see the box) and there was the inevitable Permanent Staff versus Transit Personnel rivalry. It was often better to go out of barracks at night: if one wore uniform, entry to the Woolwich Empire cinema was half price. Entertainment on the evening before pay day was limited and was often restricted to crossing the river by the free ferry and returning by the foot tunnel, or vice versa.

The work on the construction of the new barrack accommodation behind the Front Parade began in 1964. The intention was to house 17th Training Regiment RA, The Depot and a light anti-aircraft regiment RA, although the latter plan was not carried out. In 1968, 17th Training Regiment RA moved from Oswestry, Shropshire, to Woolwich.

Royal Artillery Birthday Parade 26 May 1956

The first major parade to take place at Woolwich after the war was held to celebrate the Regiment's 240th birthday on 26 May 1956. The honour fell to the artillery of 3rd Infantry Division, consisting at that time of the following:

- 20th Field Regiment RA, 26th Field Regiment RA and 49th Field Regiment RA

- 34th Light Anti-Aircraft Regiment RA and 14th Locating Battery RA.

The guns were 25-pounders and 40mm Bofors, with the associated towing vehicles of the period, mainly Quads and Matadors. There were four Auster artillery-observation aircraft also taking part, with a low fly-past over the parade ground.

The line-up of the regiments for inspection took place on the Barrack Field and was a most impressive display. The inspecting officer was General Sir Robert Mansergh KCB,

Above: The Air OP fly-past during the parade.

KBE, MC the Commander in Chief of UK Land Forces. General Mansergh (later to become Master Gunner St James's Park) carried out the task from the back of a vehicle – given the size of the formation, it would have been both arduous and time-consuming carried out on foot!

The drive-past that followed took place on the Front Parade in front of a large crowd of spectators and was a fitting tribute to celebrate the Regiment's birthday, marking what was almost a high point in the Regiment's size, prior to the inevitable cuts that were to follow as the Army reduced in strength.

KAT

Left: A battery of 25-pounders towed by Quads drives past the saluting dais in front of the RA Mess.

Below: The entire Divisional artillery formed up on the Barrack Field for inspection.

WOOLWICH MEMORIES

Royal Artillery Barracks in 1951

Anthony J. Cooper PhD

As a National Service subaltern in 1951, I stayed in the RA Barracks at Woolwich on two occasions. I stayed there briefly in February on the way to the Far East and ten months later when I was posted there pending release.

My memory of the barracks was of looming soot-blackened buildings. They had been built, if I recall correctly, to accommodate mounted troops, so that there was as much stabling as there was barrack accommodation for the troops. Of course, by 1951 the horses were long since gone, so there must have been a lot of redundant space. Nevertheless, at that time the barracks was running with troops. I remember that there was a steady stream of Gunners crossing diagonally one of the internal courtyards so that as an officer in that area one had one's hand up at the salute nearly all of the time.

The RA Mess was almost exactly the same as it was before a start was made at dismantling it in June 2007. This is borne out by the picture of the King's Dinner in 1950. The anterooms were, however, very different. The main anteroom was about as welcoming as a departure 'lounge' in a third rate airport, being lined with leather upholstered benches. The further rooms were reserved for field officers. The room above the reception area was the television room, the TV set being between the two windows which overlook the parade. Chairs and benches had been set out like seats in a cinema for those who wanted to watch. The trouble was that every time a tram went by in Grand Depot Road the TV picture would dissolve into sparks, whereupon someone nearly always got up and fiddled with the adjustments at the back of the set, thus ensuring that very little was actually seen. Not that programmes were worth watching anyway.

The Junior Officers' accommodation was primitive, especially for those who were in transit. A batman showed me to my room up some uncarpeted stairs. The room contained several iron bedsteads and a splendid Victorian wash hand stand, complete with huge jug and slop basin. Ominously the batman told me that he would bring me my shaving water in the morning. He duly came, bearing a jug of hot water which he had brought from some distant cookhouse, there being no water laid on, except, presumably, for the latrines. The draught coming up from the cracks in the floorboards was so strong that I am sure that it would have blown out a lighted match held at shoulder height.

Caught napping! Sgt Wood of The King's Troop RHA taking a break, September 1955.

On dining-in nights many officers wore khaki service dress. Officers commissioned before the Second World War wore Patrols, the blue uniform that preceded the more formal Number 1 Dress now beginning to appear, and a few wore the new Number 1 Dress. Mess Kit was not seen.

Recollections of 20th Field Regiment RA

Colonel P. R. S. Jackson OBE

The accommodation was basic, but perhaps no worse than anywhere else at that time, and training presented problems. In a search for deployment areas other than Woolwich Common, I came across a rough area of land near Chislehurst. Having convinced the local authorities that I did not actually wish to

FREEDOM OF THE BOROUGH

As truly befits a Regiment with such strong and ancient links with its home, the Metropolitan Borough of Woolwich presented it with the Freedom of the Borough on Friday 28 May 1954.

The programme for the occasion underlines the formality of the ceremony. It began in the Council chamber at 7 pm with a special meeting of the Council 'to move the Resolution that The Royal Regiment of Artillery be admitted to the Honorary Freedom of the Borough and that a Certificate of Admission be placed in a silver casket and presented to the Master Gunner St James's Park on behalf of the Royal Regiment of Artillery'. The meeting was attended by the Master Gunner, Field Marshal The Right Honourable Viscount Alanbrooke of Brookeborough KG, GCB, GCVO, OM, DSO, accompanied by the Representative Colonel Commandant, General Sir Sidney Kirkman GCB, KCB MC, the Director Royal Artillery Major General R. W. Goodbody CB, DSO and the Commander Woolwich Garrison, Brigadier M. W. Hope DSO.

At 7.15 pm, the Worshipful the Mayor, Councillor J. W. Andrews JP, London County Council, and the Master Gunner, with their respective parties, took up their positions on the dais outside the Town Hall for the ceremony. The programme reads as follows:

- A Fanfare of Trumpets will be sounded and the Union Jack, together with the Regimental Standard and the Borough Flag, will be broken. A General Salute will then be given.

- The Mayor will address the Master Gunner and the assembled Company. He will then present the silver casket containing the scroll conferring the Freedom of the Borough on The Royal Regiment to the Master Gunner.

- A Second Fanfare will be sounded as the casket is handed over and at its conclusion the Master Gunner will hand the casket to the Commander of the Royal Artillery Depot.

- The Mayor will request the Master Gunner to sign the Freedom Roll in the name of The Royal Regiment of Artillery.

- The Master Gunner, in a speech to the assembled company, will return thanks and acknowledge the honour conferred upon the Regiment.

- The Master Gunner will invite the Mayor to inspect the Escort during which the Band will play the Regimental Slow March. While the inspection is taking place the casket will be handed over to the Officer in charge of the Escort.

- On return to the dais the Mayor will invite the Master Gunner to march representative detachments of the Regiment through the streets of the Borough with bands playing and with their guns.

- The Master Gunner will then invite the Mayor to take their salute as they pass the Town Hall. A Third Fanfare will sound and the parade will then march past the dais, the salute being taken by the Master Gunner and the Mayor. A General Salute will be given.

- At the conclusion of the parade a roll of drums will sound and the National Anthem will be played.

- The Mayor accompanied by the Master Gunner and their respective parties will then leave the dais.

The march past featured an impressive number of detachments and followed a route that went from Wellington Street via General Gordon Square, Vincent Road, Burrage Road, Herbert Road, the Prince Imperial Monument on Woolwich Common to the Front Parade, taking an hour to complete the march.

The units taking part were:

RA Mounted Band

The King's Troop RHA6 x 13-pounder guns and detachments
Field Wing, Depot RA4 x 25-pounder guns and detachments
39th Heavy Regiment RA1 x 7.2in gun and detachment
75th Heavy Anti-Aircraft Regiment RA2 x 3.7in guns and detachments

Section of the RA Band

Regimental RA Units3 Officers and 50 Other Ranks
Honourable Artillery Company3 Officers and 20 Other Ranks
292nd Airborne Field Regiment RA (TA)2 x 75mm guns and detachments
2 x 25-pounder guns and detachments
353rd Medium Regiment RA (TA)2 x 5.5in guns and detachments
567th Light Anti-Aircraft/Searchlight
Regiment RA (TA)1 x 40mm Bofors gun, driver and passenger
569th Light Anti-Aircraft/Searchlight
Regiment RA (TA)1 x 40mm Bofors gun, driver and passenger
570th Light Anti-Aircraft/Searchlight
Regiment RA (TA)1 x 40mm Bofors gun, driver and passenger
265th Heavy Anti-Aircraft Regiment
RA (TA)2 x 3.7in Mark III guns, driver and passenger

Band of the Boys' Regiment RA

Detachment of the Boys' Regiment RA
Uniformed Staff of the RA Association
Standards of the RA Association

fire my guns from the common but only to deploy them, I was informed that they spent huge sums of money each year making it look rough, but they did not want to make it look rougher through vehicles driving over it! We eventually found an area on the banks of the Thames near Plumstead sewage works which, provided the wind was blowing in the right direction, was delightful.

Unless great care was taken our radio aerials tended to short circuit the overhead power cables driving the Woolwich trams, bringing the system to a grinding halt. Vehicles breaking down in the Blackwall Tunnel were not conducive to good public relations! There was the battery learner motorcyclist who became separated from the column on the way to Larkhill and did 300 miles getting out of London. By that time he had become an expert motorcyclist! And then there was the Troop Leader who turned right on Shooters Hill rather than left, becoming mildly surprised when the houses became closer together rather than further apart and considerably alarmed when he crossed a big river. Fortunately, the days of terrorism in the UK had yet to appear and the sight of a troop of guns driving round Parliament Square did not alarm the public too much.

And, of course, London with all it had to offer was on the doorstep. Before the days of 'don't drink and drive', there were pub crawls round such as the riverside Prospect of Whitby in E1 and the Antelope in Eaton Square SW1, not to mention the music halls in vogue at that time in which nude ladies posed but were not allowed to move. But one day a lady by the name of Peaches Page ran off the stage on the appearance of a mouse. A bunch of our subalterns followed Peaches Page round the music halls of London in the hope of a repetition!

Despite the poor accommodation, the lack of purpose-built facilities and the lack of training areas, Woolwich was a grand place in which to be stationed. I am sorry we have left.

20th Field Regiment Royal Artillery, Woolwich
Colonel J. H. Browell MBE

I reported to Woolwich in the autumn of 1955. My unit, 20th Field Regiment RA, had been in Hong Kong and Korea and was sent to Woolwich as part of 3rd Infantry Division to add a bit of tone to a rather run-down depot (this was before the rebuild). The regiment was stationed in Cambridge Barracks, but the officers lived in the RA Mess. I was housed in the West Gatehouse, which looked good from outside. Rooms were off a spiral staircase. There was one bathroom, no heating but a few lumps of coal at weekends. My room was cold, dilapidated and a good walk to the Mess.

In the wine cellar was a bricked-up part. This was done to stop the Guards from drinking all our best claret at the beginning of the war. I suggested we investigate. The claret was still there (1955) but of course well past its best. We drank what was still drinkable. There was also in a rack a bottle of cognac, part consumed. I was told that the Prince of Wales on a visit had drunk from it – we drank that too!

The Mess was magnificent but a bit shabby. The inhabitants were distinctly rundown, apart from those of the regiment. I was posted to 12 Minden Battery as a Troop commander. We were armed with 25-pounder guns pulled by Quad vehicles and, having fought in Korea, the regiment was well-trained and close-knit. Soon after arrival, I took over as Adjutant.

There was quite a flourishing Saddle Club at Woolwich run by Jack Paley Johnson, a perpetual major and great character who lived for horses. The Saddle Club horses were kept in Shrapnel Barracks where there was also a Riding School, and I was soon hunting with the West Kent Hunt. The horses were taken down for the season to Greenstreet Green Camp, an old ack-ack site where Jack had converted buildings into stables.

Being so close to central London with a good train service, we were frequent visitors to the theatre and I got invited to some rather smart debutante dances. If officers spent the night in town, I insisted that all subalterns caught an early morning train *before* mine when returning to Woolwich!

Part of our task was to galvanize the Mess. This was largely done by Tom Inglis who started by making everyone wear dinner jackets on weekdays, which got rid of some of the corduroy and pullover brigade. We also ran a very successful regimental dance in the Mess Room, causing consternation as the carpet had not been up for years – dances normally took place in the very boring ballroom. It was a great success, along with other entertainments.

Training was not easy from Woolwich. The Common was very restrictive, but we found various War Department-owned areas in Kent. Otherwise, it was up to Stanford in Norfolk via the Blackwall Tunnel, or down the A30 and A303 to Larkhill (no M3 or dual carriageway in those days). In May 1956 there was a review of 3rd Infantry Division artillery on the playing fields in front of the Mess, followed by a drive past in line along the Front Parade.

We went to practice camp at Otterburn in Northumberland with the rest of the divisional artillery but had not been there for more than a few days when the Suez crisis broke. We were ordered back to Woolwich to mobilize and receive reservists. The Regiment came back to extraordinary scenes of cheering, particularly in the suburbs of London. We were going to war!

The West Gate of the Royal Artillery Barracks, also used as overflow accommodation for officers at a time when the Mess was particularly full. There were more unmarried officers 'living in' during most of the life of the Mess until the 1970s and, with a Gunner regiment in Cambridge Barracks as well, it meant that getting a room in the main Mess was something of a lottery. The West Gate itself was pulled down in the mid 1960s.

Woolwich Memories

Brigadier Robert Hall

Of many memories of Woolwich, two events in particular stand out.

Dining-in the Young Officers:

In the autumn of 1959 my Young Officers' Course went to Woolwich from Larkhill to visit The Depot, The RA Mess, The King's Troop, The Honourable Artillery Company and to be 'Dined into the Regiment'. At the Dinner I sat on the right of the Presiding Officer, Major General Kenneth 'Squirrel' Mackay Lewis CB, DSO, MC, whom I now realize must have been the Representative Colonel Commandant for 1959; my father – a retired Gunner brigadier – sat on my right. After the Loyal Toast had been drunk, the Director of Music came and sat between the General and myself and had a glass of port. After a few pleasantries he turned to me and asked me to select a tune for the Band to play. I was horrified, no tune whatsoever came into my mind, I started to stutter and then a tune came to me, 'Could you please play "I could have danced all night" from My Fair Lady?', I said. He replied, 'We have already played it once tonight'; of course, I thought, that's why it came to me! My Father whispered, 'Bonnie Dundee' and I passed my new request on and was saved. Ever since I have had 'Bonnie Dundee' up my sleeve but never been asked for a tune again.

The Director Royal Artillery's Conference

From 1977 to 1979 I was Executive Assistant to the UK's Military Representative to NATO Headquarters in Brussels – a four-star officer. As Commanding Officer-designate of 25th Field Regiment towards the end of my tour, I attended the Director RA's annual conference. One of the highlights of the conference was a talk by The Master Gunner, General Sir Harry Tuzo, then Deputy Supreme Allied Commander at Supreme Headquarters Allied Powers Europe, at Casteau (near Mons) some 40 miles from Brussels. I had met him several times in Belgium when I escorted 'great men' down to his office or when he escorted 'very great men' up to Brussels.

The Master Gunner's address turned out to be a masterly tour d'horizon of the NATO nations, all of which he had visited – some many times – and as he wound up, he saw me a few rows back and said, 'I see Robert Hall from NATO's HQ in Brussels. Have I missed anyone out, Robert?' At the start of his talk I had casually listed all NATO's, then, 16 nations and ticked them off as he mentioned them. So I had no hesitation in replying, 'Only Italy and Luxembourg, General.' I now realize he was asking one of those questions, often found in Latin, expecting the answer 'No', as he explained to me, somewhat forcefully, later that day.

Horses of The King's Troop RHA in the West square in 1955. It would be a grave error not to have space somewhere in this book to pay tribute to the horses without which the Royal Regiment could not have functioned over so many years. While most of the horses used for drawing guns were of the type also used at all levels in the carriage trade, there were times when a heavier breed was needed to draw the bigger field guns, particularly during the Great War. Officers' chargers were also larger and more powerful, but their task was different from that of the gun teams. Yet, despite their numbers, like all horses they had their different characteristics and personalities and they were much loved by their Gunner companions at arms. Mechanization, when it came just before the Second World War, was an almost traumatic moment for most Gunners, though perhaps those who remembered the courage and the carnage among the horses of the Great War appreciated that, this time, the horses would not suffer so badly.

NATIONAL SERVICE IN WOOLWICH
'... CE N'ÉTAIT PAS LA GUERRE.'

Jonathan Baldwin

Life in the late 1950s for this National Service subaltern posted to the Depot at Woolwich was certainly not warlike. Indeed, it was how I imagined life during the interwar years might have been: rather more formal than the rest of the country was fast becoming, some work, quite a lot of sport and a fair amount of leisure/pleasure.

By volunteering that I could ride a horse, I was given the job of Depot MTO (Motor Transport Officer), not least because the job came with three General Service wagons (flatbed trailers with a front bogie) each with two horses. Their justification for being on the establishment was the transfer of precious artefacts from the Rotunda to the Royal Arsenal for repairs and maintenance. So a stable with six Army horses and attendant grooms overseen by Sergeant Moy, and several private horses made for a way of life I had not been expecting. Deciding who was really in charge was an interesting exercise.

Horses at the Depot were also used to teach the equestrian arts to visiting Royal Naval officers on courses at Greenwich and Sapper officers from Chatham. This took place in the indoor riding school in the north east corner of the old barracks before they were demolished.

Life in the RA Mess was more formal than in almost all other messes. Those below field rank (major and above) had to wear uniform at all meals except at weekends, but tie and jacket were de rigueur in the Mess at *all* times, more senior members wearing dinner jacket for dinner. We soon learnt the art of the quick change after dinner from Number 1 dress into lounge suit and onto the train up to Town. Evenings in the Mess were pretty quiet because the only wireless was in the Card Room which was the preserve of field officers up till 10 pm. Then Radio Luxemburg was allowed to click in, among much mutterings.

Theatre played a surprisingly large part in our evening entertainment because the Hall Porter (the peerless Mr Lund) was also a theatre ticket agency, could obtain tickets there and then and gave his commission to members of the Mess (well, the impecunious ones, anyway). He was also an inveterate supporter of junior members. Dogs were not allowed in the Mess (fines 10 shillings downstairs, £1 upstairs ... a National Service Officer's pay was £1 per day). One day, my English setter puppy was in the front hall as the Brigadier's car approached: Mr Lund hauled him into his Hall Porter's Box and, as the Brigadier entered through the revolving door, said dog was shoved head downward in the

waste paper basket and the foot-of-Lund kept the dog's behind in place while the Brigadier swept past with a cheerful 'Good morning, Lund', 'Good morning Brigadier'. Once the coast was clear, the dog was discharged onto the Front Parade.

Guard mounting was always an Orderly officer's nightmare because there were seven guards to mount. The soldiers making up the guards were mainly in transit, often with only two or three more days of their two-year National Service to do. The variety of blanco colours, scrubbed near-white or blackened belts and gaiters meant that they were many things, but not 'uniform'. Turning out the Guard was also a tortuous affair; the route included North Gate (of the main Depot), Cambridge Barracks, Connaught Barracks, the Gun Park, Greenhill, the Royal Army Ordnance Corps bakery next to the stables (now the site of the new Queen Elizabeth Hospital) and the Royal Herbert Hospital on Shooters Hill.

The Winter Ball was a very grand affair. In the manner of the day, the local Parks Department was called upon to provide potted palms of every size and colour, the Mess kitchens supplied endless varieties of exquisite food and these balls were the only ones attended when we all had dance cards. I suppose the Duchess of Richmond's Ball before Waterloo was grander but I happily settled for the Royal Artillery Winter Ball. My whole time at Woolwich (to echo General Pierre Bosquet's famous comment on the Charge of the Light Brigade) ... *était magnifique mais ce n'etait pas la guerre,* but someone had to do it!

Gun teams being watered in the West Square of the RA Barracks.

The Woolwich 'At Home' Events

During the post-war years, Woolwich Garrison staged a series of 'At Home' events, when the Regiment showed itself off to the civilian population. They were popular occasions, attended by large crowds and particularly popular with families because they offered such a wide range of entertainment.

There was always a wide variety of the Regiment's current equipment on display, with exhibits from the Rotunda alongside the latest and most sophisticated pieces in service at the time. There was always a parachute-jumping tower for the more adventurous visitors and arena displays by The King's Troop RHA competed for excitement with the Regiment's motorcycle display team. The RA Band provided a popular performance of music and marching, the marquees housed refreshments of all kinds and there was an air of enjoyment like that of a county 'show'. They were a wonderful way of keeping the Army in the public eye and, in particular, to allow the Regiment to keep in harmony with the local population.

Sadly, like the Tattoos, these became difficult to stage with the pressures of events and the worsening security problems of the 1970s, and now remain, like the church parades of the interwar years, almost a folk memory for the people of Greenwich borough. Those members of the Regiment who attended the final ceremonies on 26 May 2007 might have recognized the general atmosphere, with its parades, music and arena displays, as an echo of the 'At Home' events, but the day lacked the weather and the crowds that had thronged the Barrack Field on those invariably sunny, summer days.

KAT

The King's Troop RHA performing its famous musical drive during an 'At Home', together with examples of the programmes for these events.

VISIT BY THE CAPTAIN GENERAL IN 1969

On 27 March 1969, Her Majesty The Queen paid her second visit to Woolwich, the first having taken place in 1958. The Master Gunner, the Director Royal Artillery and the Representative Colonel Commandant accompanied Her Majesty. The visit began with a parade accompanied by a static display of equipment then in service with the Regiment, followed by a march past and drive past. During the parade, the music was provided by the Royal Artillery Massed Bands.

The parade consisted of representative guns and equipment drawn from across the whole spectrum of the Regiment's deployment, with detachments from:

British Army of the Rhine
Army Strategic Command
Air Defence Group RA
School of Artillery, Larkhill
School of Artillery, Manorbier
Trials Establishment RA
Territorial and Army Volunteer Reserve

The Guard of Honour was provided by 1st Regiment Royal Horse Artillery. The march past consisted of:

The King's Troop RHA
Guard of Honour
Detachments of 17th Training Regiment RA
The Band of the Junior Leaders Regiment RA

This was followed by a Drive Past consisting of:

Composite Battery from 7th Parachute Regiment RHA
38th (Seringapatam) Light Battery RA
7th (Sphinx) Commando Light Battery RA
49th (Inkerman) Medium Battery RA
30th Light Air Defence Battery (Rogers' Company) RA
Composite Battery from 2nd (Field) Regiment RA

At the conclusion of the parade, The Captain General took lunch in the RA Mess and then visited the Warrant Officers' and Sergeants' Mess and the Junior Ranks' Club, meeting a large number of members of the Regiment and their families. Despite the formalities, it had been a thoroughly enjoyable visit and was much appreciated by all those who had the honour of taking part in it.

KAT   *HM The Queen reviews a parade in her honour during her visit to Woolwich in 1969, the march past being led by The King's Troop RHA.*

1970s Recollections of Woolwich and The Depot Regiment

Brigadier Tim Thompson MBE

My family's involvement with Woolwich goes back to 1913 when my father, the late Brigadier L. F. Thompson CBE, MC was a Gentleman Cadet at 'The Shop', as the Royal Military Academy Woolwich was known. After service in the two World Wars, which included command of the Gunners in the siege of Tobruk, he retired in 1946 and was appointed Secretary of the Royal Artillery Institution, based in part of the now vacant buildings of the Academy.

My first memory of Woolwich is a visit during my father's six-year appointment, and I well remember being overawed when taken to lunch in that magnificent dining room of the RA Mess; I was 12 years old and it was that moment that clinched my determination to follow my father into the Royal Regiment.

In 1971, I was appointed to command 24 (Irish) Battery, one of the two in 17th Training Regiment which had moved to Woolwich from Oswestry, Shropshire, a few years before. This was a rather more pleasurable tour with that battery, in which I had done my basic training before going to Sandhurst.

The Depot Regiment 1975–76

After its move to Woolwich from Oswestry, 17th Training Regiment was collated with the RA Depot and, during Colonel John Mayo's tour in command, the two units were combined and titled somewhat cumbersomely '17 Training Regiment and Depot RA'. Shortly after I assumed command in August 1975, the title was changed to 'The Depot Regiment', but its main role continued to be the initial training of all adult recruits to the Royal Regiment. It also included the RA Band, a Women's Royal Army Corps battery and the Depot; a further dimension was added to the Commanding Officer's responsibilities when he was appointed President of the Mess Committee of the RA Mess.

In the autumn of 1975, recruiting for the Army generally received a significant boost and it soon became clear that the resources of the five training Troops would be inadequate. Cap in hand, the Commanding Officer explained his problem to that imposing, but kindly Director RA, General 'Tim' Morony, who ordered up reinforcements in the form of sergeants and bombardiers from several regiments. Their COs were naturally reluctant to send of their best to Woolwich for three months at short notice, but we were well provided for and coped with the recruiting 'bulge'.

The Depot Regiment came under command of London District, which was not greatly interested in non-Household Troops. However, their apology for a serious 'cock-up' was as surprising as it was bizarre. Our Adjutant, Tim Stokes, was informed – incorrectly as it turned out – that he had passed the Staff College entrance exam. As an apology, we were offered a three-week exercise in, of all places, Bermuda – quickly accepted, of course. We decided that the training troop whose recruits were nearing the end of their course should form the main body of the exercise, but it was surprising how many other officers and senior non-commissioned officers persuaded me that their participation was essential! The Regimental Sergeant Major (RSM), Pat Lewis, was concerned that the standard of drill might slip with the passing-out parade only a week after the recruits' return to Woolwich. As the Commanding Officer was expected to visit the exercise for a week, he could hardly turn down the others. Needless to say, we all enjoyed Bermuda, but poor Tim Stokes never got there.

The Potential Officers' Wing was affectionately known as the 'Plonks' and had been an important part of the regiment for many years. These young men completed recruit training before joining the Wing, where their leadership skills were honed, both at Woolwich and in the much more rugged conditions of Snowdonia (North Wales), where the regiment had established a training hut. Although by no means all the Plonks passed the Regular Commissions Board, many did and have provided valuable service to the Royal Regiment. I have no doubt that they all benefited from the experience.

During the summer of 1977, the Queen's Silver Jubilee was celebrated and a medal was struck to commemorate the anniversary. Only three of those medals were issued to the Depot Regiment; whether this reflected our esteem in London District's eyes is not known, but as Commanding Officer, I was ordered to give myself one of the three and face the difficult task of deciding who should receive the others, among a strength of some 1,000 men and women. The RSM, by then Mr Waterland, was a fairly easy choice and, after much discussion, the third was awarded to our best training bombardier, whose name sadly escapes me.

The three weekly pass-outs were always great occasions: a formal parade against that magnificent backdrop of the RA

A BIRD'S EYE VIEW OF THE MESS AT WOOLWICH

Mrs Jean Darmody

As a naive girlfriend, wife to be of a Gunner officer in the early 90s, the Mess at Woolwich was a revelation and an opposing view of my commercial world outside military life.

I was invited by my future husband to a regimental dinner at his regimental headquarter mess in 1991. I gladly accepted; it sounded wonderful and indeed was an amazing experience with many more to come; reviews, assemblies, race days, Chelsea Hospital, corporate events, remembrance ceremony. It opened up another world of regimental heritage, friendship and civility sadly lacking in the world of 'outside'.

Arriving at the guard room on the appointed time, my car was checked over very thoroughly with mirrors, the boot opened, the bonnet opened, all very politely and carefully. I was then directed to the rear of the Officers' Mess, a dreary and austere building of the 1960s era. It belied the grandeur of the formal rooms of the Officers' Mess – the entrance off the front parade, the ante rooms, the staircase, the portraits and artefacts were so impressive.

After introductions, pre dinner drinks and a feel for the formality of what I was a part of, my first sight inside the dining room was something I shall never forget. The sheer size of it, the grandeur, the tables set for dinner, the silver – masses of it shining in the candle light – looking up to see those magnificent chandeliers. I must have been a very quiet companion to my fellows on right and left, just taking it all in. The abiding memory of a mass of candle-lit beautiful silver pieces I had never thought existed in such quantity and in one place, the chandeliers, the music was almost too much. History has never been my strong subject, but this had it all. The King's Troop sounded the dinner call, bless them. A huge lump always came into my throat when the RA band soloist trumpeters played the Post Horn Gallop faultlessly. Then the mood changed, the table cloth rolling began. Until it is seen it is not believed, every time it worked – amazing.

Next morning the whole room was transformed back to everyday normality. The staff was bright and attentive; breakfast was served as in the best hotels. Some of us the worse for wear after a very late night in the bar, outlasting the younger element who were off to bed long before us.

Men are never good at defining the ladies' dress for occasions such as this and on these first forays into this new world of military splendour I am sure I must have got 'the dress' wrong many times, but one soon learnt. There was always good conversation amidst the candle light and delicious food expertly served by well trained and kind staff. They looked after my husband as a live-in officer during the week for many years and he still yearns for such expert service each morning in our 'help yourself' busy breakfast time.

I remember the dread of having to get up in the middle of the night (inevitable after all that liquid) to find the ladies' lavatories in the long corridor on the top floor. The floors were bare: it was just like the school facilities of long ago, with huge baths and communal showers, very sixties and not what I or indeed any of us non-military girls were used to.

All this was a period of life we both have been very privileged to have enjoyed. Woolwich, the buildings, the Mess, the length of the facade and the parade ground and the people it represents is something very special none of us will ever forget. Long may it stand and give hopefully as much pleasure and security to the people soon to inhabit it.

Barracks façade, with the participation of the RA Band, was followed by an impressive display in the Gymnasium, but what really made the day was the huge turnout of friends and relatives of the recruits. They travelled from all parts of the UK, often overnight, to support their young men and invariably marvelled at their transformation in only 13 brief but action-packed weeks. The dedication of their instructors to this rewarding task was superb.

Reluctantly, I handed over command to the late Colonel David Evans in August 1977. He and the regiment were shortly to be faced with the daunting task of fire-fighting during the strike that autumn and their outstanding performance was widely praised.

17TH TRAINING REGIMENT AND DEPOT 1990–2

Lieutenant Colonel Ashley Manton RA

It had been a while since I stayed in the RA Barracks at Woolwich, and that was when I was serving in the RA Presentation Team with the late Brigadiers Robin Duchesne and then Giles Arnold. Our frequent trips around UK meant we were seldom in the Barracks and so I had not appreciated the full extent of the facilities available within the regimental estate. In 1990 I assumed command of 17th Training Regiment RA and Depot (the title at the time) and became aware of the enormous potential of those facilities. Raising

funds for the RA Museum Project gave us the opportunity to make use of them. Captain Simon Crane spearheaded the competition called 'Combat Challenge' in which teams representing top City of London companies descended on the regiment for a challenging, fun day's event, for which privilege they contributed significant sums. At the end of the day, hundreds of 'City slickers' marched onto the Front Parade accompanied by the RA Band for the presentations and awards ceremony.

The Royal Artillery motorcycle display team, 1992.

WOOLWICH DÉBUT

Sophie Huthwaite

In September 1991 I arrived at Woolwich after a rollercoaster ride at Larkhill involving changes in the areas of Gunnery in which I was allowed to qualify and much tweaking of uniforms. As the first female to be commissioned into the Royal Artillery it had been both an exciting and a trying time. However, I had made it and all the hurdles were in the past. The dining-in to the Regiment at Woolwich was the culmination of our training and the signal that we would be released into the Royal Artillery community to try out and hone our skills.

The dining-in was an incredibly special and poignant evening not only for me, but also for my father, Richard Wigglesworth. As a retired Gunner officer, my father might have visualized attending a dining-in at Woolwich with a son, but here was his daughter, the youngest of his four children, at her dining-in

singing 'The Screw Guns' with gusto. I had been adamant that I would go into the Gunners from the word go, despite my father's numerous explanations that the Royal Artillery did not cap badge females.... How times change!

I was to have the opportunity to enjoy the Mess properly when I was posted to 17th Training Regiment RA. Although certain aspects of the Mess were beginning to show their age, this was more than compensated for, certainly for Rachel Cane and me when we discovered that we could sunbathe in total privacy on long hot summer days on the balcony outside Rachel's room overlooking the Front Parade. There was also something about running one's BFT (basic fitness test) around the parade ground in front of the imposing exterior of the Mess. It was certainly something to look at. The problems arose when one wanted guaranteed hot water or a cockroach-free room!

The black-tie 'Survivors Ball' in the RA Mess was the culmination of a most memorable day. The regiment raised thousands of pounds for the Museum Project and there was little doubt that the Royal Artillery was the talk of the City that week.

The prime task of the regiment was recruit training, this comprised of Phase 1 – a ten-week 'Common Military Syllabus' training course – followed by Phase 2, a four-week Trade training course: 24 and 59 Batteries ran the Phase 1 training alternately and HQ Battery's Training Wing ran Phase 2. Similar courses and pass-out parades were also run for the Territorial Army.

Just prior to my handing over command in late 1992, the pass-out parade of 59 Battery's recruits was the last time the whole regiment was on parade at Woolwich, as shortly afterwards 59 Battery transferred to the newly formed Army Training Regiment at Pirbright, Surrey, where Phase 1 training would continue in an 'All Arms' environment.

The period also saw the demise of the Women's Royal Army Corps (WRAC). The occasion was marked by a parade on the Front Parade. A number of WRAC attached to the regiment at the time became RA cap-badged and a larger number who were drivers in our attached sub-unit of 56th Transport Squadron, Royal Corps of Transport (RCT), became RCT cap-badged.

As with all regiments at the time, the First Gulf War in 1991 affected 17th Training Regiment in many ways. First, the RA Band deployed to Iraq in its stretcher-bearer role and this prompted a visit to the regiment by Prince Charles to meet the wives of those deployed. Second, and in response to the threat by Saddam Hussain to inflict massive casualties on our forces, we prepared several barrack blocks as overflow wards for the Queen Elizabeth Military Hospital. Third, as we might have been required to train a mass of battlefield replacements, the regiment was brought up to full strength (unusual at this time for those regiments not deploying to Iraq). There was an agonizing wait during the 48-hour 'media blackout' period at the start of the offensive, for news of whether Saddam had in fact been able to carry out his retaliatory threat – fortunately, as we now know, the contingencies were not required.

The Depot played host to many RA sporting activities and was the location for several RA finals. The regiment became the

Army hockey winners and a recruit boxing competition was also re-introduced with great success, despite the reservations of the regimental doctor!

The Display Troop, comprising the Motorcycle Display Team and the RA Parachuting Team, continued to entertain the crowds and help in recruiting. The RA Band was in constant demand in support of the Royal Regiment and in providing regular concerts in the Barracks and for local events such as the Leeds Castle open-7air concerts. The Warrant Officers' Course, Potential Officers' Course and Pre-Regular Commissions Board assessments were part of the normal routine of the regiment, as were the firing of Royal Salutes and the organization of the annual Remembrance Day Parade at the RA Memorial at Hyde Park Corner.

Our activities in support of our Freedom of the Boroughs of both Bexley and Woolwich were frequent and our links with the Mayoral Offices were extended to include the City of London when Sir Brian Jenkins became Lord Mayor. As he was an ex-member of the Regiment, our guns participated in the Lord Mayor's Show and he attended many events in the regiment during his year of office, including taking the salute at a pass-out parade.

Another regular event was our support for the London Marathon: we fired the guns for the start of the race on Blackheath, and the recruits handed out water to the runners as they rounded the Barracks' perimeter.

Apart from the in-house RA Conferences such as the Director RA's annual conference, we also hosted other military conferences and dinners for Army Board members. The RA Mess was used by the odd outside organization: for instance the Variety Club of Great Britain held dinners to raise money for the Army Benevolent Fund and Prince Philip was a guest on one such occasion. Later the Woolwich Mayor borrowed the Mess to host a visit by the President of Slovenia.

Sadly my tour concluded in November 1992 when I handed over to Lieutenant Colonel John Gibbon: it had been an enormous privilege to have commanded such professional officers, non-commissioned officers and soldiers and it was the most enjoyable and memorable of all my postings.

The 200th anniversary of the formation of the Royal Horse Artillery in 1993

Major Denis Rollo

This was a much larger event than the Royal Regiment's 250th birthday celebrations of 1966, which took place in central London. It was a Royal Review in which The King's Troop, Royal Horse Artillery (RHA), and every RHA battery, Regular and Territorial Army took part. The main event took place on the Front Parade and each battery paraded with 105mm Light Guns drawn by Land-Rovers, with their detachments. In front was a Royal Guard of Honour, of three officers and 100 Other Ranks, mounted by 1st Regiment RHA. Behind the spectator stands, which faced the Barracks, the King's Troop was in action waiting for the order to fire the Royal Salute.

The parade was brought to attention and as the royal car appeared the first round was fired and the salute proceeded. Her Majesty, the Captain General, was received at the saluting base by the Master Gunner, General Sir Martin Farndale, and the Director Royal Artillery, Major General M. T. Tennant. Accompanying Her Majesty was another Gunner, Major-General B. T. Pennicott, a Gentlemen Usher to Her Majesty. A Royal Salute was then ordered, the Guard of Honour presented arms and the Massed Bands of the Royal Artillery played the National Anthem. The Captain General, on foot, inspected the Guard of Honour, following which Her Majesty inspected the main part of the parade from a vehicle. The parade ended with a mounted march past by The King's Troop RHA and then the main body of the parade with its guns.

In the afternoon there was a garden party on the Sports Ground attended by all those who had taken part in the parade and the spectators. Just before Her Majesty left the massed bands played the National Anthem but with a difference, it being accompanied by a rafale of 21 guns, the number usually fired for a Royal Salute.

HM The Queen inspects a Guard of Honour formed by 1st Regiment Royal Horse Artillery.

*Above: The Queen signs the Visitors'
Book in the RA Mess.*

*Top right: The Guard of Honour on the
Barrack Field facing the parade ground
during the drive past of the RHA
batteries.*

*Right: The Parade formed up on the
Front Parade, with all of the RHA
Batteries together with those which still
have 'letter titles' despite now being RA
and those from the Territorial Army
which served as RHA at some point in
their history. Each battery is represented
by a section of three guns drawn by
Landrovers.*

16TH AIR DEFENCE REGIMENT RA

At the close of a long tour in Dortmund, Germany, 16th Regiment held a farewell parade on 12 July 1995 and prepared for a move back to England. The journey took many forms, but the main body of vehicles and equipment went by road and sea, arriving at Deptford and driving to Woolwich. There it was given a rousing welcome, as recorded by the Commanding Officer, Lieutenant Colonel S.M. Gledhill RA:

I am certain, the marvellous welcome which the regiment has been given by the people of Woolwich will ensure that it will be a happy and successful posting for many years to come. Who can forget the cheering crowds, with children waving Union Jacks, as we marched and drove through the town past the Mayor, on the Parade, to both welcome the regiment to Woolwich and reaffirm the Royal Regiment of Artillery's Freedom of the Borough of Greenwich. It was a great honour for us, and I am sure that many people felt as I did, that we were coming home.
(Extract from 16th Regiment Journal)

and the Master Gunner, General Sir Martin Farndale, addressing the Regiment that day on parade:

Your arrival here is of the greatest importance and significance to the Royal Regiment. Your arrival has saved Woolwich for the Regiment … All Gunners come here for visits, reunions and parades. It is still the Regimental HQ of the Regiment …. There is another reason why you are so very welcome. You will have seen today as you marched with such style through the Borough of Woolwich exercising our right as Freemen of Woolwich to do so, how the population turned out in their thousands and decorated the streets, so delighted are they at your arrival.

Sadly, the prediction of saving the Woolwich 'home' was not to be, but 16th Regiment made sure that its time there was as packed with events as that of any of its famous predecessors.

The decision to put a service regiment with so much equipment in Woolwich had been taken at short notice and, on arrival, there was insufficient accommodation in the RA Barracks to house the offices and equipment. The regiment had to await a rebuild which was to take nearly three years to complete, housed meanwhile in the Royal Arsenal. Its new Regimental Lines were built on the old Repository site

alongside the Rotunda Museum and were formally opened as Napier Lines at the beginning of July 1998.

At this point there was a regimental HQ, headquarters battery, three missile batteries and a workshop, all of which had the difficult task of maintaining their operational capability while being called upon to undertake an extraordinary variety of activities. Indeed, 16th Regiment spent much of the next 12 years away from its Woolwich base. In common with all serving regiments these days, there were seldom days in any given year

16th Regiment RA formed up on the Front Parade with its equipment.

The Commanding Officer inspects a cadre course – part of the training for young NCOs making their first important step up from Gunner to Lance Bombardier.

in which to relax and the programme of events spanned an enormously wide range of tasks and locations.

It would take a much longer article than this even to list them all, let alone go into details, but a selected few may give some idea of the life of a service regiment at the turn of the 21st century.

Tours in Northern Ireland were still a factor until the peace process was completed, and the regiment was in County Armagh from October 1998 for six months, with further shorter tours later. It had barely returned before it was off to Cyprus for another six month tour in the United Nations' peacekeeping role – another place it was to return to for shorter tours later. Returning from Cyprus, the regiment planned to go to Texas in the USA for a major exercise; in the event, it was represented in Texas by only a small number of key personnel. Instead, it found itself deployed on duties connected with the disastrous outbreak of foot and mouth cattle disease, with soldiers deployed in many different parts of the country, from north to south.

There were duties in support of the Fire Service during a firemen's strike; an exercise in Poland; frequent long trips to the Outer Hebrides to fire their Rapier missiles, though a firing camp at Castlemartin in South Wales gave some relief from that long, 600-mile road and sea journey. 'Dry' training on Salisbury Plain, in Wales, at Stanford (Norfolk), Otterburn (Northumberland), the northwest coast of Scotland and many other places kept the batteries on their toes. In between all this were the adventure training exercises, which included trekking in the Himalayas, hiking the 73-mile length of Hadrian's Wall, sailing and skiing.

The spectacular 'Music of the Night' event, staged in the Royal Arsenal in the summer of 2001, was largely the work of 16th Regiment, which also had to provide gun detachments – an interesting retraining exercise for missile-trained soldiers who had not had previous experience of gun drill. This also came in useful to support the annual Leeds Castle musical event, providing 'cannons' for the sound effects in the *1812 Overture*. The regiment even found itself standing in at short notice for the Scots Guards who were in Northern Ireland: the Guards had had to bow out of plans to support the Chinese community in London at the Dragon Boat races in Docklands.

Top: The Battery Commander of 32 (Minden) Battery RA presenting Minden roses to his battery – an annual ceremony recalling the Battle of Minden in 1759 at which the battery played a significant part.

Above: The unusual sight of an officer in the Royal Air Force inspecting a Guard of Honour during a visit as the officer commanding the UK Ground Based Air Defence organization in which 16th Regiment plays an important role.

The Gunners stepped in and even managed an overall win, only to lose it on a re-run. A 'home-grown' pantomime rounded off their cultural activities that year.

Another impressive parade exercising the Royal Regiment's Freedom of Greenwich took place in July 2004. Meanwhile, 16th Regiment had gained a fourth battery in April 2004 when further changes in the Army's organization took place, but this put even more pressure on accommodation. Nonetheless, training continued, both in Woolwich and in the many other venues around the country. Woolwich Common was the obvious local site for deploying the firing units. The aircraft flying into Heathrow and the City Airport always provided something for the radars to track, though these would have been easy meat for a system capable of tracking high-speed ground attack aircraft.

One wonders what the 18th-century Gunners who trained on the Common would have made of their 21st-century successors, but they would surely have applauded their professionalism and spirit as they dealt with all the problems they faced in such a busy and demanding life.

KAT

161

THE ROYAL ARTILLERY INSTITUTION

Colonel M.J.N. Richards

(based on an historical note by Brigadier P. W. Mead, published in 1972)

The 1958 Reorganization and the Last Half of the 20th Century

As the British Army re-organized following the end of the Second World War and with the gradual demise of the British Empire, the Royal Regiment's domestic affairs came under close scrutiny. In 1956 a special committee was set up under the chairmanship of Major General B. P. Hughes, which made proposals for a major reorganization that were accepted and implemented in 1958.

As a result, previously independent funds, such as the Master Gunner's Fund, the Headquarters Officers' Mess Fund, the RA Band Fund, the Sports Fund, the Warrant Officers' and Sergeants' Headquarters and Central Mess Funds, together with many smaller funds, were concentrated within the framework of the RA Institution. Although this hugely simplified the control of subscriptions and the planning of Regimental expenditure, it did mean that a legal scheme was needed to ensure equity between past assets and future income, as well as to set up a means for future control. During these proceedings the RA Institution, somewhat to its surprise, became a charitable trust. Its governing body became the Council of the Royal Artillery Institution under the Master Gunner's chairmanship and the office of 'Controller of the Charity' was established, to be generally responsible to the Council for the administration and management of the Charity. General Hughes himself became the first Controller.

Also in 1958, as part of other major War Office reorganizations, authority was given for a Regimental Headquarters Royal Artillery to be established. The bulk of the Institution's staff, hitherto paid by the Regiment, were promptly transferred to the Regimental Headquarters establishment, with the Secretary being regarded as the officer in charge of the latter. This arrangement gave rise to some tensions: whereas the Charitable Scheme made clear the Institution's staff was responsible only to its Trustees, the responsibility of the Regimental Headquarters staff (usually the same individuals) was less clearly defined in War Office instructions. This led to one Director Royal Artillery (DRA) deciding not to press his claim that the Regimental Headquarters staff were responsible solely to him.

To some extent these changes overshadowed the Institution's long-standing functions and responsibilities. In particular the control, management and allocation of all the Regiment's charitable funds (other than the welfare funds managed by the Royal Artillery Charitable Fund and the Royal Artillery Association funds) has tended increasingly to preoccupy the Institution's Trustees and staff over the past half century. Charitable spending to support the extra-mural and sporting life of the serving Regiment has grown, but the Institution's traditional responsibilities have nevertheless been maintained, albeit that the emphasis has altered somewhat. The *RA Journal* continues to maintain in each edition a high percentage of historical articles alongside those covering current operations, strategy and tactics, current and future equipment, as well as more light-hearted articles on Regimental life. The Institution also continues to make annual awards in recognition of academic and scientific achievement.

Neither did the demise of the printing press mean the Institution abandoning its long tradition of publishing, although costs have continually risen since the 1960s. The *Journal* and the Blue List have been published routinely using contract printers, while a whole series of important books have been commissioned through different publishing houses on an 'as required' basis. The most notable of these has been the ongoing volumes of the Regimental History covering the period from the start of the First World War. Individual authors have also been supported either with financial grants or in some cases with the Institution taking direct responsibility for commissioning a book.

It is the arrangements for meeting the Institution's historical responsibilities that have changed most over the past 50 years or so. From a high point around the the outbreak of the First World War in 1914 there is no doubt that, with a few notable exceptions, only lip-service was given to the care of the Regiment's history until the early 1960s, when the Royal Artillery Historical Affairs Committee was formed to address the problem. By 1965 this had become too large to be effective and it was expanded to form the RA Historical Society open to all Gunners. The Historical Affairs Committee reverted to a select committee of the Institution to advise the Master Gunner and the DRA on historical matters. In 1960 the first Historical Secretary RAI was appointed.

This new Historical Secretary also became the Curator of the Regimental and Rotunda Museums, although the RAI Trustees retained overall responsibility for the Regimental historical collections until 1990, when the Master Gunner's Committee handed over that responsibility to the Trustees of

Maj-Gen B.P. ('Bil') Hughes CBE, who had a distinguished war record, especially in anti-aircraft operations, is remembered as much for his extraordinary historical knowledge of the equipment and tactics of the Peninsular War as for his long service as a reforming Controller of the Royal Artillery Institution. Among other works, he was the author of Honour Titles of the Royal Artillery *and of the much-prized* Regimental Heritage *book published in 1984.*

the Royal Artillery Historical Trust. This Trust had been first established in 1981, principally as a vehicle to apply for appropriate museum-related grants.

It was also during the 1980s that there was a growing realization that the facilities available in the Royal Military Academy and the Rotunda were not only wholly inadequate for the purpose of housing the Regimental Collections, but also with the impending closure of the RMA buildings, half of those facilities would disappear anyway. Accordingly in 1990 Royal Artillery Museums Ltd was set up by the Master Gunner's Committee as a charitable company owned by its members, with the aim of establishing a new museum to properly house all the Regimental Collections. The Royal Artillery Institution provided a seedcorn grant for work to start to identify a suitable site for the new museum and to raise the necessary funds to build it. Subsequently, the decision was taken for it to be established in the Royal Arsenal as soon as sufficient funds had been raised.

The Last Decade

For most of the 50 years since the RA Institution became a charitable trust in 1958 and some of its original staff assumed appointments in Regimental Headquarters, its relationship with the Headquarters is perhaps best described as being 'at arms length', principally because of physical dislocation. The Secretary and his staff remained in the offices in the Royal Military Academy, as did the Historical Secretary and his staff, while the Regimental Headquarters itself was established in Government House with the Garrison Headquarters, and indeed a few individual staff officers actually worked in Headquarters Director Royal Artillery on the Front Parade.

The impending move of that last body from Woolwich to Larkhill in the early 1990s was the catalyst for a further change, which saw the – by then – Regimental Colonel as head of a reorganized Regimental Headquarters responsible to the Director Royal Artillery for all regimental matters. The Institution's staff was fully integrated into the new Headquarters, and the Secretary also became Regimental Secretary as head of a newly formed Regimental Secretariat

with the staff of the Royal Artillery Charitable Fund and the Royal Artillery Association. The Secretariat's role was to provide coordinated support to all the regimental committees from the Master Gunner's Committee downward, although of course the appropriate staffs retained their responsibility to the trustees of the various different charities, and the Controller remained responsible for the general administration and management of all the charities.

The new Regimental Headquarters started work in 1993 and, when Headquarters Director Royal Artillery moved to Larkhill in 1994, it moved into offices on the Front Parade, with all its staff together except for the Historical Secretary and his staff, who for the time being remained with the Museum and Library in the Royal Military Academy.

This reorganization was also inevitably used by the Ministry of Defence as a way of reducing costs: the number of MOD staff posts serving all the Regimental charities, including the RA Institution, was gradually reduced from 1994 onwards. Its principal effect on the Institution was the establishment of a single finance department within the Secretariat responsible for the day-to-day administration of all the Regiment's charitable funds, and the combining of all publishing responsibilities under the Editor of *The Gunner* magazine. Despite the reduction in staff posts, these arrangements have generally worked well over the past decade and, of course, the Secretary of the Institution in his role as Regimental Secretary retained management oversight for both of the new finance and publishing departments. He also retained his overall responsibility for editing the Royal Artillery Journal, which dated from the original publication of the *Proceedings and Minutes* of the RA Institution in 1858.

Once the decision had been taken on a site for the new museum and as it became clear that there would be sufficient funds to build it, the Historical Secretary became increasingly involved with the mammoth task of planning and developing its detailed layout and the subsequent move of the collections themselves. In the event, the new Museum opened on 26 May 2001, with the bulk of the collections together on one site having been moved from their various disparate locations in the RA Mess, the Royal Military Academy and the Rotunda. The Historical Secretary became the curator of the new RA Museum when it opened, although he retained his responsibilities to the RA Institution for regimental historical matters.

In 2004 the Regiment took the decision that it was now the right time to move its home from Woolwich, where it had been since 1716, to Larkhill which had clearly become the centre for all Regimental professional and 'family' activities, and was a much more natural home in the 21st century. Accordingly plans were put in train to move the Regimental Headquarters and, as part of that move, the Royal Artillery Institution finally closed its offices on the Front Parade of the RA Barracks on 30 November 2005, 151 years after it had moved into its first purpose-built offices in the Barracks.

Unfortunately, for personal reasons, none of the Woolwich-based staff, most of whom had been loyal servants to the Institution for many years, were able to move to Larkhill. This meant that their collective expertise was lost, but any concern which was felt at the time has proved to be groundless. The RA Institution in its new home at Larkhill and with its new, equally dedicated staff has continued to fulfil its long-standing and traditional roles to the Regiment.

THE REGIMENTAL HEADQUARTERS

Major Denis Rollo

By the end of the 1930s, Woolwich had been regarded as the headquarters of the Regiment for well over 200 years, but at no time was there one officer who could be said to be head of the Regiment other than the Master Gunner St James's Park. There was a Director of Artillery in the War Office, but he was a technical staff officer working under the Master General of the Ordnance. There was an Inspector of Artillery, a War Office appointment, who worked to the Military Training Directorate of the War Office. In the old days there had been an Adjutant General RA and then a Deputy Adjutant General RA, but by 1939 this post had been reduced to a Colonel who represented the Regiment in the Adjutant General's Department.

So what was the Headquarters of the Regiment at Woolwich just before the outbreak of war in 1939? It could only have been a combination of the Royal Artillery Institution under the Master Gunner and the Secretary, together with the Commander of the Royal Artillery Depot, Brigadier The Honourable T. P. P. Butler, Commanding 1st and 2nd Training Brigades and the Depot Brigade, and 1st and 2nd Boys' Batteries. The training brigades and the Boys' batteries left Woolwich shortly after the outbreak of war as part of an Army plan to take the training establishments into safer areas. The Depot remained as such for the whole of the war and continued in this role for some years.

The lack of a professional head of the Regiment was remedied in May 1942, when the appointment of Arms Directors in the rank of Major-General for Armour, Artillery, Engineers and Infantry, was approved. The first Director Royal Artillery was Major-General W. J. Eldridge who had been holding the post of Director Anti-Aircraft and Coast Defence Training and Organization in the War Office. Major-General Eldridge was relieved by Major General O. M. Lund in February 1944. The job, however, remained in the War Office until 1964, when all the Arms Directors were rusticated to make way for the new Ministry of Defence (MOD).

The Gunner decision was to move HQ Director Royal Artillery to Woolwich and it occupied the North-West Tower Block at the Royal Military Academy for a while until the accommodation in the Barracks, overlooking the Front Parade was ready. The Commander 18th Training Brigade RA moved to Government House, beside the Common: this was also HQ

Woolwich Garrison, with the same commander. This officer also held the post of Regimental Brigadier for some time. The War Office then noticed that there were three 'red hats' (Army slang for officers of 'star' rank, who wore a red band around their service dress caps) in Woolwich and summoned a deputation to Whitehall to explain itself. The third 'red hat' was the Deputy Director RA, a brigadier. The War Office ordered

that the red hats at Woolwich were to be reduced to two and that the post of Deputy Director was to go.

In 1985, the future of Woolwich was under discussion, as was the future of barracks in London District. There was a view that Chelsea could be sold off, that the occupants, the Foot Guards, could move to Woolwich and the Gunners could go to Larkhill. This will sound a familiar story to those who now know that something approaching this happened, over ten years later. In the event, the 1985 plans were dropped.

In 1993–4, the Army Department of the MOD laid plans for the formation of Arms Centres and the RA Arms Centre was to be at Larkhill. It was then agreed that HQ Director Royal Artillery should move to Larkhill as part of the Centre, all of which would result in manpower savings. At the same time, the rank of Arms Directors was reduced from Major-General to Brigadier and, in the Gunner case, the rank of the Commandant of the Royal School of Artillery was reduced to Colonel. The author of this article was due to retire as a Staff Officer Grade 2 (SO2) Staff Duties and this, rather miraculously, was to take effect at the same time as the move of HQ Director Royal Artillery. When the move day came the SO2 still had two weeks to serve and, in good soldier fashion, decided to stay till the end to direct mail and answer the telephone. On the second Monday he sat down at his desk and lifted the telephone, only to find that it had been cut off.

What might then have been the final blow to Woolwich was an MOD Army Department decision to disband Arms Training Regiments and group them into Army Training Regiments. (In other words, instead of each Arm training its own recruits under its own arrangements, they were all to go through the same basic training together.) It was considered that Arms Depot Regiments were superfluous. Accordingly, on 31 March 1995 the Depot at Woolwich was disbanded, its functions, according to the MOD, having ceased, and the RA Training Regiment facility moved to Pirbright to join the Guards Training Regiment. However, the Master Gunner, General Sir Martin Farndale, wanted to avoid the risk of losing the RA Barracks and asked that a Gunner service regiment be moved into Woolwich: to the surprise of many, this was agreed. In September 1995, 16th Regiment Royal Artillery arrived and 'Gunner Woolwich' got a further reprieve, which lasted 12 years.

While suburban London was not thought to be particularly suitable for an Air Defence Regiment, in true Gunner style 16th Regiment settled into the area well and its soldiers made good use of the excellent travel facilities and entertainment available on their doorstep. The regiment's move to North Luffenham, Rutland, will certainly provide a marked contrast to Woolwich, leaving the Front Parade to look forward to the sound of foot drill commands and the tramping of infantry boots.

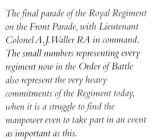

The final parade of the Royal Regiment on the Front Parade, with Lieutenant Colonel A.J.Waller RA in command. The small numbers representing every regiment now in the Order of Battle also represent the very heavy commitments of the Regiment today, when it is a struggle to find the manpower even to take part in an event as important as this.

END OF AN ERA

The final day of the Regiment at Woolwich was, appropriately, 26 May 2007 and the format was reminiscent of the 'At Home' events of yesteryear. For security reasons, it was an all-ticket affair, but there was a large gathering of Gunners past and present who made the effort to be present at the farewell. They were rewarded by displays in the arena by The King's Troop, Royal Horse Artillery, re-enactions of period artillery, motorcycle dare-devilry and impressive parachuting, together with the usual refreshment marquees and performances by the Royal Artillery Band.

After lunch the main event got under way on the Front Parade in front of massed stands of spectators. Despite heavy operational commitments, over 400 serving officers and soldiers marched onto the Front Parade. They were accompanied by a large contingent from the Retired Regiment who, led by the Controller, Maj-Gen Mike Shellard, and with their Standards flying, marched proudly past the inspecting officers, FM Lord Vincent and The Master Gunner St James's Park, Gen Sir Alex Harley.

In a final poignant act, the Union Flag and Regimental Standard – flown proudly over the South Arch for the past 291 years – were slowly lowered to the haunting notes of 'The Day Thou Gavest' and the Last Post, after which they were folded and handed for safekeeping to the GOC London District and the Director Royal Artillery respectively. Then, with the sound of their final gun salute still echoing among the deserted

buildings, The King's Troop, Royal Horse Artillery, rode slowly and quietly off the Front Parade, the final formal act of closing the Regimental Home at Woolwich.

The weather had been dull most of the day, but it started to drizzle during the parade: by the time of the final gun salute, the heavens had opened and the rain fell in earnest, creating a sad and solemn scene, somehow fitting for the Royal Regiment's farewell to its home for so many years.

KAT

All: The King's Troop RHA marches past, the final event marking the closure of the Royal Artillery 'home' on 26 May 2007. The stiff breeze shows the Union Flag to advantage, but the drizzling rain dampened the spirits and added to the sense of sadness at the end of a long era.

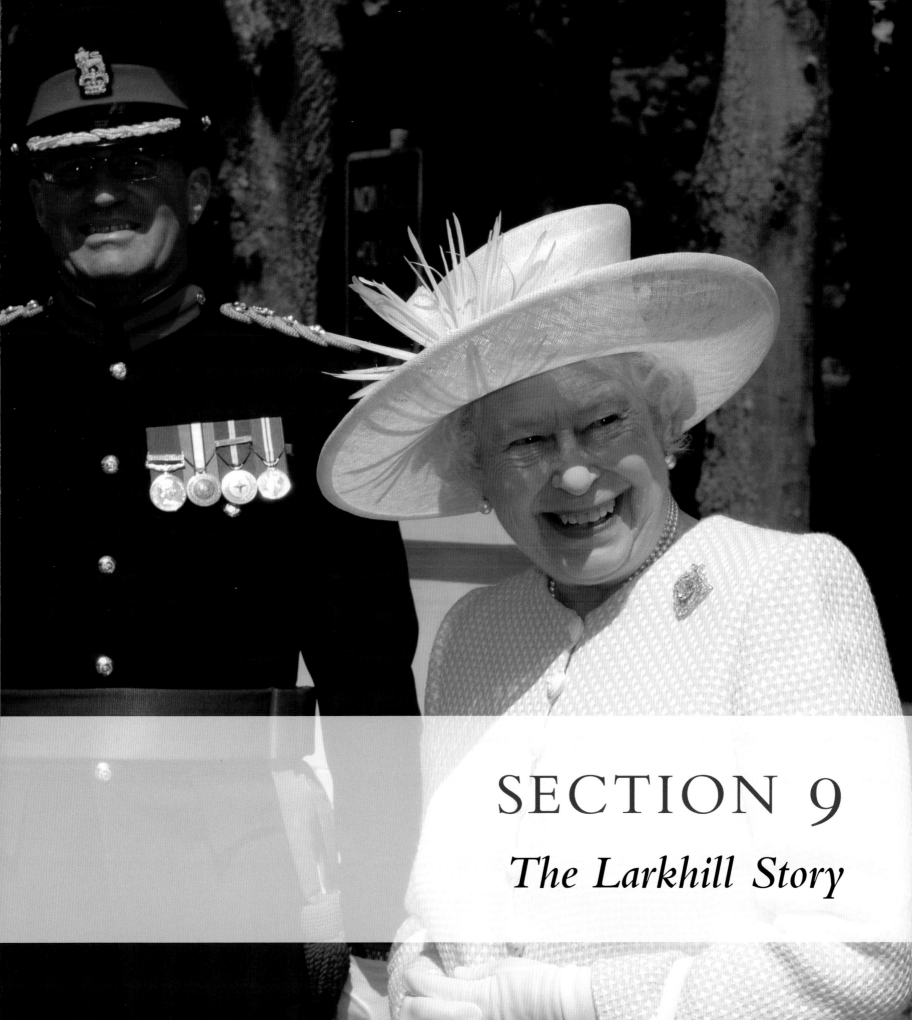

SECTION 9
The Larkhill Story

MOVE OF THE REGIMENTAL HOME

Major Edward Ellis Jones MBE

Headquarters Director Royal Artillery (HQ DRA) moved from Woolwich to Larkhill in the summer of 1994 under the then Director of Royal Artillery, Major-General Ian Durie. This left Regimental HQ RA and the Charities at Woolwich on their own and at that time there were no plans to move the Royal Regiment of Artillery as a whole from Woolwich to Larkhill.

However, after a Defence Estates Review by the Ministry of Defence, the Secretary of State announced in September 2003 that Woolwich was to close by April 2008. Following a decision taken at the Master Gunner's Committee on 19 November 2003, the Master Gunner wrote to the Chief of the General Staff and declared the Gunners' strategic intent to embrace Larkhill as the future location of our Regimental Home.

The Regiment had been in Woolwich since 1716 and had accumulated vast amounts of property, including the stored items from disbanded units and units in suspended animation. The real estate occupied by the Regiment in Woolwich had afforded the space required to display and store such items with relative ease and security. It was now obvious that all this property would have to be appropriately accounted for, moved, stored or displayed at Larkhill, where space was at a greater premium.

A Project Officer, initially Lieutenant Colonel Tony Mott, was appointed and five boards were formed, headed by retired senior officers of the Regiment to examine the following areas:

- Regimental property such as monuments and guns within the RA Barracks and the immediate vicinity
- RA Disbanded Units Property
- BRA Officers' Mess, Woolwich
- RA Institution Property
- Warrant Officers' and Sergeants' Mess, Woolwich

Lieutenant Colonel Tony Mott handed over his duties to Lieutenant Colonel Phil Everitt in March 2005, and the work was completed by November 2005.

Under the Regimental Colonel, Lieutenant Colonel James Gower, RHQ RA completed its move to Larkhill in December 2005, and was swiftly followed by the Royal Artillery Institution and the Royal Artillery Association, which were both installed at Larkhill next to the Director's Headquarters. At the same

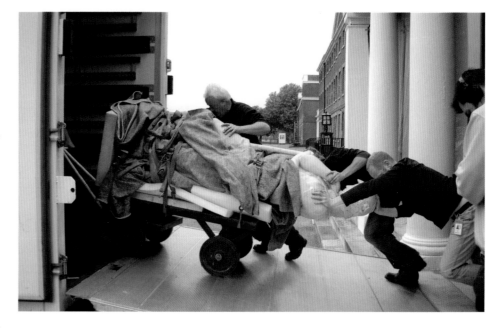

Wrapped up for the journey, Armed Science on her way to Larkhill.

time, the Regimental Secretary, Colonel Nick Richards, retired and his post was taken up by Colonel Nick Quarrelle.

With the work of the Regimental Boards complete, the Regimental Home Committee was constituted in March 2006 to oversee and direct all aspects of the move of the Regimental Home from Woolwich to Larkhill, under the direction of The Master Gunner.

The Move

During the summer of 2005, the move began with the gradual transfer of Regimental property from Woolwich. In late 2005 and early 2006, the property of the Disbanded Units and Regimental Artillery Institution was moved into a purpose-built secure store at Larkhill. During 2006, two valuable stained-glass windows were also removed from the Chapel of St Michael and All Angels at the Old Royal Military Academy and installed in the Church of St Alban the Martyr at Larkhill. Pews and other artefacts were also removed from the Chapel prior to the old Royal Military Academy site being sold for development.

Following the 'Farewell to Woolwich' Parade on 26 May 2007, the move began in earnest. The four large dining tables in the Officers' Mess were dismantled the very next day in preparation for the removal of the chandeliers and the statue

Above: The new Silver Room at the RA Mess, Larkhill.

Bottom right: Armed Science in her new home in the Mess Room, Larkhill.

Armed Science. The property to be moved was not just limited to the furniture and artefacts normally housed in the Headquarters Officers' Mess and Central Warrant Officers' and Sergeants' Mess at Woolwich; some significant and extremely large pieces of Regimental heritage were to be relocated to the new Regimental Home at Larkhill. The movement of property involved both Regimental personnel and, for the more complex and valuable items, specialist contractors. Some of the highlights of the move of Regimental property are covered in greater detail below.

Chandeliers

Any visions of a comedy fiasco (remember that *Only Fools and Horses* television episode?) during the removal of the five large chandeliers, which hung in the Dining Room of the Officers' Mess, were quickly dispelled. Experts whose pedigree included chandelier removal at Westminster Abbey, the Vatican and the White House, painstakingly dismantled each chandelier piece by piece, carefully cataloguing and wrapping each component prior to their going for extensive cleaning and the subsequent move and installation at Larkhill.

Regimental Silver

Before the Royal Artillery Mess Silver Collection could be brought to Larkhill a purpose-built secure silver room was needed in the Officers' Mess. This was completed in August 2007, with the funding for the build being met by Headquarters Land Command. Shortly afterwards, the entire collection was moved to Larkhill amid great security. It must be emphasized that unlike most museum exhibits which remain solely on display, a large quantity of the silver is put to almost daily use both in the Royal Artillery Mess and elsewhere.

'Armed Science'

The marble statue Armed Science was commissioned by Colonel R.A. Shafto Adair (later Lord Waveney) who commanded the Suffolk Artillery Militia. He presented it to the Royal Artillery Mess in 1855. As the statue had been in its place at Woolwich since 1862, very little was known of its construction and configuration until dismantling began. To the contractors' relief, Armed Science came apart relatively easily in a series of manageable pieces for the move and subsequent installation in the dining room of the Headquarters Royal Artillery Mess, Larkhill.

Antique Ordnance

The collection of antique ordnance comprising eight cannon and two mortars that lined the far edge of the Front Parade at Woolwich has now been relocated to various positions at Larkhill. Due to the age and delicate nature of this ordnance, specialist contractors and equipment were used for the move. The largest piece of ordnance, the Bhurtpore Gun, which was captured at the storming of the Indian fortress of Bhurtpore in 1826, weighs 21 tonnes.

Kettledrum Banners

This pair of kettledrum banners, dating from the early 18th century, is among the oldest possessions of the Royal Artillery, and is considered unique as a surviving pair of this age. Banners such as this would be draped around the kettledrums that were used to control the trains of artillery in the field. This particular pair of banners was in the procession at the funeral of the Duke of Marlborough, Master General of the Ordnance, in 1722. The delicate condition of these banners necessitated some major conservation work before being moved to Larkhill. The fully restored kettledrum banners are now displayed in the Royal Artillery Headquarters Mess.

Dickson Memorial

Three memorials were also on the removals manifest, the largest – weighing approximately 70 tonnes – being the Dickson Memorial. Dedicated to the achievements of two of the Regiment's Master Gunners, Major General Sir Alexander Dickson and his son General Sir Collingwood Dickson VC, this memorial stood at the southern edge of the Front Parade. For the contractor tasked with the move there were a few unknowns as to the actual weight of each stone and what might be at the core of the memorial. These were only answered once the memorial was being dismantled for the move to Larkhill.

Above: The dining room in the RA Mess at Larkhill, showing the Georgian chandeliers, furniture and pictures from Woolwich, with Armed Science in place at the far end of the room.

Top right: The kettledrum banners, now on the staircase leading from the entrance hall to the dining room in the RA Mess (See page 9).

Right: The Dickson Memorial on the approach road to the Headquarters at Larkhill.

Left: The 18-in howitzer ordnance being lowered onto its mounting, following its move to Larkhill. The ordnance alone weighs almost as much as two battle tanks.

Below, left and right: the set of Florentine guns and the Bhurtpore gun in their new positions.

Bottom: An aerial view of the Larkhill garrison, looking west. The RA Mess complex is in the centre of the picture.

Railway Gun

Of all the items of Regimental property, the move of the 18-inch 'Railway Gun' required the most planning due to its size and weight. With a total length of almost 16 metres and an all-up weight of 180 tonnes, the move involved the services of a myriad of agencies to get its transportation to Larkhill under way. This piece of ordnance is the sole survivor of five built from 1917 for service on the Western Front. They were the largest pieces of ordnance to enter Land Service. This particular howitzer was completed in 1919, too late for the First World War and strictly speaking, it is on a proof mounting rather than an operational railway mounting, It was used for proof firings at Shoeburyness (the range at the mouth of the Thames), which culminated in the firing of 1,000lb aircraft bombs in the 1940s and 1950s. The move was completed in May 2008 and the Railway Gun now sits by the sports pitches. Its arrival marked the conclusion of a complex operation and the scene was now set for the formal opening of the new Regimental Home by the Captain General.

The railway gun on its track beside the sports field at Larkhill.

HISTORY OF TRAINING AT LARKHILL

Colonel C.J. Nicholls and Major G.D. Shapland RA

Practice on the Plain c.1900, using 12-pounder rifled breech loading guns.

Right: 'A' Mess, replaced in the 1930s by the new RA Mess, but remaining in use for many years thereafter and known to many old Gunners as the Young Officers' Mess.

Far right: Heavy howitzers at practice on the Plain c.1917.

The Origins of Gunner Training

In the early part of the 19th century, gunnery training was conducted at Woolwich, with live firing taking place on Woolwich Common. By 1860 the conduct of live firing was restricted to Plumstead Marshes at Woolwich and the School of Gunnery at Shoeburyness (at the mouth of the Thames), established on 1 April 1859. The need for more training areas was identified in the latter half of the 19th century, with the result that Okehampton Camp (Devon) was established in 1875. By 1899, 22,000 acres had been acquired in Wiltshire on Salisbury Plain and the first practice camp had taken place.

The typical rolling countryside of the Plain proved ideal for the purpose of training field gunners. Generations of them have struggled with map-reading their way around its perimeter as

they search for gun positions and observation posts from which to engage targets in the 'Impact Area'. The daunting vista of bare ridges littered with odd bits of scrap, old tank hulls, bushes and white shell scrapes meant that, in the past, few were able to dispense with the traditional 'ranging' or 'adjustment of fire' in order to get their guns on target: modern technology has changed all that. In the distance, woods on the skyline provide reference points for instructors to indicate targets, while the many curiously shaped plantations become 'wagon lines' or offer shelter for those needing to 'hide' from all-seeing aircraft or unmanned air vehicles. In wet weather, driving off road can be a real challenge in the deep, clinging mud and, in the dry, white chalk dust seems to coat everything and everyone.

Larkhill is aptly named and the sound of birdsong fills the air. Far from city pollution, the atmosphere is clear and, on a sunny day, the panoramic views are breathtaking. (On an inclement day, views can be very short range and the rain is often horizontal!) There is an amazing amount of wild life on the Plain, too, much of it surviving unscathed within the Impact Area, despite the constant deluge of shellfire. Strenuous attempts are made to maintain the ecology, not least in reintroducing the famous great bustards, although they are hard to spot and are easy prey for foxes.

Early Days

As early as 1900, the value of the new training area on Salisbury Plain had been identified and a proposal to move the School to Netheravon village on its east side had been approved by the Adjutant General and the Secretary of State. However, objections

from Shoeburyness delayed the move and it was not until 1915 that the School of Gunnery for the Royal Horse and Royal Field Artillery moved to Larkhill. The staff under the first Chief Instructor, Brevet Lieutenant Colonel W. Ellershaw RA, consisted of two major instructors, four captain instructors and a quartermaster.

In January 1920 the Chapperton Down Artillery School, the Heavy Artillery Gunnery School and the School for Instruction for Royal Horse and Royal Field Artillery were amalgamated to form the School of Artillery under the first Commandant, Brigadier-General H.W. Newcome DSO. In 1921 the Siege Artillery School moved from Lydd (Kent) to Larkhill. The staff by that time was made up of a commandant, brigade major, staff captain, adjutant, assistant adjutant, quartermaster, two chief instructors in gunnery, six major instructors in gunnery (artillery), two major instructors in gunnery (survey), seven captain instructors in gunnery (artillery), two captain instructors in gunnery (survey) and a superintendent of experiments. The number of courses was developed and expanded to include eight courses for officers, including the Gunnery Staff, Brigade Commanders and Counter Bombardment courses, while a further eight courses for soldiers included the Battery Staff, Permanent Staff Instructors and Survey courses.

Major-General John Younger CB (Adjutant of the School in 1921) wrote the following letter to *The Gunner* magazine in July 1971 giving us a glimpse of those days:

General Newcome was of course the creator of the School of Artillery and the founder of the great reputation which it now enjoys; he was a great Gunner and a fine administrator. He gathered in all the wartime schools like Chapperton Down Artillery School, and formed them in one Artillery School. We all loved him and were proud to have him as our Commandant. He it was who obtained Major Macleod from the Sappers to teach us about Survey; a brilliant and charming man who laid the foundations of our well-known Regimental Survey. Indeed

when saying goodbye to him some years later the Commandant remarked that he was so efficient and nice that he might almost be a Gunner.

There were no civilians at the School in those days, so the Regimental Sergeant Major had a large number of soldiers under him. One of them was the General's batman, known throughout India as 'Anderson Sahib' when the General was Major-General RA there. He was a Royal Marine formerly, but was mobilized into a field battery and given a pair of horses to look after. He said 'Beg pardon Sergeant but how do I go about these 'ere, there weren't any of them in my last ship.'

We were true pioneers in those days, there were no shops at Larkhill, and the only available transport was Ranger's bus from Durrington. We did not enjoy the luxury of today, life was more simple, but we were very happy.

Above: HM King George VI, accompanied by Queen Elizabeth, watching practice on Salisbury Plain in April 1941. Judging from the Queen's protective hands and the direction of their Majesties' gaze, it was probably an anti-aircraft engagement.

The Second World War

The 1939–45 war saw the next major change to the School, when it was decentralized and the Wings were formed. By 1942, the School was made up of the following:

Headquarters Wing
Gunnery Wing
Air Wing
Anti-Tank Wing
Tactics Wing
Survey Wing
Equipment Wing
(A 'Young Officers' Wing was added shortly after the end of the war).

Their Majesties King George VI and Queen Elizabeth visited the School on 3 April 1941 and spent the morning looking at the ranges, Gun Park and miniature range. As it had snowed the previous night, they were transported round the ranges in a staff car with chains, rather than run the risk of getting the royal vehicle stuck. In April the following year, the Prime Minister, Mr Winston Churchill visited the School, chiefly to see the 6-pounder anti-tank gun in action.

From the 1960s to the Millennium

The year 1961 saw the adoption of the crossed cannons surmounted by St Edward's (or the Queen's) Crown as the official insignia of the School. It was also in the 1960s that, at long last, the buildings at Larkhill were transformed from long, wooden huts to their modern, much smarter style, including new offices, instruction facilities and gun parks. The building containing the main lecture theatre was appropriately named Newcome Hall after the first commandant.

Knighton Down, on the northwest corner of the garrison area, became well-known as a demonstration area for the general public as well as for visiting courses from other arms schools. With tiered seating and space for arena displays of equipment and clear views across a specially cleared impact area for demonstrations of firepower, there was a constant demand for visiting regiments and batteries to make up the required numbers to put on an impressive show. The facility remains, but the costs have risen enormously since the days of the 25-pounder and the huge surplus of ammunition remaining after the war, so there have been no such grand displays since 2002.

In 1970, the 50th anniversary of the School of Artillery, Her Majesty the Queen conferred upon the School the title 'Royal

Left: The RA Mess, seen against a background of Knighton Down and the training area.

Below: The Royal Artillery Hunt meets.

School of Artillery'. On 3 April 1973 The Captain General visited Larkhill, looking around the Gun Park and the workshops before having luncheon in the RA Mess. She spent the afternoon at the RA Point-to-Point (cross-country horse steeplechase).

In 1971 the School of Anti-Aircraft Artillery at Manorbier, in South Wales, closed and was relocated at Larkhill, bringing with it the development of a large new facility. (The range at Manorbier is still used.)

By 1983, the School looked more like today's establishment with the headquarters (including Developments, the Battlefield Artillery Target Engagement System Military Team and the RA Mounted Band) and the following wings:

Gunnery
Tactics
Guided Weapons
Signals
Royal Electrical and Mechanical Engineers (REME)
Young Officers
Support Regiment
Locating Battery

Since shortly after the establishment of the School, the provision of personnel and equipment to support courses and to run the range had been the responsibility of a regular regiment posted for that purpose to Larkhill for a fixed period. The first unit to carry out the role of Depot Brigade was 15 Brigade Royal Field Artillery, and 17 brigades or regiments held the appointment until 1982, when the Support Regiment, Royal School of Artillery was formed. It was renamed 14th Regiment RA in October 1984, and the regiment has fulfilled the task to this day.

There were two significant changes in the 1990s. First, the consolidation of the various ranges and training areas on

Salisbury Plain into the Army Field Training Centre Salisbury Plain in 1991, marked the end of Gunner 'ownership' of the Plain. Indeed, extensive use of the Plain for manoeuvre training means that the School now has to compete directly with other users for range space. Second, the School was joined by HQ DRA in 1994. This coincided with wider changes that put training on a more formal footing, on a pan-Defence basis, which led to the arrival of Royal Artillery Training Policy Branch at Larkhill, were the beginnings of the integrated structure that is in place today.

The 21st Century

The final change occurred in 2004, after an MOD study, which was designed to identify the benefits, or otherwise, of Directorates operating more closely with their Schools. Larkhill was the trial site, and the main thrust of the study was a reorganization of responsibilities, for example, the Commandant became the focus for all artillery training and was far more closely aligned with HQ DRA. The trial resulted in an increased synergy between training policy and delivery and kept training firmly in the Regiment's eye.

Today, the School comprises the following elements under the Headquarters:

Targeting Branch
Strike Branch
Artillery Command Systems Branch
Young Officers Branch
14th Regiment RA, with
A Firing Battery (34th (Seringapatam) Battery RA)
An Equipment Battery (1st Battery RA 'The Blazers')
A Phase 2 Training Battery (24th (Irish) Battery RA)
REME Wing

So much, for policy and organization – what about delivery of training?

Training Delivery

The 17th Training Regiment ceased training soldiers at Woolwich in 1994. Army policy directed a centralization of soldiers' Phase 1 (recruit) training, which is now conducted at Harrogate, Pirbright or Winchester, where Gunner recruits rub shoulders with peers from across the whole Army. Subsequent individual training is carried out at Larkhill, namely Phase 2 (initial individual special to Arm) training and Phase 3 (individual career) training. 24 (Irish) Battery RA became the Phase 2 training battery in 1994 and continues in that role today.

Below: A firing demonstration in progress, with 105mm Light Guns alongside a battery of 155mm AS90 self-propelled guns.

Below right: Fitness training, the Gunners shown here manhandling a Light Gun.

The content of initial special to Arm Individual training has evolved in parallel. Perhaps the most radical change is also the most recent, implemented on 1 April 2008. The new Phase 2 training syllabus comprises a ten-week 'one size fits all' package, which provides a soldier who is both a driver and communicator. All initial platform (gun, missile, radar, etc.) training is conducted in regiments. While this might seem heresy to some, the new package has been well received by regiments, who send their soldiers back to the School for subsequent training on equipment.

Contemporary Training

Cooperation between the Services has never been at a higher level and this is reflected in training. Not only must the contemporary Gunner be master of his/her artillery speciality, but he/she must be able to bring to bear artillery skills in a Tri-Service ('Joint') environment and indeed learn how the other Services operate.

A good example is to be found in Ground Based Air Defence (GBAD). It is only the Gunners who are now equipped with a surface-to-air missile system, but the single regiment (16th Regiment RA) is commanded by a Joint HQ, established at High Wycombe, Buckinghamshire, in 2005. Although training on the equipment (Rapier Field Standard C) is delivered by the Royal School of Artillery personnel permanently stationed with the Regiment, training objectives satisfy both Army and RAF requirements and the rigorous evaluation regime is based largely on former RAF practice.

Simulation is being used more and more in training at the School as technology improves. The School is equipped with a variety of systems, which can represent the capabilities of all RA equipment as well as relevant systems from the rest of the Army, the Royal Navy and RAF. Students can be subjected to high-pressure training and then be shown how they fared on 'playback'.

That said, live firing remains a vital element of most courses. A typical year sees the firing of over 22,000 rounds of 105mm and 155mm, together with 15,000 rounds of 14.5mm sub-calibre ammunition. Additionally, some 5,000 81mm mortar rounds will be fired by the Infantry in support of the School. The total cost is in the order of £15 million.

In parallel to military training, increased attention has been directed to providing opportunities for RA soldiers to gain

nationally recognized civilian qualifications. These include apprenticeships and a range of academic qualifications. There is relevance both to a soldier's military role and subsequent civilian career, which is an incentive for retention. The Regiment provides the Army standard; the Royal Artillery Centre for Personal Development was established as a Gunner charity in 1998 and has been recognized nationally. Its main HQ is at Larkhill, where Phase 2 soldiers develop and support their literacy and numeracy skills, prior to their first posting. It has also established a learning centre in each Gunner regiment, managed by qualified teachers, exporting training to where the soldier lives, which is a concept also used by the School for some military courses, to reduce turbulence between operational tours.

The Influence of Operations

The high level of commitment by the Regiment to current operations is recorded elsewhere. The School has been proactive in learning lessons from returning regiments and batteries and indeed has sent instructors to theatres of operation.

New courses have been devised to meet the requirement for the control and coordination of fire support from aircraft of all nations, as well as land-based systems (known as 'Joint Fires'). The Forward Observation Officers (FOO) Course has been developed to meet the needs of Fire Support Team (FST) Commanders, who conduct this task on operations.

Further new courses have been written to prepare soldiers to deploy with equipment that has been rapidly procured under 'Urgent Operational Requirement' procedures, such as Unmanned Air Vehicles (UAVs), and radars. Finally, many regiments have re-roled, for instance from air defence to UAV and from 155mm self-propelled artillery to 105mm towed artillery.

In Summary

The Royal School of Artillery is certainly smaller than in the past, but its personnel deliver a more diverse range of training than ever before and to a wider audience – the Regiment, the Army, the other UK Services and to personnel drawn from a variety of nations, some of whom would have been part of 'red forces' in exercises held earlier in its history. Life is, as ever, a balance: in addition to the core activity of military training, sport and extramural activities, including for example the RA Hunt, are pursued with enthusiasm as a counterbalance to the demands of operations and the associated training.

Demand for training has increased hugely, but the challenges described above and indeed many others have all been met and overcome, often at very short notice, by a mix of professionalism and determination. The Royal School of Artillery approaches its Centenary in high spirits and with optimism, as part of the Regimental Home.

Future instructors undergoing training on the High Velocity Missile air defence system.

The Regiment Today

Colonel C.J. Nicholls

Above: Counter Rocket Artillery and Mortar (C-RAM) system deployed in Iraq.

Far right: Lightweight Counter Mortar Radar (LCMR).

consequence of the very high operational demands on the Regiment, deployment in what was called the *secondary* (infantry) role, in which Gunners performed with distinction for the duration of operations in Northern Ireland and latterly in Iraq, is not undertaken today.

Contemporary terminology describes our roles as *primary* or *tertiary*. The former describes situations such as when a Light Gun regiment deploys with its Light Guns or a Surveillance and Target Acquisition regiment deploys with its usual equipment. The latter covers situations when a regiment re-roles to another artillery equipment, such as an AS90 self-propelled gun regiment deploying with Light Gun, or a Close Air Defence regiment deploying with mini- Unmanned Air Vehicles (UAVs).

The seven TA regiments continue to provide vital support to their Regular counterparts as follows: close support – 100th, 103rd and 105th Regiments RA (Volunteer); WLR and MLRS – 100th Regiment RA(V); Air Defence – 106th Regiment RA(V); Surveillance & Target Acquisition patrols, which provide intelligence from behind enemy lines, and HQ liaison parties – the Honourable Artillery Company (HAC).

Size, Shape and Location

The Royal Artillery of 2008 has an establishment of approximately 7,000 and hence represents about 7 per cent of the Army. There are 15 Regular regiments, 7 Territorial Army (TA) regiments, together with The King's Troop RHA and the Royal Artillery Band, who remain central elements of national pageantry. Those who remember the concentration of regiments in the British Army of the Rhine may be very surprised to know that, by the autumn of 2008, only two regiments will remain in Germany – 3rd Regiment Royal Horse Artillery in Hohne and 26th Regiment RA in Gütersloh. By contrast, those who remember a regiment permanently based in Northern Ireland (22nd Light Anti-Aircraft Regiment left Omagh in September 1959) may well be glad to know that 40th Regiment RA is now based in Lisburn.

Roles and Equipment

The Regiment conducts a wide variety of roles; 40 per cent of deployable regiments do not serve guns and the Army is most grateful for the capabilities that we provide. Indeed, as a

However, the prevailing situation is not that simple. New requirements have arisen from the demands of current operations. Several new and significant pieces of equipment were introduced into service in 2007 in less than six months.

The Guided MLRS provides much longer range and pinpoint accuracy with rockets guided by global positioning technology; fewer rockets are needed to defeat targets, while the risk of collateral damage is reduced. The Counter Rocket Artillery and Mortar (C-RAM) capability uses a rapid firing cannon to defeat the indirect fire threat to bases.

Unmanned Air Vehicles (UAVs) are remotely controlled and provide commanders with high-quality visual and electro-optical live pictures of the battlefield 'over the hill'. There are two variants, the Hermes 450 TUAV, and the Desert Hawk III Mini UAV. The former flies for longer and requires a runway to take off and to land, while the latter cannot stay aloft for as long and is launched by hand from forward areas. Another high-technology surveillance device is the Lightweight Counter Mortar Radar, which detects mortar baseplates in any direction.

We are leading the Army's development of Fire Support Teams, which provide critical support to operations through the coordination and integration of mortars, guns, rockets,

If regiments deployed in primary role only, the equipment manned by Regular regiments of the Royal Artillery is:

Light Gun (105mm towed gun)	7 (Para) Regt RHA; 29 Cdo Regt RA; 40 Regt RA
AS90 (155 mm self propelled howitzer)	1RHA; 3 RHA; 4 Regt RA; 19 Regt RA; 26 Regt RA
Rapier (Medium altitude Surface to Air missile)	16 Regt RA
High Velocity Missile (Close Air Defence missile)	12 Regt RA; 47 Regt RA
Multi Launch Rocket System (MLRS – Surface to Surface missile)	39 Regt RA
Weapon Locating Radars (WLR), Advanced Sound Ranging, Surveillance & Target Acquisition patrols	5 Regt RA
Tactical UAV (TUAV)	32 Regt RA
Almost all of the above (for training support)	14 Regt RA

helicopters and fixed-wing aircraft. They have been equipped with a variety of new equipment to supplement the already highly computerized command and control systems operated by the Regiment.

AS90 self-propelled guns on exercise on Salisbury Plain.

Right: Afghanistan – a rocket being fired from a Guided MLRS launcher.

Far right: The Falklands – a Rapier missile being fired in practice.

Below right: Weapon Locating Radar.

Below far right: A Tactical Unmanned Air Vehicle (TUAV), Hermes, on the runway.

Operations

The RA contribution to Operation 'Telic' in Iraq remains significant. Primary roles were used to great effect during the invasion, after which regiments deployed in the secondary (infantry) role. This ceased in 2007 and the RA presence now provides essential force protection and intelligence, surveillance and target acquisition support, comprising both mini and tactical UAVs and weapon-locating radar. There is also a strike capability with a troop of AS90 self-propelled guns to engage firing points and C-RAM to engage munitions in flight.

Over the past 12 months, Operation 'Herrick' in Afghanistan has witnessed an increase in deployed RA personnel, with a

Training Fire Support teams at Larkhill.

continuous Light Gun presence of two gun batteries, an HQ battery and additional fire support teams. It is worth noting that since the initial deployment of six light guns with 7th Parachute Regiment RHA in the middle of 2006, when it was hoped by politicians that we would not have to fire a shot, as at March 2008, we have fired some 25,000 rounds of 105mm ammunition.

Guided Multi Launch Rocket System is now in theatre with 39th Regiment and has fired in support of both pre-planned operations and, due to the precision achieved by the rockets, very close to troops in contact. Mini and tactical UAVs again provide remote imagery of wide areas of the areas of operation, to supplement intelligence gained by the Lightweight Counter Mortar Radar and the men of the surveillance and target acquisition patrols. Personnel from 16th Regiment RA are deployed as part of the Recognized Air Picture Troop, which provides essential information to staff coordinating the use of airspace by manned aircraft, unmanned air vehicles, helicopters and various munitions. At times, the old adage of 'big sky, small bullet' is far too simplistic a statement. These initiatives complement and supplement existing capabilities, which have themselves been developed and refined. All in all, the RA now provides commanders with significant additional combat power.

Finally, in both theatres, Gunners are instructing local forces to conduct operations themselves. One interesting example is the training of soldiers from the Afghan National Army to operate the 122mm Soviet D-30 howitzer, many of which were ranged against us across the North West German Plain not that long ago! Obtaining the relevant firing tables and gun drill books was an interesting challenge for the Sergeant Major Instructors in Gunnery.

Not to be forgotten is the enduring requirement to provide Rapier air defence cover to the Falkland Islands. This is provided by the one unit across the three Services to be

An AS90 155mm self-propelled gun on operations in Basra, Iraq.

equipped with this system (16th Regiment), in addition to its commitments in both Iraq and Afghanistan. This is but one example of the pressures facing regimental commanders today and the times between tours are well below 'government guidelines' of 24 months. This has been the case for some time and will remain so for the foreseeable future.

Consequently, the need for the TA has been reinforced. The TA continues to provide essential support to operations; the requirement to provide 68 personnel per operational rotation is a challenge, but one that it is relishing. TA soldiers are being deployed increasingly in their primary role and close links are being forged between the TA and the regular regiments they support, which is excellent – the TA is being ever more closely integrated into our regular Order of Battle. The year 2008 will see formed gun detachments from the TA close support regiments deploy in support of Operation 'Herrick' for the first time.

Unfortunately, our success on operations comes with a human cost; 6 Gunners have been killed and 30 wounded on operations over the past 12 months [AQ2]. The Regimental charities are fully involved in providing benevolence and welfare; through their actions, over £2 million was made available to deserving cases, both to the old and the not so old in 2007.

Conclusion

To conclude, the Regiment has been fully involved in every Army deployment since the end of the Cold War. In 2008 batteries or regiments are deployed in the Falkland Islands, Iraq and Afghanistan. Personnel are deployed as individuals more widely still. Between tours, regiments and batteries must return to the primary role, which requires individual and collective training, better to qualify people who are the lifeblood of the Royal Regiment. Additional tasks such as Ceremonial Duty at Buckingham Palace, St James's Palace and the Tower of London are given to batteries and discharged with style. Sport is still played; expeditions are still mounted – 'all work and no play' is not the way ahead.

The Regiment is proud of its past; its recent contributions to the Army and to Defence are highly relevant and widely valued – the operational awards list and recent citations bear witness to that. Yet every member constantly looks to the future, to new organizations, new tactics, new equipment and new opportunities.

The Regiment's mottoes 'Ubique' (Everywhere) and 'Quo Fas et Gloria Ducunt' (Where Right and Glory Lead) are as relevant now as they have ever been and will continue to be so.

Left: Observation Party on operations in Afghanistan.

Below: A Light Gun in action.

THE QUEEN'S VISIT 2008

On June 12, 2008, The Queen, Captain-General of the Royal Regiment of Artillery, formally opened the new regimental home of the Royal Artillery during a visit to the Royal Artillery Barracks, Larkhill.

This was an occasion rich in ceremonial and symbolism. After a Royal Salute fired by The King's Troop Royal Horse Artillery, Her Majesty unveiled a new entrance stone before becoming symbolically the first person to enter to the newly named Royal Artillery Barracks.

Having inspected a Guard of Honour to the accompaniment of the Regimental band, Her Majesty went on to meet with soldiers who have had recent operational experience in Iraq and Afghanistan along with those who have been on deployment in other parts of the world.

Far right: HM The Queen inspects the Guard of Honour provided by 1st Regiment Royal Horse Artillery.

Below: HM The Queen arrives by helicopter.

Below right: A salute by The King's Troop Royal Horse Artillery.

After lunch in the Officers' Mess, where the Royal Standard flew from the masthead, Her Majesty sat for photographs with the RA Senior Command as Captain-General, before joining a Garden Party attended by serving and retired Gunners and their families, along with guests from Canada, Australia and New Zealand.

A splendid day culminated in The Queen signing the Visitors' Book before being driven off to a waiting helicopter. With Her Majesty on board, the helicopter performed a farewell circuit of the ground – an unforgettable conclusion to this key moment in the Regiment's evolution.

KAT

Scenes during HM The Queen's visit to Larkhill, unveiling the new entrance stone, being shown displays of equipment and ending in her enjoyment of an informal all-ranks garden party amid a large gathering of Gunners from far and wide. The silver vase (top right) was presented to Her Majesty to mark the occasion.

LIST OF SUBSCRIBERS

This book has been made possible through the generosity of the following subscribers. The suffix RA or RHA after an officer's name denotes a serving officer; the word 'retired' has been omitted for officers throughout the list as it is required only in official documents.

106 Regt RA (V)
206 (Ulster) Battery RA(V)
207 (City of Glasgow) Battery RA(V)
212 (Highland) Battery RA(V)
3rd Regiment Royal Horse Artillery
47th Regiment, Royal Artillery
P.E. Abbott Esq.
Lieutenant Colonel H.C. Abela MBE
Brigadier K.D. Abraham
B. Adamson Esq.
Lieutenant Colonel The Hon.
  L.R. Addington DFC
Captain R.P. Agombar TD CG
P. A'Hearne Esq.
J.G. Aird TD
F. Allen Esq.
Major N. Allen
The Honourable Sir Peter Allen
Major D. Allmond
Major (QM) J.T. Anderson
Brigadier M.G.R. Anderson MBE
Captain R.C.R. Anderson
T.S. Archer Esq.
Major D.F.M. Archibald
Bombardier J.E. Armitage
Sergeant S.I. Arnold
Colonel W.H. Atkins OBE
Major J.C. Auckland-Lewis
Lieutenant Colonel G. Avery
Mrs L.A. Ayers
Lieutenant Colonel R.C. Ayers OBE
C.E. Bacon
Lieutenant B. Bader
Lieutenant Colonel J. Bagshawe-Mattei
Major General J.B.A. Bailey CB MBE
Brigadier D.A.T. Baines MBE
D.R. Baker Esq.

R. Baker Esq.
J.D. Baldwin TD DL
A.W. Ball Esq.
P.E. Ballard Esq.
R. Ballentine Esq.
D.M. Barnard Esq.
Lieutenant Colonel M. Barnes OBE TD
Major A.J. Barron TD
Major General R.L. Barrons CBE
P. Batterbury Esq.
Fife-Major J. Bayne
M.J. Beaver Esq.
Lieutenant Colonel I.R. Bell RHA
T. Bell Esq.
Colonel A.D. Bennett
J.A. Bennett Esq.
Colonel J.S. Bennett OBE
Ex Bombardier B.N. Bentley
Major General G.W. Berragan
J.H. Bessell Esq.
Lieutenant Colonel J. Biles MBE
Captain J. Binzer
M.A. Birch Esq.
J.A. Bird Esq.
P. Bishop Esq.
M.C. Black Esq.
H. Blackham Esq.
L/Sgt H.G. Blackham
P.W. Blackwell Esq.
N.C. Bladon Esq.
In memory of Lieutenant Colonel
  K.M. Blanchard RA
Captain R.S. Blandford
S.J.W. Blofeld Esq.
S.A. Blyth Esq.
Captain D. Boehm
J.R. Booth Esq.

F.D. Bottomley TD
Lieutenant Colonel C.J. Boulter OBE MC
G.H. Bowthorpe Esq.
T.V.C. Boxall Esq.
W.C. Boyles MSM
Major J.D. Braisby
Colonel J. Brake
Colonel William J.F. Bramble OBE
B. Brealey Esq.
Colonel R.M. Brennan
D. Brighton Esq.
D. Broad Esq.
Major E.G. St J. Brockman
Brigadier E.C. Bromby
Mrs E. Brooke
D.R. Brooks Esq.
Lieutenant Colonel P.C. McE. Brooks
  MBE
Colonel J. Browell MBE
WOI (SMAC) G. Brown
Lieutenant Colonel M.C. Brown
Major A.J. Bruce TD MA CANTAB
Captain I. Bruce-Russell
W.A. Buckley Esq.
D. Budd Esq.
Captain N.J.M. Budd RHA
P. Budd Esq.
S. Burgess Esq.
General Sir Edward Burgess
R.M. Burns Esq.
Brigadier C.R. Burson CBE
Lieutenant General Sir Edward Burton
  KBE
Stephanie Butcher
T. Buxton Esq.
A.G. Cage Esq.
G. Caldwell MSM

Colonel D.J. Cameron TD
C. Campbell Esq.
W.J. Capstaff Esq.
L/Cdr Walter Carney
Colonel J.C. Carter
Colonel M.G.J. Carter
Colonel P.W. Cartmel
Sergeant A.J. Cartwright
Colonel J. Cater
Colonel D. Challes
C. Chambers Esq.
R.G. Chandler Esq.
D.W. Chapman Esq.
Lieutenant Colonel G.J. Charge
WOI SMAC (Retd) M. Charlton
J.B. Charman Esq.
S.G. Johnson Esq.
D. Chillingworth Esq.
WOII V.J. Chivers
Brigadier A. Clark
G.K. Clarke Esq.
Major W.G. Clarke
Brigadier R.A. Clay CBE
Brigadier T. Clay
D. Clewlow Esq.
Brigadier N. Clissitt
Ex Staff Sergeant T. Clocomb
E. Clowes Esq.
WOII (TRQMS) F.G. Cole
Lieutenant Colonel G. Cole RA
Major General G. de E. Collin
  CB MC DL
J.R. Collinge Esq.
Lieutenant Colonel (TIG) M. Comben
M. Conkerton Esq.
Major D.E. Cook TD
WOII G. Cook

A.J. Cooper TD RD PLD
Colonel M.B. Cooper
F.J. Corbett Esq.
Staff Sergeant G. Cordery
Major General J.E. Cordingley OBE
W.J. Corkish Esq.
D.C. Corney Esq.
Colonel T. Cornick
Major General B. Cornock
Major General C.G. Cornock CB MBE
Major J.B. Corrigan KSG
Brigadier H. Cotesworth Slessor
Major J.B.S. Cottam
R.G. Cowlishaw Esq.
A.P.W. Cox Esq.
E. Cox MBE
Lieutenant Colonel L.A.A. Cox OBE
V. Cox MBE
G.H. Coxhead Esq.
J. Craven Esq.
Major D. Crawford BEM
Mrs J. Credland
Brigadier D. Creswell
Lieutenant Colonel R.F. Crimp
J.H. Crompton Esq.
M. Cross Esq.
Major General R.J. Crossley CB CBE
Colonel B.G. Crowe OBE
B. Cubbon Esq.
S.L. Cunningham Esq.
Major W.E. Cunningham
Captain C.L. Dalley BSc RLC
Major M.J. Dalley MBA FInstAM
K.W.G. Dampier Esq.
N.A. Daniel Esq.
W.J. Darlington Esq.
Lieutenant Colonel M. Darmody
C.J.R. Davies Esq.
Major J.H. Davies MBE
Lieutenant Colonel M.F. Davies
Colonel N. Davies LVO JP DL
Major General B.W. Davis CB CBE
Lieutenant Colonel G.R. Davison MBE
Brigadier R.C. Davison
A.A.B. Dawson Esq.
J.F. Dawson Esq.
C.G. Day Esq.
J. Day Esq.
Mrs N.M. Day
T. Day Esq.
R.N. Dean
Lieutenant Colonel P.C. Deane MBE
Captain A. Dewey
W/Bdr S.G. Dickinson
Major J.B. Dingle
Major R.M. Dingwall
Major M. Dix
G. Dixon Esq.

N. Dixon Esq.
S.N. Dixon Esq.
Major R.G. Dodds
P.A. Dornan
Brigadier M.G. Douglas-Withers CBE
Major G.M. Down
Lieutenant Colonel B.R. Downs
Major P. Dowse MBE
D.A. Drinkwater Esq.
K. Dudman Esq.
D. Dulson Esq.
A. Dunn Esq.
J. Dunn Esq.
Sir Robin Dunn
Durkan Estates Ltd
Colonel J.R.W. Dutton
T. Dwyer Esq.
Ms P. Dyer
J.J. Eales Esq.
F.E. Easton Esq.
Major R.S. Eastwood
A.R. Edge Esq.
Lieutenant Colonel M.C. Edmunds
C. Edwards Esq.
R.K. Edwards Esq.
Brigadier N.H. Eeles
C.P. Ellis Esq.
Captain J. Ellis
R. Elston Esq.
Major M.R. Elviss
M. Embleton Esq.
D. Ensom Esq.
Captain R.M. Esden MBE
P.F. Etherton Esq.
Mrs S.K. Evans
T.P. Everett Esq.
Major M.A. Everitt MBE
Major A.J. Every
Lieutenant Colonel M. Ewence
R.R.D. Ewing Esq.
Captain B.W. Exley
Brigadier A.J. Faith CBE
Captain A.J. Faith
Colonel C.S. Faith OBE
Lieutenant Colonel S.A. Faith
R. Fallas Esq.
Major M. Fallon
Lieutenant Colonel J.F. Falzon BEM
Major D.J. Farley
G. Farr Esq.
F. Fazackerley Esq.
M.G. Felton Esq.
A.W. Fernie Esq.
D.K. Fiddes Esq.
Major R. Field
P.I. FitzGerald Esq.
T. Fitzpatrick Esq.
P.J.P. Fletcher Esq.

B. Flight Esq.
The Reverend Canon V.R.P. Flinn
R.A. Flory Esq.
Major M.C. Fluckiger-Paine
H. Forwood Esq.
Lieutenant Colonel N.J. Foster
Lieutenant Colonel A.P.H.B. Fowle
    MC
Major C. Fowler
Brigadier I.B.R. Fowler
K.P. Fox Esq.
Brigadier P. Fox
Captain S.K.S. Fraser
Major L. Le B. Freeman MBE
Colonel N.W. Frend
S.A.J. Froud Esq.
P.J. Furse Esq.
J.T. Gall Esq.
M. Gammon Esq.
D. Garnier Esq.
Bombardier P. Gauci
R.A. Geeson Esq.
Lieutenant Colonel J.D. Gibson
Colonel G.E. Gilchrist TD
D.M.H. Gill Esq.
B. Gillions Esq.
M. Gilman Esq.
W.J. Gladden Esq.
Colonel A.A. Glenton
Major D. Goddard MBE
A. Goodman Esq.
Lieutenant Colonel G.H.W. Goodman
Major General J.C.M. Gordon CBE
Brigadier A.F. Gordon
G. Gorman Esq.
G. Goulette Esq.
Lieutenant Colonel J.R.M. Gower
Lieutenant Colonel E.C. Grace
A. Graham Esq.
Major P. Graham TD
General Sir Timothy Granville-
    Chapman GBE KCB ADC Gen
B.W. Gray Esq.
M.D. Greaves Esq.
In memory of Sergeant W.J. Green
Greenwich Council
L. Grinrod Esq.
Brigadier J.C. Groom CBE
Major S.A. Guild TD WS
Lieutenant Colonel R.J. Guille MBE
T. Guinan Esq.
Major M. Hadfield
P.P. Hall Esq.
Miss P. Hall
Brigadier R.W.S. Hall
Major B.C. Hallett
C.J.M. Hamilton Esq.
K.E. Hammond Esq.

Lieutenant Colonel R.A. Hamzat RA
Major R.D. Hancock TD
Bro. J.H. Hands ROH
D. Hardie Esq.
Major G.W.C. Harding
W. Harding Esq.
Colonel R.J.H. Harding-Newman
D. Hardy CVO K St J TD
General Sir Alex Harley KBE CB
M. Harper Esq.
A.R. Harris Esq.
P.R. Harrison Esq.
Major R.F. Harrison
A.D. Hart Esq.
Brigadier H.L. Hartley
Major B.G. Harwood
Capt J.K. Hassell
L. Hawker MC
Lieutenant Colonel G.D. Hayes
Lieutenant Colonel D.L. Haynes MBE
Captain P. Head
Major P. Headey
Lieutenant Colonel M.R. Healey RA
Major J. Heaney
Brigadier Sir Gilbert Heathcote Bt CBE
Lieutenant Colonel R.J.G. Heaven MC
D. Hendry-Keerworth Esq.
R.J. Hennessey Esq.
Major A. Henry
Major D.J. Hercus
Majors C. and E. Hewitt
Major C.P.R. Hill
Major R.J. Hill MBE
Lieutenant Colonel J.E.T. Hoare DFC
Brigadier D.H. Hodge OBE
Lieutenant Colonel G.A. Hodkinson
Mrs E. Beryl Holder (née Betty Lewis)
Dr A. Holdes
Lieutenant Colonel R.D. Holl
B.H.J. Holloway Esq.
Major T.S.H. Collins
F. Honey Esq.
Lieutenant Colonel D. Hopkins
J.F. Hopkins Esq.
Captain P.D. Horne
Brigadier and Mrs G.B.R. Horridge
Major A.C.S. Holtom AFC
K. Houldey Esq.
R. Howard Esq.
Colonel P.G. Howard-Harwood
    MBE DL
Brigadier J.H. Howarth
L. Howey Esq.
R. Howick Esq.
D. Hudson Esq.
J. Hughes Esq.
P.C. Hughes Esq.
W.D. Hughes Esq.

J.W. Humphreys Esq.

A. Hunter-Choat Esq.

Colonel P.R.S. Jackson OBE

WOII Stephen R. Jackson

Lieutenant Colonel J.M. Jago OBE

D.H. James Esq.

T.D.R. James Esq.

M. Jamieson Esq.

Colonel R.R. Jammes

I.D. Jefferson Esq.

Colonel M.T. Jefferson

B. Jenkins Esq.

G. Jervis Esq.

P.J. Jobson Esq.

Captain W.J. Johnson

Colonel E.A. Jolley TD DL

Lieutenant Colonel D.A. Jones

F.C. Jones Esq.

The Reverend Captain I. Jones

Miss L. Jones

Lieutenant Colonel M.E. Jones

P.J. Jones Esq.

R.C. Jones Esq.

Major S. Jones

Major J. Jordan

R. Jordan Esq.

Major M. Joslyn

Major G.W. Joyce TD

A.G. Kavanagh Esq.

Mrs D. Kavanagh

D.F.G. Kay MBE

Lieutenant Colonel M.J. Kelly RA

B. Kelly Esq.

E.R. Kelly Esq.

Major R.D. Kelly TD

Major J.B. Kennedy

P.A. Kennedy Esq.

S.T. Kent Esq.

Lieutenant Colonel D.A. Kernohan

Colonel G. Kerr

G. Kerr Esq.

Brigadier J.E. Killick

Mrs J. King

Brigadier B. Kingdon

Colonel J.A.B. Kinloch TD

R.W. Kinsley BEM

Colonel C.A. Knightley

S. Krone Esq.

Major B.R. Lacock

R.V. Lalabalvu Esq.

Sergeant D. Lamb

Lieutenant Colonel J.S. Landau

Major C.F. Lane

Captain C.M. Lane RHA

P.R.L. Lane Esq.

W.N. Lang Esq.

Colonel The Lord Langford OBE DL

Lieutenant Colonel D. Langford

E. Lapham Ex ATS

Lieutenant Colonel T.F. Law RA

Major R.S. Laws

Major L.J. Le Besque TD

B.J. Leadbetter Esq.

Lieutenant Colonel J.J. Learmont RHA

General Sir John Learmont KCB CBE

Captain J.P. Lee TD

R.W. Leigh Esq.

Lieutenant Colonel W.J. Lemon

W.R.A. Lennard MBE

Captain D.H.J. Lester

Major J. Lewis

Lieutenant Colonel N. Linge MBE RA

Lieutenant Colonel K. Litt

C.D. Livett BEM

Mrs M. Lochhead

R.J. Lodge Esq.

R. Lodge Esq.

Lieutenant Colonel A. Logie

Major M.J. Long TD

Captain J.S. Long

T.R.W. Longmore Esq.

B. Longrigg Esq.

Lieutenant Colonel I.D. Lonsdale TD

Captain M.A. Loughlin FLIA

Major C. Lovick RA

Major C. Steadman

G.A. Lowthian Esq.

Lieutenant Colonel D.W. Luck

Major T.E. Luker

Brigadier C.D. Lunn

D. Lusty Esq.

R. Lyall Esq.

Colonel C.J.A. Lyne-Pirkis

Major General R. Lyon CB OBE

Lieutenant Colonel A.M. MacFarlane

Major J. Machin TD

I.M. Macleod Esq.

Lieutenant Colonel T. Major

I.W. Mallory Esq.

M.C.D. Malone Esq.

Major General W.D. Mangham

A. Manson Esq.

Colonel M. Manson

D. Marbeck Esq.

W.A. Markham Esq.

Sergeant T. Marks

F. Marle Esq.

J. Marment Esq.

Lieutenant Colonel A. Marsden

Mrs A.L.R. Martin

Major A.T. Martin

Colonel P.H. Marwood BSc ARCS

Hazel Mason

Major R.H. Matthews MC

WOI ASM R.N. Mawdsley

R. Mawson Esq.

Major A.L. Maxwell TD

Major D.C. Maxwell

Major B.A. May

Colonel J. Mayo

Lieutenant Colonel M.C. McCabe RE

Lieutenant Colonel C.C. McCarthy

P. McComas Esq.

Major (QM) R.A. McCudden

The Reverend R.A. McDowall

Major General B.P. McGuinness CB

Major L. McIntosh

Lieutenant Colonel I.K. McKay

Lieutenant Colonel R.A. McPherson

S.J. McSorley Esq.

M.D. Miller Esq.

Major P.N. Miller

Major R.P.A.V. Miller

Brigadier M. Milligan

Major General J. Milne CB

Colonel K.A. Mitcheson OBE

W.T. Monaghan Esq.

Brigadier L.W. Monk

Major H.R. Montgomerie

Colonel A.L. Moorby

Colonel R.G. Moore MBE TD

Major General W.H. Moore CBE

C.G. Morgan Esq.

I.J. Morgan Esq.

I.P. Morgan Esq.

Lieutenant Colonel J. Morkham RFD

Colonel A.D. Morris

Lieutenant Colonel B. Morris

M. Mortimer Esq.

A.P. Moss Esq.

P. Mount Esq.

D.J. Moyle Esq.

Major G.F.A. Munns

Lieutenant Colonel J.D. Musgrave RA

D.J. Nanson Esq.

Major D.E. Naylor MBE

Captain A.S. Neagor

J.H. Neale Esq.

R.J. Nerney Esq.

Major H.G. Newcome RA

Major General H.W. Newcome

Major J. Newcome

Major W.D. Nichol

Colonel C.J. Nicholls

A.W. Nicol Esq.

Lieutenant Colonel J. Nicol RA

Ms E. Noon

Captain B.A.J. Normington TD

T.A. Norris Esq.

Lieutenant Colonel (TIG)
    G.W.A. Norton

Brigadier R. Nugee MBE

Officers' Mess, 105 Regt RA(V)

The Reverend E. Ogden

S.J. O'Gorman Esq.

Major A.R. O'Hagan TD DL

T. Oldfield Esq.

P. Orchard-Lisle Esq.

Colonel D.R.M. Owen DSO OBE

E. Owen Esq.

Brigadier J.L.A. Painter

P. Painter Esq.

L.C. Palmer Esq.

L.G. Palmer Esq.

Ex Gunner C. Parr

Brigadier B.A.H. Parritt CBE

J. Parrott Esq.

B. (Taff) Parsons Esq.

Major G.S.E. Paske MC

S. Paske Esq.

Lieutenant Colonel H.C. Paterson TD

J. Pattinson Esq.

M. Pawley Esq.

A.D. Phillpots Payne Esq.

J.R. Pearson Esq.

R.T. Pearson Esq.

Major J.H.H. Peile

B.J. Pelmore Esq.

M.W. Pendergast Esq.

Major General B.T. Pennicott CVO

Captain C. Percival QVRM

K.T. Perry Esq.

J.M. Peters Esq.

Major H.C. Phillips

Colonel J.M. Phillips

J. Phipps Esq.

Major W.D. Pickett MBE

I.R. Picton MBE

The Right Honourable Sir Malcolm Pill

W. Platts Esq.

D. Poole Esq.

P. Pope Esq.

Major C.P.R. Postlethwaite

Major H.J.F. Potter MBE DL

Brigadier D. Potts

Brigadier M.N. Pountain CBE

G. Poynton Esq.

A.J. Price Esq.

H. Price Esq.

O., Y. and R. Probert

Lieutenant Colonel R.H.C. Probert
    OBE DL

Brigadier R.W.H. Purdy OBE

Lieutenant Colonel D.R. Putney USAF

N.G. Quarrelle Esq.

J. Quinn Esq.

A.C.M. Raven Esq.

R. Rayer Esq.

Lance Bombardier F.W. Raymond

G. Raynor Esq.

In memory of Lieutenant R. Raynor

Lieutenant Colonel D.R. Reavill

J.A. Rees Esq.
Captain W.E. Rees
Major (QM) J.H. Reynolds
R.J. Reynolds Esq.
T. Reynolds Esq.
General Sir David Richards
   KCB CBE OSO ADC
Colonel M.J.N. Richards
Major General N.W.F. Richards
T. Richardson Esq.
I.M. Rickard Esq.
Major F.A. Rigby TD
Dr F.N. Rigby
Brigadier J. Rigby
Major General A. Ritchie CBE
Colonel A.C. Roberts
   OBE TD ADC DL
Major A.P. Roberts
Lieutenant Colonel J.R. Roberts LGM
K. Roberts Esq.
Major P. Robinson
Sergeant A.J. Rogers
Sergeant A. Rogers
Mrs L.A. Rollo
R. Rouse Esq.
Captain A.J.W. Rozelaar
Colonel J.A. Rozelaar
Lieutenant Colonel P.A. Salisbury
Lieutenant Colonel P.C. Salloway
A.E. Salmon Esq.
Brigadier H.L.B. Salmon OBE
Ms N.K. Sandars
B.J. Sanders Esq.
Major J. Sandys-Renton
Captain G.A. Sargeant
Major M.J. Sargent RA
K.L. Saward Esq.
Major H.V. Sawyer
D.C. Scholfield ISM
Brigadier F. Scott
Major T.E. Scott
Colonel P. Seabrook
L.J. Seatherton Esq.
Major D. Sebag-Montefiore
Major J.A.F. Sewell MC (HAC)
Colonel P. Sexstone
Captain M.R. Shallcross
Major G.D. Shapland RA
A.W. Sharman Esq.
Lieutenant Colonel W.E. Shaw
L.G. Sheldrick Esq.
Major General M.F.L. Shellard CBE
Captain D. Shenton RHA
M. Shenton Esq.
Major M.R. Shephard
M.S. Sheridan Esq.
M.J. Sherriff Esq.

R.S. Shooter Esq.
Major P. Shovelton CB CMG
C. Shuter Esq.
Lieutenant Colonel D.W. Sibley
Colonel and Mrs D. Sime
Major A. Simmons RHA
G. Simpson Esq.
Lieutenant Colonel T. Simpson
Mrs A. Skinner
A.E. Skinner Esq.
B. Skinner Esq.
B.J. Skinner Esq.
D.M. Skinner Esq.
P.J. Skinner Esq.
R.J. Skinner Esq.
M.D. Slade Esq.
G. Smith Esq.
Major J.B. Smith
J.M. Smith Esq.
M.J. Smith Esq.
Mrs M.M. Smith
Captain P.G.W. Smith MBE
P.J. Smith Esq.
P.R. Smith Esq.
Brigadier R.J.S. Smith OBE QGM
Ex/Sergeant J. Smith
P.K. Snook Esq.
J. Southgate Esq.
Colonel G.T. Spate OBE TD DL
P. Spens Esq.
Major R.L. Spiller
K.G. Spiret Esq.
Colonel R. Squires
W.G.R. Standen Esq.
Colonel J. Starmer-Smith OBE
Major General R. Staveley
Colonel J.M. Steele CB OBE TD DL
Major General M. Steele
Major General J. Stephenson
Colonel D. Stevens
R.D. Stevens Esq.
Lieutenant Colonel and
   Mrs K.A.P. Stevenson
T.W. Stimson Esq.
Major W.R. Stirling
W.J. Stocker Esq.
Lieutenant Colonel T.O.G. Stokes
Major General A.C.P. Stone CB
R. Stoodley Esq.
N. Strachan Esq.
I. Straker Esq.
B.M. Strickland Esq.
Lance Bombardier J. Sturge
G. Suddaby Esq.
T. Sweet Esq.
R.A.P. Swinhoe-Standen Esq.
Major J. Sworder

Major General R.M. McQ. Sykes
Brigadier C.W. Tadier CBE ADC
Mrs J.W. Talbot
J.M.A. Tamplin Esq.
Major I.E. Tate
D.A.J. Taylor Esq.
H. Taylor Esq.
Colonel M.J.E. Taylor MBE TD DL
Colonel R.A. Taylor
Captain S.E. Taylor
M.A. Taylor-Smith Esq.
Captain D.R. Thatcher
P. Theobald Esq.
Captain D. Thirkhill
C. Thomas Esq.
K. Thomas Esq.
R.C.C. Thompson Esq.
Brigadier T. Thompson MBE
Brigadier J.R. Thomson QVRM TD
L. Thorne Esq.
Major J. Thorneloe
Lieutenant Colonel M.J. Thornhill
Major J.W. Timbers
Brigadier K.A. Timbers
Ms N. Timbers
Major S.R. Timbers
Colonel I. Tinsley
L.C. Tofts Esq.
G. Tooley BEM LRRG
Lieutenant Colonel W.A.H. Townend
Lieutenant Colonel (Quartermaster)
   S.K. Tullett MBE
B. Turner Esq.
Major J. Turner
Major J.E. Tye MBE
Lieutenant Colonel S.N. Upton
Lieutenant Colonel M.D. Valenzia RA
E. Varley Esq.
Colonel S. Vasey
I.R. Ventham Esq.
I.R. Vernon Esq.
Lieutenant Colonel D.D. Vigors
Field Marshal Lord Vincent
Colonel M. Vincent
T. Vincent Esq.
J.F. Voce Esq.
Lieutenant Colonel Gordon
   W.C. Waddell RA
Major A.J. Walker TD
WOI (RSM) J. Wall
Major M. Wallace
Colonel Norman Wallace
Lieutenant Colonel A.J. Waller RA
Brig. H.J. de W. Waller MBE MC
S.C. Walter Esq.
G. Cecil Ward Esq.
Major R. Warne

D.N. Warner Esq.
Major General G.H. Watkins
Mrs R. Watson
R.M. Watson Esq.
S. Watson Esq.
Lieutenant Colonel J. Watts
Colonel A.S. Weatherhead OBE TD
Major L.R. Weaver
Major General Sir Evelyn Webb-Carter
   KCVO OBE
Major N. Webber
WOII W.M. Webster
Captain R.J. Weedon
Brigadier R.P.M. Weighill
Colonel W.P. Weighill
C. West Esq.
J. West Esq.
Major D.J. Westmoreland TD
Major J.F.T. Wheen
Lieutenant Colonel D.V. Whelan RA
J.L. Whistance Esq.
Lieutenant Colonel A.J. White RA
R.J. Whiteway MBE
G. Whittaker Esq.
H.F. Whybro Esq.
The Reverend H.L. Whyte OCF
R. Wigglesworth Esq.
Lieutenant Colonel D.A. Wilcox
S.R. Wild Esq.
General Sir Michael Wilkes KCB CBE
Lieutenant Colonel G.P. Wilkinson RA
Colonel I. Wilkinson
Major R.J. Wilkinson
Valerie Wilkinson
Lieutenant General Sir Michael Willcocks
M. Williams Esq.
Lieutenant Colonel P.J. Williams RCA
Major B. Willsher
B.M.E. Wilson Esq.
Major J. Wilson
Captain P.R.D. Wilson
Major T.A.K Wilson TD JP
Lieutenant Colonel R.A. Winchester
B. Winfield Esq.
WO and Sgts Mess, 105 Regiment RA(V)
Captain C.J. Wood
C.M. Wood Esq.
L.C. Wood Esq.
P.F. Wookey Esq.
Lieutenant Colonel T. Wordsworth RA
G. Wormald Esq.
Major A.H.Q. Wright
D.J. York Esq.
Major General E.J. Younson
Major General David T. Zabecki

INDEX

Index of Contributors

All articles signed KAT are by Brigadier Ken Timbers.
The article signed TMI is by Third Millennium Information Ltd.

Picture Credits

Unless an acknowledgement appears below, the illustrations in this volume have been provided by Royal Artillery, Woolwich. Every effort has been made to contact the copyright holders of all works reproduced in this book. However, if acknowledgements have been omitted, please contact Third Millennium Publishing. The publishers would also like to thank Roy Fox and Peter Ashley for their work on this volume.

Alan Godfrey Maps: Maps – 32, 35 and 45; **Michelle Bowen**: Map 79; Playbills (x3) 80; **Corbis**: Prince Rupert 17; **Crown Copyright**: ©1966 – all images 158–9, ©1995 – all images 160–1, ©2007 – all images 164–6, ©2008 – all images 167–85, barring those indicated in the table below; **English Heritage**: Grand Depot Barracks 75, Connaught Barracks, Cambridge Barracks 76, Red Barracks 77; **Getty Images**: Staff outing 107; **Greenwich Heritage Centre**: Woolwich ferry 107, Beresford Square 108, **Greenwich Visitors Centre**: The Clock Tower 140, Freedom of the Borough 147; **Courtesy of Mrs G.P. Hale**: 17th-century view 8, RA Barracks 30; **David Hodge**: Rushgrove House 32; **Sophie Huthwaite**: Sophie Huthwaite 157; **Imperial War Museum**: Crimean soldiers 8, Woolwich Barracks 112; **National Maritime Museum**: Royal Laboratory (southern entrance) 13, Great Harry 14, Greenwich Palace 15, Royal Dockyard 16, Royal Laboratory (southern end) 19, Woolwich 19, Cadet barracks 25, Gentleman cadets 26, The Warren 28; Blitz aerial 113; **National Portrait Gallery**: John Churchill 23, Charles Lennox 37; **David Rowlands**: Rocket Troop 85; **Copyright Royal Artillery Institution**: Maj-Gen B.P. Hughes CBE 163; **Ken Saward**: Snuff box 129, **Ken Timbers**: Mary Rose 15; Old RMA building 24; Academy Room and Board Room 25; Mallet's Mortars 60; Royal Garrison Church 74; Greenhill Schools 102; **Matthew Wilson**: Map, 61

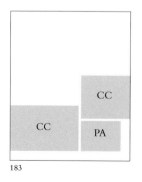
183

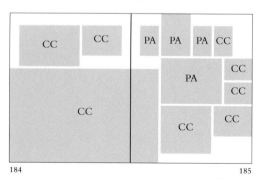
184　　　　　　　　　　　185

CC = Crown Copyright　　　PA = Peter Ashley